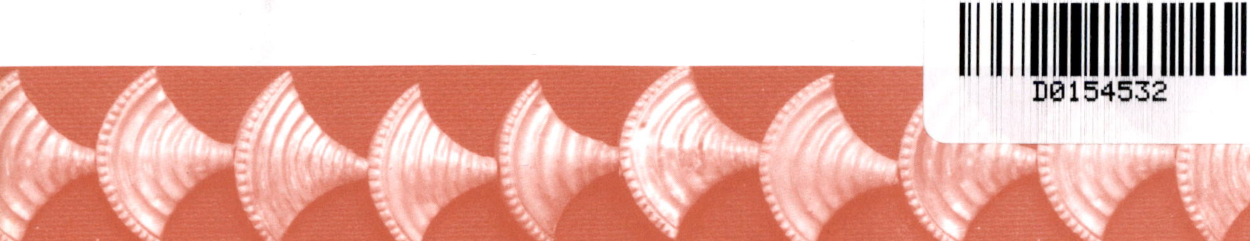

Milatos
Knossos
Archanes
Karphi
Plati
Psychro Cave
Lato
MT JUKTAS
LASITHI
Myrtos (Phournou Koryphi)
Myrtos (Pyrgos)
Palaikastro
Petras
Petsophas
Zakros
Praisos
Ziros

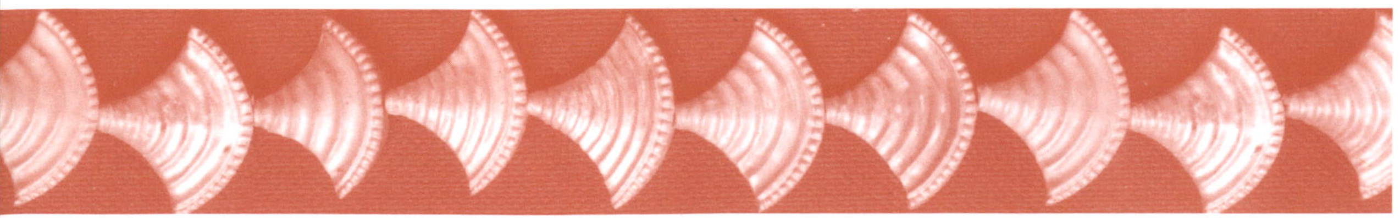

CRETAN QUESTS

CRETAN QUESTS

British Explorers, Excavators and Historians

Edited by

DAVINA HUXLEY

BRITISH SCHOOL
AT ATHENS
2000

Published and distributed by
The British School at Athens
Senate House
Malet Street
London WC1E 7HU

ISBN 0 904887 37 5

Typeset by
Cambrian Typesetters, Frimley, Camberley, Surrey
Printed by Bookcraft Ltd, Midsomer Norton, Somerset

CONTENTS

FOREWORD

The centenary of Sir Arthur Evans's starting excavations at Knossos in 1900 is a good occasion to review British scholarly achievements in Crete over the last century and earlier. That is the purpose of this collection of essays which the British School at Athens offers in homage, gratitude and affection to its many members from Britain and elsewhere who have worked in Crete and, to a far greater degree, to our hosts, colleagues and friends in Crete and from the rest of Greece.

Dilys Powell called one of her books about Greece *An Affair of the Heart*. How much more that title holds for British experiences in Crete. It has been a passionate involvement imbued with a strong sense of the spirit of place and of the continuity of human adaptation to the physical fact of Crete with its bleak mountains, upland plains with their swallow-holes, dry torrent-beds enlivened in the summer heat by stands of pink oleander, ancient olive groves and lush lowland valleys. The endless variety of Cretan scenery seems to demand a commitment from all who pass through.

Many of us who have been lucky enough to work in Crete when young have a sense that this is where we grew up, through exposure to the place and the Cretans and traditions that seem to transcend the millennia and bring us almost into direct contact with the people of any age of Crete's great and long history. If at times it has been painful when we have recognised our feeble perceptions of the Cretan sense of honour and our inadequate responses, we may set against that those who have fought for Crete and its – and our – freedom.

Shaped by this love for Crete, British research in the island has been another way of repaying our debt to Cretans past and present, for their constant hospitality and their generosity in setting straight our fuzzy thoughts on their heritage and helping us have a sharper sense of what it all means. The result has been a story we may be proud of, as the contributors to this book aim to show and explain. It is a story we may expect to continue, probably more often nowadays through formal collaborations with our colleagues in Crete when in the past the scholarly arrangements tended to be looser. But neither formality nor informality will dampen the intellectual friendship. It is hard to envisage what a book such as this will contain in 2100 but, provided enough of the young still have the chance to learn to love Crete, I have no doubt there will be plenty of work of value to report.

GERALD CADOGAN

INTRODUCTION

This book, in honour of work by British scholars in Crete, gathers together contributions from twenty-two people. That not all of them are British seems appropriate. They were encouraged to treat their subjects as they saw fit, and were offered freedom from any predetermined structure, once they had agreed to write about a particular period or topic.

The book is divided into two sections. The first studies the work of British travellers and archaeologists against the background of more than a century of discovery in Crete. The second part examines in turn each chronological period or specialised subject to assess the British contribution to the present knowledge of it. Added to this is an account of the responsibilities of the British School at Knossos; there are also some agreeable reminders of people whose work on excavations is essential, but may not always gain enough recognition – we have called them Artists and Craftsmen.

We do not intend the book to be a comprehensive work of reference, but rather a series of essays with some brief bibliographical pointers to further study. In a few cases where the subject is less well known, more complex, or more controversial, the number of citations at the end of each section has been allowed to swell somewhat. Repeated general references in the bibliographies to the standard works such as Evans's *The Palace of Minos* or Pendlebury's *The Archaeology of Crete* are often omitted.

In the first half of the twentieth century most people referred to themselves in print by their initials and surname. The editor has respectfully kept to this usage in general, while allowing much more use of first names after about 1950, but inconsistencies are inevitable. Even more so is this the case in the thorny subject of the transliteration of Greek: in the published titles of books or articles, or in direct quotations from them, the original spelling is kept. An attempt is made to find consistent forms for use elsewhere, in some cases traditional ones.

Grateful acknowledgement is due to many people, among them the friends and colleagues of the contributors for any advice they have given; to Deborah Harlan who calmly organised the texts, the editor, and her computer with enviable efficiency; and the late Lady Waterhouse who offered the run of her library and much useful conversation about the School. Finding illustrations would have been far harder without the invaluable help of Dr Susan Sherratt of the Ashmolean Museum with the Museum's photographic service, and of Dr Elisabeth Waywell (Secretary of the School) with the photographic department of the Institute of Archaeology, University College London. Dr John Bennet and Robert Wilkins of the Institute of Archaeology at Oxford, Dr Hector Catling (in very difficult circumstances for him), Mrs Lilah Clarke, Dr Dominique Collon, Professor John Killen, A.H.S. Megaw, Mrs Alicia Pauling, Stuart Thorne and Dr James Whitley all gave willing assistance. Ann Sackett was able to make available material from the riches of the British School Archive in Athens. Andrew M. Tomko III kindly gave permission to use his map.

Many of the photographs reproduced were taken by the contributors or their colleagues. Acknowledgement is made also to the Ashmolean Museum Oxford (especially for access to the Evans Archive), the British Library, the University of Birmingham Library, the Fitzwilliam Museum, Cambridge, and the Herakleion Museum.

Generous donations from the Marc Fitch Fund and the Jowett Copyright Trustees, together with the expertise and guidance of Roy Stephens of Leopard's Head Press, have made this publication possible. George Huxley showed great patience and resourcefulness under a long barrage of questions; there was much enjoyable discussion too, both with him and all those involved in the project.

DAVINA HUXLEY

ABBREVIATIONS

Periodicals and series

A. Delt.	Archaiologikon Deltion
AF	Archäologische Forschungen
AJA	American Journal of Archaeology
Ant. J.	Antiquaries Journal
AR	Journal of Hellenic Studies Archaeological Reports
ASA	Annuario della R. Scuola Archeologica di Atene
BAR	British Archaeological Reports
BCH	Bulletin de correspondance hellénique
BCH supp.	Bulletin de correspondance hellénique, supplément
BICS	Bulletin of the Institute of Classical Studies, London
BSA	Annual of the British School at Athens
BSA supp. vol.	Supplementary volume of the Annual of the British School at Athens
BZ	Byzantinische Zeitschrift
CAH	Cambridge Ancient History
CAJ	Cambridge Archaeological Journal
CMS	Corpus der minoischen und mykenischen Siegel
GRBS	Greek Roman and Byzantine Studies
JHS	The Journal of Hellenic Studies
JRGZM	Jahrbuch des Römisch-Germanischen Zentralmuseums, Mainz
Kr. Chron.	Kretika Chronika
Mon. Linc.	Monumenti antichi pubblicati per cura della Accademia Nazionale dei Lincei
Op. Ath.	Opuscula Atheniensia
OJA	Oxford Journal of Archaeology
PCPS	Proceedings of the Cambridge Philological Society
PPS	Proceedings of the Prehistoric Society
Röm. Mitt.	Mitteilungen des Deutschen Archäologischen Instituts, römische Abteilung
SIMA	Studies in Mediterranean Archaeology
SMEA	Studi micenei ed Egeo-Anatolici

Books, symposia, articles etc.

Ayiopharango (1975)	D. J. Blackman and K. Branigan, 'An Archaeological Survey on the South Coast of Crete, between Ayiofarango and Chrisostomos', *BSA* 70 (1975)
Ayiopharango (1977)	D. J. Blackman and K. Branigan, 'An Archaeological Survey of the Lower Catchment of the Ayiofarango Valley', *BSA* 72 (1977)
EILAPINI	*EILAPINI. Tomos timitikos yia ton kath. N. Platona* (Iraklion, 1987)
Fauna and first Settlers	D. S. Reese (ed.), *Pleistocene and Holocene Fauna of Crete and its first Settlers* (Madison, 1996)
Greek Prehistory	E. B. French and K. A. Wardle (eds.), *Problems in Greek Prehistory: Papers presented at the Centenary conference of the British School of Archaeology at Athens, Manchester, April 1986* (Bristol, 1988)
KNC	J. N. Coldstream and H. W. Catling (eds.), *Knossos North Cemetery. Early Greek Tombs* (BSA supp. vol. 28, 4 vols., 1996)
Labyrinth	D. Evely, H. Hughes-Brock, N. Momigliano (eds.), *Knossos: a Labyrinth of History. Papers presented in honour of Sinclair Hood* (London, 1994)
Minoan Palaces	R. Hägg and N. Marinatos (eds.), *The Function of the Minoan Palaces. 4th International Symposium at the Swedish Institute in Athens, 1984* (Stockholm, 1987)
Minoan Society	O. Krzyszkowska and L. Nixon (eds.), *Minoan Society. Proceedings of the Cambridge Colloqium, 1981* (Bristol, 1983)
PM	A. J. Evans, *The Palace of Minos at Knossos* i–iv (London, 1921–35)
Sanctuaries and Cults	R. Hägg and N. Marinatos (eds.), *Sanctuaries and Cults of the Aegean Bronze Age. 1st International Symposium at the Swedish Institute in Athens, 1980* (Stockholm, 1981)

LIST OF FIGURES

CRETAN CHRONOLOGY

(Adapted from *The Aerial Atlas of Ancient Crete*)

All dates are approximate

NEOLITHIC	Aceramic	7000–6500 BC
	Early Neolithic I	6500–5000
	Early Neolithic II	5000–4700
	Middle Neolithic	4700–4400
	Late Neolithic	4400–3700?
	Final Neolithic	3700?–3400
PREPALATIAL	Early Minoan I	3400–3000/2900
	Early Minoan II	2900–2300/2150
	Early Minoan III	2300/2150–2160/2025
	Middle Minoan IA	2160/1979–20th century
OLD PALACE	Middle Minoan IB	19th century
(PROTOPALATIAL)	Middle Minoan II and Middle Minoan IIIA?	19th century–1700/1650
NEW PALACE	Middle Minoan III	1700/1650–1600
(NEOPALATIAL)	Late Minoan IA	1600–1480
	Late Minoan IB	1480–1425
	Late Minoan II	1425–1390
	Late Minoan IIIA1	1390–1370/60
POSTPALATIAL	Late Minoan IIIA2	1370/60–1340/30
	Late Minoan IIIB	1340/30–1190
	Late Minoan IIIC	1190–1070
	Sub-Minoan	1070–970
IRON AGE	Geometric	970–700
	Orientalizing	700–630
ARCHAIC		630–480
CLASSICAL		480–330
HELLENISTIC		330–67
ROMAN		67 BC–AD 330
EARLY BYZANTINE		330–824
ARAB		824–961
LATE BYZANTINE		961–1204
VENETIAN		1204–1669
OTTOMAN		1669–1898

BRITISH RESEARCH IN CRETE

EARLY TRAVELLERS FROM BRITAIN AND IRELAND

With its commanding position on the great sea route from Italy and the Adriatic to the eastern Mediterranean Crete attracted scores of travellers before the major researchers of the nineteenth century, Sieber, Pashley, Raulin and Spratt. The island was not, however, the sole object of the earlier journeys; until the mid-sixteenth century these comprised mainly pilgrimages to the Holy Land and thereafter wide antiquarian and scientific travel. This last objective had, indeed, brilliant thirteenth and fourteenth century forerunners such as Simon Corda of Genoa and Cristoforo Buondelmonti from Florence. The visitors, together with a few of the many merchants, have left highly interesting records of Cretan society, political conditions, economic activity, natural environment and antiquities. At the same time we should note that these valuable contributions are matched or even outshone by the reports and letters of sixteenth and earlier seventeenth century resident Italian officials, engineers, humanists and scientists such as Barozzi, Castrofilaca, Foscarini, Basilicata and, most brilliant of all, the polymathic Onorio Belli from Vicenza.

Among the travellers was a small number from Britain and Ireland. They have left a variety of informative and sometimes dramatic records of an island under Venetian and Ottoman colonial rule (1204–1898). Harsh though fiscal and service imposts on the population of some 200,000 (in the decades around 1600) were, the fertility of most of the island was never in doubt, trade was strongly promoted and foreign contacts not discouraged.

Among the many medieval pilgrims voyaging to the Holy Land, and our first traveller, was the Irish monk Symon Simeonis, from Clonmel, who visited in 1323. He observed Khania surrounded by cypresses of great height, 'nemore cipressino gloriose ac magnifice dotatum', but Candia (Herakleion), though well defended, 'civitatem muro fortissimo circumcinctam', had vile, narrow, dirty and tortuous streets, entirely unpaved. Italian wives shimmered with gold, pearls and gems but when widowed were black-veiled and avoided the society of men as of serpents. The island abounded in excellent wine, cheese (both much exported) and fruits, among them pomegranates, lemons, figs, grapes, melons, water melons and gourds. Symon also describes an encampment of gypsies, who observed the Greek Rite, apparently the earliest record of their movement through to Europe. After an anonymous fourteenth century English pilgrim whose account in verse confirms Candia as 'A faire toun, and stron of valles' (FIG. 1), while the island grows 'alle the Malvesy that men have', our next pilgrim, William Wey (1458, 1462), a Fellow of Eton College, concentrates on currency exchange rates.

A first antiquarian note is sounded by Sir Richard Guylforde and his chaplain, again bound

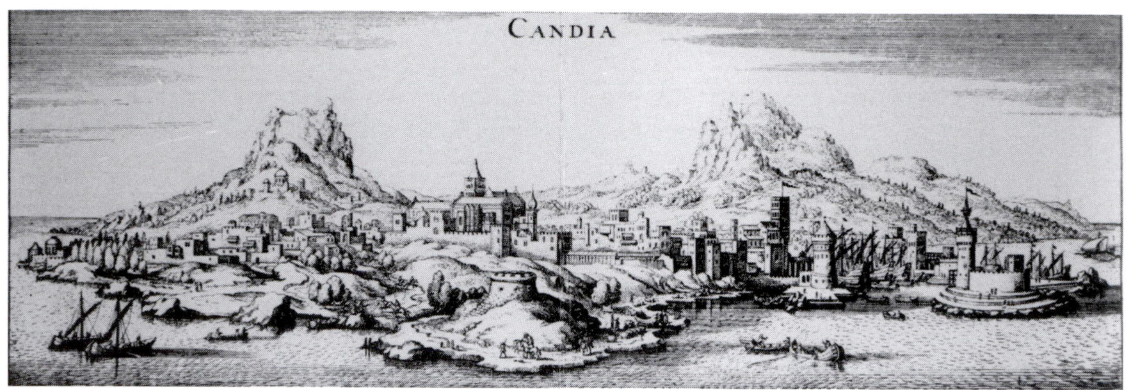

FIG. 1 Candia. 16th century (Frans Hogenberg, after B. de Breydenbach, 15th century)

for Jerusalem. Despite the observation that in Crete 'There be ryght eveyll people' they saw the church and grave of Titus at Gortyn in 1506 and they knew that the city of Candy 'was sometyme the habytacle and lordshyp of ye kynge Mynos'. Much of Guylforde's chaplain's text is soon used by the next English pilgrim whose account survives, Sir Richard Torkington in 1517. He met several English merchants in Candia, who filled his bottles with Muskadell. He was shown the head of St Titus, covered with silver and gold, and he had heard that there was 'an old brokyn Citee which was callyd Cretina' (Gortyna); but his chief concern, though he did not leave the city of Candia, was the hot and cloudless weather. Our last pilgrim, John Locke, who left England on the *Mathew Gonson* in March 1553, noted the quality of Cretan archers, who 'shoot neere the marke', even though he did not land during his voyage along the south coast.

Torkington met English merchants already in 1517. There had in fact been English trading ships in the eastern Mediterranean in 1446 and 1457 and from 1511 they had 'an ordinarie and usuall trade to Sicilia, Candie, Chio, and somewhiles to Cyprus' and the Levant. The first English consul at Candia, Censio de Balthasari, was appointed in 1522 and the first Englishman to hold the post seems to have been Denis Harrys, a London merchant, in 1530; in 1540 he was succeeeded by George Petrocochino. Cretan wine and oil were the main exports. At almost the same date as pilgrim Locke, Roger Bodenham voyaged to Crete and Chios in 1551. He is our first informative merchant. As well as noting that Turkish ships had brought wheat to sell in Crete he describes the appearance of a large force of heavily armed Cretans banished to the mountains but called to serve against a Turkish threat, 'good archers, every one with his bowe and arrowes, a sword and a dagger, with long haire, and bootes that reach up to their grine, and a shirt of male. . . . They would drinke wine out of all measure'. He loaded it to take to England.

In the fifteen years from 1596 to 1611 came the first British visitors who, like Symon Simeonis nearly three hundred years earlier, travelled in the island and have left extended accounts. The time was one of extreme contrasts, from the glories of the Cretan Renaissance in sacred painting and poetic drama to the plagues and earthquakes which afflicted the population.

Fynes Moryson arrived on the south coast from Iskanderun (Alexandretta), sick with dysentery, in 1596. Proceeding with great difficulty, 'like a snaile', he reached Mone Odhegetria above Kaloi Limiones (Fair Havens). He then passed near 'the Monument famous for the love of the Kings daughter *Ariadne* to Theseus, called the Laberinth of *Crete*'. Pliny (*Nat.Hist.* 35 xix 85) had described the construction in detail despite the fact that in his day 'nulla vestigia exstant'. The underground site near Ambelouzos had been visited since the twelfth century (Eustathius) by travellers and Venetian officials, but was recognized by Francesco Suriano before 1514 to have been the stone quarry for building adjacent Gortyna. Arrived at Candia, Moryson was checked for infectious disease; the officials 'caused ropes to be hanged acrosse our chamber, and all things we had, yea, our very shirts, to be severally taken out, and hanged thereupon, and so perfumed them with brimstone, to our great annoyance', before giving him freedom to go wherever he wished. In the city he lodged with Richard Darson, merchant, who was 'wel acquainted with the best courses of living in *Candia*'. Like all others he notes the abundance of red wines, cereals, pulses, oil, meat, sugar, honey, 'Cedar trees' (juniper), cypress trees and the chests made therefrom, medicinal herbs and 'coloured dyings'. He left for Constantinople on a Greek ship loaded with wine, lemon juice and onions.

Three years later, in July 1599, the violent Sir Antony Sherley and party arrived from Zante *en route* to Persia for diplomatic purposes. They were admirably treated by the Duke of Candia and by the gentlewomen who 'oftentimes did make us banquets in their gardens, with music and dancing'.

The Scot William Lithgow spent fifty-eight days in Crete in 1609, part of a vast exploration described in his famous book of 1632, *The Totall Discourse, Of the Rare Aduentures, and painefull Peregrinations of long nineteene Yeares Trauayles*. . . . His extraordinary style, at the same time loquacious, exaggerating, vivid and pungent, is of a piece with his travels themselves, full of incidents and detailed topographical, social and environmental information. Robbed on the road, yet given a clay sealing for identification to prevent any such repeated usage, he went on to enjoy Canea (Khania) with its castle and ninety-seven palaces. Travellers recognise the landscape with 'the prickles of a kind of Thistle wherewith the Countrey is overcharged . . . marvelous sharpe, and offensive unto the inhabitants, whereof, often a day to my great harme, I found their bloody smart'. The armed Greeks resemble those of Bodenham, helmet and shield replacing the mail shirt. Women's dress is also described, its wearers 'insatiably inclined to *Venery*, such is the nature of the soyle and climate'.

Agricultural production was as abundant as Moryson had found: 'the best *Malvasy, Muscadine* and *Leaticke* wines', oranges, lemons, melons, citrons, grenadiers (pomegranates), *Adams* apples (limes), raisins, olives, dates, honey, sugar, three kinds of grapes, 'medicinable hearbes'. Cereals, however, were imported yearly, though the plain of Khania was full of wheat and other crops, 'the garden of the whole universe: being the goodliest plot, the Diamondsparke, and Honny Spot of all Candy'. Passing along 'the skirt of Mount *Ida*' he was shown the Idaian cave, the temples of Gortyna (one 'as yet undecayed') and the entrance of the labyrinth. He offers a splendid description, concluding that here Theseus 'did enter and slay the *Minotaurus*, who was included there by Dedalus: this *Minotaure* is said to have been begot by the lewd and luxurious *Pasiphae*, who doted on a white Bull'.

George Sandys, son of the Archbishop of York and a man wholly different in personality from Lithgow, travelled widely in the Turkish empire, including Egypt, before sailing west from Cyprus in 1611. He has left a full description of Crete in his book of 1615, packed with Classical scholarship and ancient history, including moralizing personifications: 'Notorious is the adultry of *Pasiphae*, with the General *Taurus*; which gave unto the Poets the invention of their *Minotaur* (so called they the bastard)'. He describes the ruins of Gortyna, the labyrinth (of which he heard from an English merchant), the summit of Ida and its church, wild fauna, the wines and special grapes from Chios, and herbs, including cistus in great quantity; from this plant ladanum was gathered, as Belon had first described some sixty years earlier. Most interestingly he provides unique testimony of the survival of a particular placename: Knossos had long since 'left but a sound of the name; a little village there standing, called Cinosus'. He also describes a remarkable armed dance, with bows bent ready, quiver on the back and sword at the side, recalling (or maintaining) the ancient *Pyrricha*. But women's dress did not attract him, they 'only wearing loose veils on their heads, the breasts and shoulders perpetually naked, and dyed by the Sun into a loathsom tawny'. Despite Sandys' social and topographical detail it is not at all clear that he actually landed on the island; rather he seems to have sailed along the southern coast, proceeding west towards Sicily.

When Bernard Randolph explored Crete in 1680 the island had been eleven years under Turkish control, since the end of the long siege of Candia; of this an anonymous British volunteer on the Venetian side in 1668 has left a lively account in a book published in London in 1670. Randolph had no serious interest in antiquity; he set out to describe the condition of the island as he found it, from Siteia to Khania. In Candia public buildings had been repaired, but outside the walls the scene was still rubble strewn and grim: 'All the plain for above two miles without the walls is like a new plow'd field, where you cannot walk, but must see pieces of dead men's bones'.

In the country agricultural production remained strong; as well as vineyards olive groves now appear more prominent, as in the plain of Hierapetra, and there were huge, square, wooden vats at Khania. Sugar and cheese were abundant and wheat was sold for export at Siteia. This last contrasts with previous times, but it may have been simply the local Turkish leader desiring profit. The gathering of ladanum continues and a range of wild plants provided food. The south side of the Lasithi range had 'an abundance of *Cyprus* trees'. The descriptions of Rethymno (FIG. 2) and Khania (FIG. 3) indicate well built, thriving towns. This last aspect, however, is rather contradicted soon afterwards by Ellis Veryard, a medical doctor who travelled in Crete in 1686. He found the towns in a state of decay, while noting that the chief commodities were oil, sugar, honey, wax, excellent wines and an abundance of choice fruits. After leaving Crete for Alexandria he recounts his dramatic capture by Algerian pirates.

Just over fifty years later, in August 1739, Dr Richard Pococke landed on the Sphakian coast, having sailed from Rhodes in a Scottish ship. His travels (1739–40) were motivated by a genuine spirit of enquiry, to see 'every thing that was curious'. He was elected a Fellow of the Royal Society and became a senior ecclesiastic with successive bishoprics in Ireland. His monumental and much translated book, *A Description of the East* . . . I (1743), II (1745), in its Cretan section as in others, inaugurates British exploration of antiquity on a new scale. His topographical studies and identifications of the Diktynnaion, Polyrrhenia, Aptera, Panormos, Gortyna

FIG. 2 Rethymno. *c.* 1700 (J. P. de Tournefort, *A Voyage into the Levant* . . . I (1718) pl. 4)

FIG. 3 Canea. *c.* 1700 (J. P. de Tournefort, *A Voyage into the Levant* . . . I (1718) pl. 10)

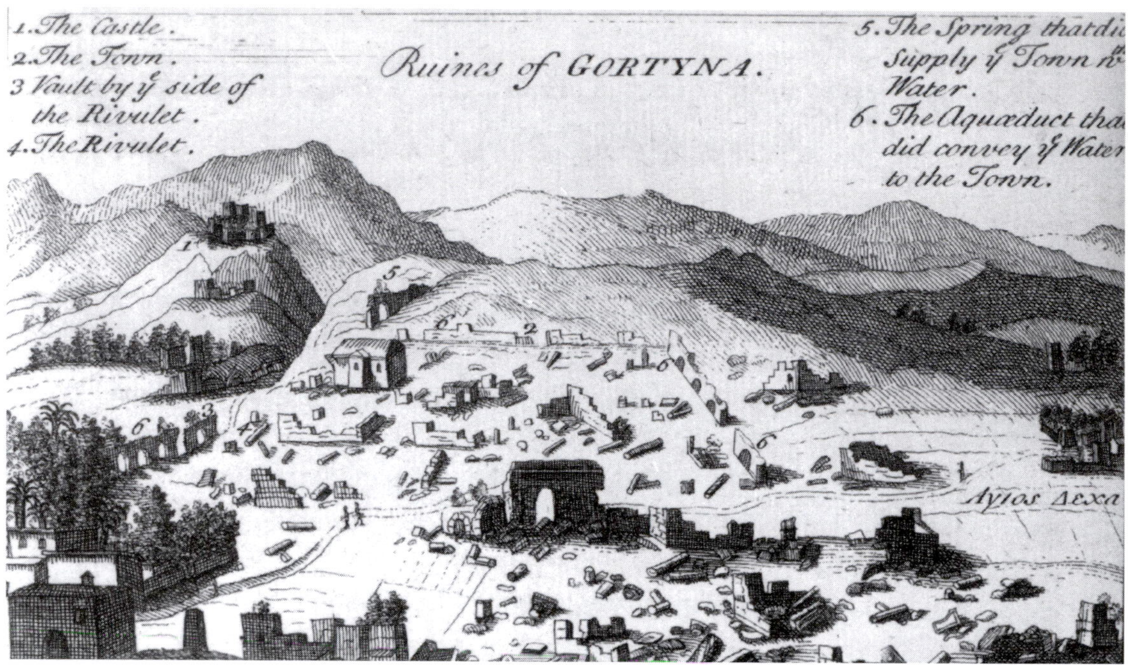

FIG. 4 Gortyna. *c.* 1700 (J. P. de Tournefort, *A Voyage into the Levant* . . . I (1718) pl. 12)

(FIG. 4) and the reputed (at least since Buondelmonti) tomb of Caiaphas at Knossos are clear forerunners of Robert Pashley's brilliant and still fundamental work nearly a hundred years later.

Like the earlier travellers Pococke has much on agricultural products and export trade, oil to France for soap-making and to Germany and England, a little silk, wax and honey, much strong and cheap wine, raisins, figs and almonds. He has lengthy descriptions of people, manners and dress, of pottery making at Margarites, of the town of Candia, now well built, with broad and handsome streets though with desolate parts near the walls, much as Randolph had found. He has details on wild herbs and the poisonous spider. He climbed Mount Ida, where shepherds placed snow on stones in the sun, 'receiving water in their bottles as it melted'.

Pococke well exemplifies eighteenth-century spirit, sympathetic, curious for polymathic observational detail, lightly moralistic in social and religious comment, staid alongside Lithgow or even Sandys. Much more than his predecessors he describes administrative and political as well as fiscal structures. In this he allows us to recognise the limits of earlier travellers' contributions, highly informative of everyday life, of the people, their customs and beliefs, of agricultural production and natural environment. They also sometimes include valuable comments on the remnants of ancient Crete. To all this Pococke adds awareness of other major dimensions, primarily political, ecclesiastical and historical. This fuller view of affairs begins to relate to the large actuality (and even larger bibliography) of Cretan political and economic history in the Venetian and Ottoman periods.

British and Irish travellers, including others

not described here, make up only about eleven per cent of those who have left accounts. Many other European and occasional Turkish nationals contribute a large fund of significant information. Buondelmonti, Belon and Tournefort among these other visitors, the great Italian inspectors for the Serene Republic in Crete and Belli, resident doctor at Khania, are the outstanding figures before Pococke; Meursius and Dapper are the most informative of those who wrote on Crete from home. After Pococke, among late eighteenth-century travels, the visit of Sibthorp in 1786 should be noticed, the fruit of which was the inclusion of three hundred and thirty plant species in his, Smith's and Lindley's sumptuous and magisterial ten-volume *Flora Graeca Sibthorpiana* (1806–40).

In the nineteenth century four travellers carried exploration and publication on Crete to a wholly new level. Each presents a wealth of information based on direct observation, varying according to their individual interests but at a standard far exceeding previous work. First came the Austrian Sieber, in Crete throughout 1817, whose work of over nine hundred pages, *Reise nach der Insel Kreta* . . ., appeared in 1823. His interests were the Cretan environment, especially flora, archaeology, economics, ethnography, folklore and demography. The Frenchman Raulin, in the island throughout 1845, has left an unsurpassed account, in over a thousand pages, of the Cretan environment, botany and agriculture in his *Description physique et naturelle de l'ile de Crète* (1869). The other two travellers were British, Pashley, in Crete in 1834, and Spratt, who worked offshore to produce the Admiralty Charts and onshore for his geological map of the island, in 1851–3 and 1858–9.

Pashley's *Travels in Crete* (1837) brilliantly applies knowledge of ancient Crete to identification of ancient cities on the ground, as well as displaying mastery of Venetian sources and of modern Cretan Greek, which he uses in recording many *mantinadhes*, songs and sayings, and bringing his own training as an economist to bear on Cretan population and production statistics, imports and exports. The condition of the island, at a low point in its history even by the dismal standards of late Ottoman control, is graphically and perceptively observed.

Spratt's emphasis some twenty years later is different, but equally invaluable. A natural scientist, like Raulin a few years before him, he concentrates on the physical geography and geology, in the process ascending Mt Ida with his instruments and observations. His *Travels and Researches in Crete* (1865) also tackles many problems of ancient topography, based again on personal exploration (and occasionally in disagreement with Pashley), as well as describing the condition of the people as he found them. Excellent illustrators accompanied both Pashley and Spratt, as brilliant botanical artists had drawn for Sibthorp and Sieber. But the prize for nineteenth-century visual representation of the island, actually following a long and rich tradition, must go to Edward Lear, who made nearly two hundred sketches on his visit in 1864. These were rapidly turned into water-colours upon his return to England. His delightful, grumbling, informative and personal journal was completed in 1867, but not published until 1984 (Rowena Fowler (ed.), *Edward Lear, the Cretan Journal*), including over thirty of his paintings.

The major British contributions to published knowledge of Crete thus came in the nineteenth century, leading up to the first travels of Arthur Evans in 1894. But our earlier writers, pilgrims, merchants, botanists, enquiring travellers and their illustrators, have left much precious and often original information and insights into the Great Island.

PETER WARREN

The bibliography of early east Mediterranean travel, even just that which includes Crete, is very large. Details of the primary sources cited and of information given may be found in the following brief selection of secondary works.

E. Angelomati-Tsoungaraki, 'I Kriti sta periigitika keimena (teli 17ou–arches19ou aiona)', *Pepragmena tou 6 Kritologikou Synedriou* 3 (1990), 9–37.

H. Gaspares, *Physiko kai agrotiko topio sti mesaioniki Kriti 13os–14os ai.* (Athens, 1994).

R. Hakluyt, *The Principal Navigations Voyages Traffiques and Discoveries of the English Nation Made by Sea or Over-land to the Remote and Farthest Distant Quarters of the Earth at any time within the compasse of these 1600 Yeers* (Glasgow, 1904), v.

D. Hemmerdinger Iliadou, 'La Crète sous la domination vénitienne et lors de la conquête turque (1322–1684). Reseignements nouveaux ou peu connus d'après les pélerins et les voyageurs' *Studi Veneziani* 9 (1967), 535–623.

D. Hemmerdinger Iliadou, 'La Crète sous la domination vénitienne et lors de la conquête turque (1322–1684)', *Studi Veneziani* 15 (1973), 451–584.

W. R. Lowder, 'Candie Wyne. Some documents relating to trade beween England and Crete during the reign of King Henry VIII', *Ellenika* 12 (1952), 97–102.

E. Platakis, *Xenoi physiodiphai, geographoi kai periigitai peri Kritis kata tous 12–19 aionas* (Aghios Nikolaos, 1973).

W. G. Rice, 'Early English Travelers to Greece and the Levant', in *Essays and Studies in English and Comparative Literature* (Ann Arbor, 1933), 205–60.

K. Simopoulos, *Xenoi taxidiotes stin Ellada 333 m.Ch.-1700* (Athens, 1970).

J. P. A. van der Vin, *Travellers to Greece and Constantinople. Ancient Monuments and Old Traditions in Medieval Travellers' Tales* (Istanbul, 1980) I–II.

P. M. Warren, '16th, 17th and 18th century British travellers in Crete', *Kr. Chron.* 24 (1972), 65–92.

P. M. Warren, 'Early Irish and British travellers to the island of Crete', *The Anglo-Hellenic Review* 14 (1996), 15.

S. H. Weber, *Voyages and travels in Greece, the Near East and Adjacent Regions made Previous to the Year 1801* (Princeton, 1953).

A. M. Woodward, 'The Gortyn "Labyrinth" and its visitors in the fifteenth century', *BSA* 44 (1949), 324–5.

S. Yerasimos, *Les voyageurs dans l'empire Ottoman (XIVe–XVIe siècles).* (Publications de la Société Turque d'Histoire Serie VII no. 117) (1991).

EVANS IN CRETE BEFORE 1900

Arthur Evans's intellectual journey to Crete began long before 1894 when he first visited the island. By then he was familiar with the work of other scholars in the field of Cretan archaeology, particularly those who identified Crete as a possible source of ancient seals. Already in 1889 the Ashmolean Museum had acquired a four-sided inscribed sealstone said, erroneously, to be from Sparta (FIG. 5). Evans corresponded with Fürtwangler, an authority on sealstones, and learnt that similar seals in the Berlin Museum came from Crete. He started recording seals with a Cretan provenance some of which he saw on a visit to Athens in 1893; he learnt of others from his colleague J. L. Myres, who visited Crete in the same year on his advice. After studying these Evans was able to announce that he had recorded some sixty symbols. Furthermore far from being random they represented a system of writing.

Evans was drawn to Crete primarily to search for engraved seals as further evidence of his theory. His meeting, in 1892, with Federico Halbherr, an epigraphist, who had been working in Crete since 1884 discovering many sites and conducting small excavations, widened his interests (FIG. 6). Evans hoped to discover further sites particularly those belonging to the 'Mycenaean' period, and to excavate.

The importance of Knossos, as the site of a 'Mycenaean Palace' had been established long before. Evans knew of the excavations by Minos

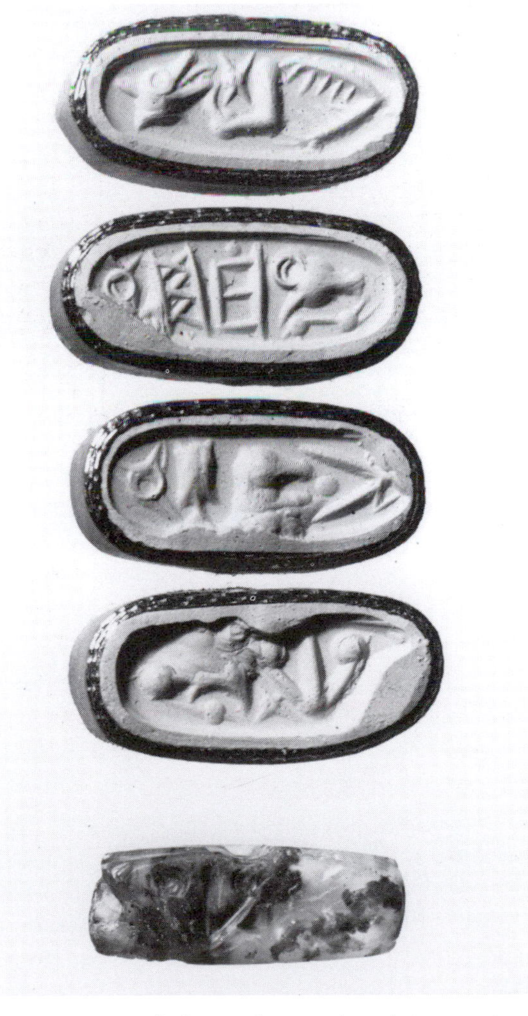

FIG. 5 Four-sided carnelian seal and impressions from it. Kenna no. 148. (Ashmolean Museum Oxford)

FIG. 6 *Seated left to right,* Evans, Hazzidakis, Halbherr. *Standing,* Savignoni, Mariani.

Kalokairinos at Knossos in 1878–9. A pithos from these excavations had been given to the British Museum and Evans, a frequent visitor to the Museum, would have seen it there. He might also have been given some account of Kalokairinos's trials by W. J. Stillman, a personal friend since 1877. He would also have known of the unsuccessful attempt of the latter to resume excavations at Knossos in 1881. Stillman was followed by other would be excavators, H. Schliemann, A. Joubin and above all J. L. Myres who had discussed his plans at length with Evans. Although Myres's own plans came to naught, in the face of opposition from Crete, Evans would not be put off so easily.

Evans arrived at Herakleion on 15 March 1894, with two clear aims: firstly to track down sealstones for his own research and to acquire objects for the Ashmolean Museum of which he was Keeper; secondly to find new sites and to excavate. In Herakleion he was supported by the small group of scholars already working in the field, Halbherr and his Italian colleagues and most importantly Dr Joseph Hazzidakis, President of the *Philekpaideftikos Syllogos* (Society for the Promotion of Education) in Herakleion. Evans intended to stay only a fortnight on the island and within a few days of his arrival he was taken out to Knossos by Minos Kalokairinos. What he saw there confirmed his decision to chose Knossos for his excavation. In consultation with Hazzidakis he began the protracted negotiations that were to lead eventually to the purchase of the site, a necessary prelude to excavation. The land on which the site stood belonged to several different Moslem proprietors and although Evans managed to acquire an unspecified plot in 1894 it was not until 1900 that he was able to complete the transactions. His Oxford colleagues, knowing Evans's mercurial temperament, feared that he would alienate his Cretan colleagues. However Evans was prepared to be patient. He recognised that in the political climate at the time it would be impossible to excavate. Fearful that any objects discovered would be exported to Turkey the Cretans would never have agreed to such a proposal. There was a further problem; Joubin had an outstanding claim for the French School at Athens to excavate at Knossos. However Hazzidakis backed Evans's plans wholeheartedly and 'pooh-poohed' the petition of Joubin whose reservation of Knossos he deemed to have lapsed.

Having confirmed the choice of Knossos as his proposed excavation site, Evans set out to pursue his other aims. His travels took him from Herakleion to Rethymno, south through the Amari valley, then parallel to the south coast as far as Makryialos before turning north. He visited many little-known sites in the Siteia district before returning to Herakleion along the north coast. His success in fulfilling his aims owed a great deal to Alevisos Papalexakis, his guide and muleteer. Alevisos had already accompanied Joubin and the Italians on their travels and had made contact with the peasants on whose land sites were to be found. Everywhere he went Evans purchased antiquities, particularly sealstones, from the dealers and villagers. He was an instinctive recorder of what he saw and did, his mind and eye were as likely to be engaged by the contemporary scene, not least its politics, as its antiquities. During his visit Evans kept a detailed diary which also partially covers later visits in 1896 and 1899; a second diary which once existed has not been traced. A series of small sketchbooks record inscriptions, objects and site plans. His travels lasted, not the fortnight he originally planned, but six weeks. Later in the same year Evans wrote an article, published in *The Journal of Hellenic Studies*, on Cretan Scripts where for the first time he used the term 'Minoan', which K. Hoeck had introduced in his three-volume history of Crete. However Evans continued more usually to write 'Mycenaean' to describe the civilization he had realised preceded that prehistoric period on the mainland.

Evans paid a second visit to Crete in 1895 with his friend Myres. They visited the sacred cave above the village of Psychro (FIG. 7), the source of ancient bronzes bought by Evans the previous year, and conducted a small dig. After crossing the Lasithi and Katharo plains Evans and Myres travelled down to Kritsa. On the way they visited a number of ancient sites with substantial remains. These they called 'forts' and they published their discoveries in a joint article

FIG. 7 Villagers at the Psychro Cave, excavating in 1895. Photographed by J. L. Myres. (Ashmolean Museum Oxford)

in *The Academy* entitled 'A Mycenaean Military Road'. These structures have not yet been fully investigated. Evans was photographed at the most important known as Akhladies which he

FIG. 8 Evans, wearing a silk-swathed pith helmet, photographed by J. L. Myres at Akhladies, 1896. (Ashmolean Museum Oxford)

wrongly called the Kitten's Cistern (FIG. 8). He was anxious to show Myres the great city of Goulas (Lato), which he believed dated to the prehistoric period and an entrance of which he likened to the Lion Gate at Mycenae. Myres photographed and drew plans and subsequently Evans published an article on the site.

On a second visit to the Psychro Cave the following year Evans acquired a fragmentary offering table engraved with signs which he was later to call Linear A (FIG. 9). He then made his way to Omales on the northern slopes of Mount Selena where he was excited to find a 'Town of Castles', each building placed on a rocky knoll (FIG. 10). These structures have yet to be investigated. Many more sites were visited in the Siteia region and notes published in *The Academy*, where Evans again used the term 'Minoan'. He visited Ligortyno and studied the material which had recently been discovered in tholos tombs. He sketched several objects which were subsequently acquired by the Louvre (FIG. 11).

In 1897 Evans visited North Africa. He returned to Crete in 1898, travelling mostly in

FIG. 9 Fragment of a table of offerings from Psychro, with Linear A inscription. (Ashmolean Museum Oxford)

FIG. 10 'Ellenika', one of the 'Castles' on the north slopes of Mt Selena. Sketched by Evans. (Evans Archive, Ashmolean Musem Oxford)

the east of the island, revisiting the sites he had seen in 1894 and 1896 and finding new ones. Much of his time was taken up with politics and he recorded his views in letters to *The Manchester Guardian*. By the end of 1898 the political position had been resolved, most of the Turkish troops had left the island and Prince George, second son of the King of Greece, had been appointed High Commissioner. In 1899 Evans returned to Crete with D. G. Hogarth, the Director of the British School at Athens. The two men travelled round east Crete, earmarking sites for future excavation by the British School. In that year petitions to excavate were presented by the Italians, French and British. The British were favoured by both Hazzidakis and the Prince and it was agreed that Evans should excavate at Knossos independently from the British School, which was to be granted other sites. Both Evans and Hogarth were instrumental in helping Hazzidakis and his colleagues to formulate a new antiquities law.

During his long exploratory forays in the last decade of the nineteenth century Evans's travel diaries, notebooks, letters and published articles record his growing knowledge of the island and its civilization. He had gone to Crete to find a form of writing, and his work was to reveal three scripts which he was to call the Hieroglyphic, Linear A and Linear B. He had discovered numerous sites and had acquired by purchase the land on which the well-known site of Knossos stood. Although many of Evans's 'discoveries' were not original, he recognised their importance and had the gift of communicating his ideas to scholars and the general public in both articles and in lectures. In 1894 Evans had told the Abbot of the Monastery of

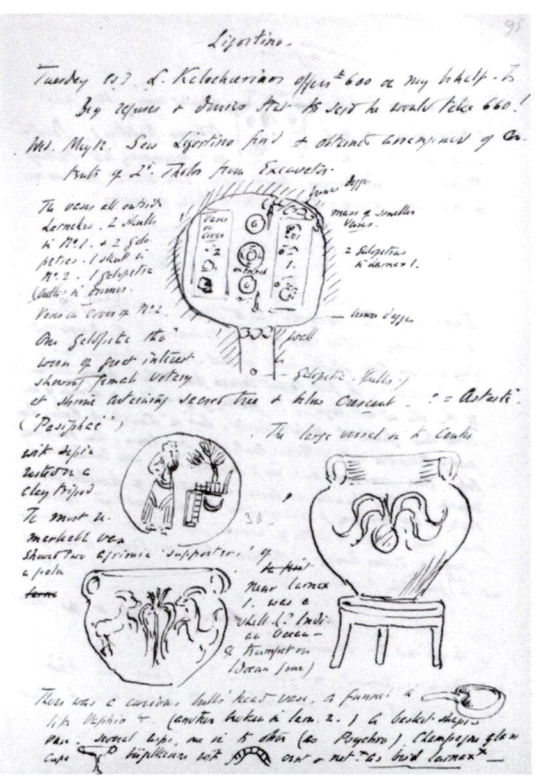

FIG. 11 Page from Evans's diary, 1896, showing position of objects (now in the Louvre) found in a tholos tomb at Ligortyno. (Evans Archive, Ashmolean Museum Oxford)

Arkadia that 'the world belonged to those who know how to wait'. In Crete his patience in the face of many difficulties was to be amply rewarded.

ANN BROWN

A. Brown, *Before Knossos . . . Arthur Evans's Travels in the Balkans and Crete* (Oxford, 1993).

A. J. Evans, Travel Diary for 1894, part of 1895 and 1899. Notebook C. Evans Archives, Ashmolean Museum. Sketches in subsidiary notebooks.

A. J. Evans, 'Primitive pictographs and prae-Phoenician script from Crete and the Peloponnese', *JHS* 14 (1894), 270–372.

A. J. Evans, 'Explorations in Eastern Crete, I. – A Mycenaean Dedication', *The Academy*, 13 June 1896, no. 1258.

A. J. Evans, 'Explorations in Eastern Crete, II. – A Town of Castles', *The Academy*, 20 June 1896, no. 1259.

A. J. Evans, 'Explorations in Eastern Crete, III. – Mycenaean Dikta', *The Academy*, 4 July 1896, no. 1261.

A. J. Evans, 'Explorations in Eastern Crete, IV. – Above the Libyan Sea', *The Academy*, 18 July 1896, no. 1263.

A. J. Evans, 'Goulas: the city of Zeus', *BSA* 2 (1895–6), 169–94.

A. J. Evans, *Letters from Crete, reprinted from the Manchester Guardian of May 24, 25, and June 13th, with Notes on some Official Replies to Questions asked with reference to the above in the House of Commons*, privately printed. (Oxford, 1898)

A. J. Evans and J. L. Myres, 'A Mycenaean Military Road', *The Academy*, 1 June 1895, no. 1204.

K. Hoeck, *Kreta*. vol. 2 of 3 (Göttingen, 1823–9).

THE PIONEERS: 1900–1914

When Arthur Evans began excavating on the Kephala hill at Knossos on 23 March 1900, the British School was already at work in exploring the surrounding country. Ten days earlier, D. G. Hogarth, Director of the School and later Director of the Arab Bureau in Cairo during the First World War where the archaeologist T. E. Lawrence was among his subordinates, had started a fairly fruitless hunt for the early tombs of Knossos. 'In the event I found what I had not expected, namely a well-preserved early town', he wrote in his preliminary (and only) report in the School's *Annual* for 1899–1900, where Evans also published his first report on the Palace.

Both Evans and Hogarth were working under the auspices of the newly formed Cretan Exploration Fund, whose patron was Prince George, the High Commissioner appointed to Crete after the island had become independent of the Ottomans (FIGS. 12 and 13). Its purpose was to promote British excavations in this fruitful new territory and, tacitly, to ensure that the sites that the British wanted did not fall to others. Knossos was the prime case, where various people had shown interest for over twenty years. They included Minos Kalokairinos of Herakleion, who first made soundings in the palace in 1878, the French School at Athens, W. J. Stillman on behalf of the Archaeological Institute of America, Heinrich Schliemann and the young John Myres in 1893, when he set about trying to organise a joint operation between the British School and the Hellenic Society. 'I propose to begin at *Gnossos*', he wrote to Alfred Biliotti, the British Consul at Khania,

The Cretan Exploration Fund.

Patron:
H.R.H. PRINCE GEORGE OF GREECE,
High Commissioner of the Powers in Crete.

Directors:
ARTHUR J. EVANS, M.A., F.S.A.,
Ashmole's Keeper, and Hon. Fellow of Brasenose College, Oxford.
DAVID G. HOGARTH, M.A., F.S.A., F.R.G.S.,
Fellow of Magdalen College, Oxford, and late Director of the British School at Athens.
R. CARR BOSANQUET, M.A., F.S.A.,
Director of the British School at Athens.

Hon. Treasurer:
GEORGE A. MACMILLAN,
Hon. Secretary of the Society for Promoting Hellenic Studies.

Hon. Secretary:
JOHN L. MYRES, M.A., F.S.A., F.R.G.S.,
Student of Christ Church, Oxford.

The Throne Room in the Palace at Knossos in course of Excavation.

The following Appeal, including a Statement of last Season's work, has been issued on behalf of the Fund:—

The preoccupation of the public mind caused by the war in South Africa made it impossible last year to press the claims of Cretan exploration. Sympathy, indeed, was not wanting. A representative Committee was formed, and we were able to initiate a Fund, to which the patronage of the High Commissioner of the Powers in Crete, Prince George of Greece, was accorded. Thanks to the good offices of His Royal Highness, a number of important sites were set apart for British excavation. But of the £5,000

FIG. 12 Title page of the brochure for the Cretan Exploration Fund, 1900. (Evans Archive, Ashmolean Museum Oxford)

FIG. 13 Evans, *right*, and Hogarth outside the rented house in Candia (Herakleion) in the first year of excavation at Knossos. (Evans Archive)

'but want to get a general leave to make trial-diggings at such other sites as I may find promising'. Myres thought it essential that the prime finds be retained in Crete by the Syllogos collection (the forerunner of today's Herakleion Museum) rather than be taken to the Constantinople Museum on the orders of the government. But he gave up the project in the light of the difficult political conditions in Crete in the last years of Ottoman rule. Then, as now, archaeology could easily become a political issue. In 1894 Myres went to excavate in Cyprus, where the British had taken over the government from the Ottomans in 1878.

Crete's independence in 1898 was a chance from heaven for foreign scholars to turn their research on the island, which had been generally confined to travels and study of objects during the 1890s and earlier, to excavation. They were encouraged by the welcoming attitude of Joseph Hazzidakis whose generous support of foreign expeditions is as important, and far too little acknowledged, a factor in explaining the explosion in knowledge of early Crete before the First World War as Vassos Karageorghis's similar approach has been in Cyprus in the years since its independence in 1960. Both scholars took the opportunity to put their countries on the world map of learning and, luckily, there were plenty of sites to go round. In Crete in 1900, besides the British working at Knossos and the Dictaean Cave under the auspices of the Cretan Exploration Fund, Luigi Pernier began at Phaistos for the Italians. The Italian Mission also turned to Gortyn in 1900, where Federico Halbherr had already worked in 1884–7 and 1894. In 1902 Stephanos Xanthoudides worked there, and Halbherr and other Italians started at Haghia Triadha.

In eastern Crete, the American Harriet Boyd (Hawes) dug at Kavousi in 1900 and started at Gournia in 1901. Other colleagues from the U.S. were Richard Seager who started in 1903 his campaigns at Vasiliki, Pseira and Mochlos and Edith Hall who dug at Vrokastro in 1910 and 1912. In the meantime, the British had turned to Zakros, Palaikastro and Praisos, while Xanthoudides worked at Chamaizi in 1903 and started many seasons of excavating Early and Middle Minoan *tholos* tombs in the Mesara plain in 1904. Hazzidakis himself began at Tylissos in 1909. It was an exciting decade whose research has stamped knowledge of Crete indelibly. Although the many new sites that have been excavated since 1960 – or old sites that have been revisited – modify our interpretations, it is still the case that all modern research derives from, even if it is at times in antithesis to, the way the discoveries at the big sites were formulated in the first heady years of Cretan freedom in the early twentieth century. Above all this holds for Knossos.

At Knossos Hogarth worked for nearly two months, moving in a circle around the Palace site searching for tombs and fine objects. On Gypsades hill to the south, following a lead that this was the place where an important Late Minoan serpentine rhyton with relief decoration (FIG. 14) had been discovered, he unearthed the Minoan houses now known as Hogarth's Houses. On the slopes of Ailias to the east, the hope that the conjectural 'lords of the Kephala Palace might have been buried across the water [meaning, across the Kairatos river] proved fallacious'. By the time he finished the chase to the north of Makryteikhos village he had dug numerous test pits, as his map in the *Annual* shows.

FIG. 14 Part of a serpentine rhyton, probably from Gypsades, bought by Evans in 1894. (AE 1247; Ashmolean Museum Oxford)

However unsuccessful the campaign was at finding cemeteries, it marks the School's first efforts to explore the Minoan settlement of Knossos. Today that is still an incomplete task. The largest lacuna in our knowledge of a site that has been occupied for at least nine millennia is the Minoan city around the Palace and the earlier settlements on the site. Researchers still have plenty of work to set the Palace in its proper immediate context and trace the earlier and later history of the settlements of Knossos and how the inhabitants have exploited, and adapted to, the Knossos valley.

Eager for finds and frustrated by Knossos, Hogarth proceeded forthwith to the so-called Dictaean Cave which is in the hills surrounding the upland plain of Lasithi, about 100 metres above the level of the plain, near the village of Psychro. Evans had searched there in 1896, following Halbherr and Hazzidakis in 1886, and followed by J. Demargne in 1897. Hogarth excavated for three weeks from 24 May to 14 June and found the goods he desired, especially in the lower cave (which he called the 'lower grot'). He worked forcefully, smashing the stalactites that had often formed around the offerings in the cave-shrine and using explosives. 'About twenty were employed incessantly till the last day of the dig', he wrote, 'in drilling the larger boulders to receive blasting charges, and in smashing up the smaller'.

The cave had been used, probably for habitation, in Late Neolithic times, perhaps running into Early Minoan, when it may have become a burial ground. From Middle Minoan I until the seventh century BC it was an important sanctuary, where plenty of bronzes and other offerings were waiting for Hogarth to find them. 'When nothing more could be seen in the crevices, which had been scrutinised twice and thrice, and we had dredged the pool's bed as far as wading men could reach, I called off the workers, who were falling sick of the damp and chill', wrote Hogarth in his memoir, *Accidents of an Antiquary's Life*; 'and two days later we left silent and solitary the violated shrine of the God of Dicte'. Hogarth's finds are in the Herakleion Museum (apart from a little pottery in the British Museum and the Fitzwilliam Museum). Evans's finds of 1896, however, and some purchases of his, are in the Ashmolean Museum.

Soon after Hogarth began his hunt for tombs at Knossos, Evans started on 'the prehistoric acropolis of Knossos', better known as the Kephala hill (while 'Acropolis' is kept

FIG. 15 Excavation of the Throne Room at Knossos. (Evans Archive)

FIG. 16 Evans and Mackenzie at the excavation of the Palace of Minos, watching workmen at the south dump. (Evans Archive)

nowadays for the hill to the west that was the classical acropolis of Knossos). His assistant was a friend of Hogarth's, Duncan Mackenzie, the skilled interpreter of the British School's prehistoric excavation at Phylakopi on Melos, where he worked from 1896 to 1899. Evans sent a telegram to Rome inviting him to work at Knossos. He replied on 16 March 1900: 'Agreed coming next boat'. On 23 March Knossos was under way. Hogarth was to write later: 'Over the very site of his [Minos's] buried Throne a desolate donkey drooped, the one living thing in view. He was driven off, and the digging of Cnossus began'. His excavation site on Gypsades offered, and still offers, an excellent view of the Palace site and any work there.

Today it is surprising to see to what an extent in that first season Evans and Mackenzie developed the interpretations and ideology of Knossos that, on the whole, are still strong. Both fresh to the site, and unimpeded by the clutter of previous interpretations (since there were not any), they worked with vigour and excitement (FIG. 15). Although, as Evans admitted, the shallow soil deposits overlying the floors made it easy to move fast, they managed to uncover virtually all the west side of the building by the time they stopped on 2 June (FIG. 16). The finds were astonishing, whether architecture, frescoes, pottery, stone vases, sealings or clay tablets inscribed in Linear B.

Evans never gives the impression of doubting that they had found a palace – and a place for a king, Minos, however mythical that king was – and heads his first report firmly: 'The Palace'. Although anyone starting afresh might hesitate today to call the Kephala building (or any of the buildings like it) a palace, the word has become a technical term in Minoan archaeology for a large and complicated structure of superior architecture, normally with evidence of archives, storage, arts and crafts and religion (including areas that seem to have been shrines), laid out around a rectangular 'central court'. (The central court is the key criterion, in present terminology, for distinguishing palaces from 'palatial buildings', however many of the other traits of a palace they may reveal in terms of architecture, room function and finds.) A better historical analogy today for these building complexes with their courts, set as they appear to be within a theocratic framework, would be a monastery such as those in western Europe in the Middle Ages or that still exist in the East Mediterranean. But, with mythical Minos in mind, Evans stuck to the idea of a palace. And that is what the great building at Knossos is still called.

Evans's approach to naming the different rooms and spaces was similarly expansive or, as some might say although I think it would be unfair, prejudicial. Unlike the Phylakopi excavation, which used a system of letters and numbers (eschewing any possibility of inherent emotive value-judgements about the function of the rooms), at Knossos Evans christened the rooms by their distinctive architectural features or contents. Although many of the names he adopted that year have been modified, terms such as 'The Corridor of the Procession', 'Long Gallery' (and its Magazines) and the 'Room of the Bügelkannes' (nowadays the Room of the Stirrup Jars) are all recognisable as continuing core elements of Knossian studies over the last century. The baroque nomenclature soon became familiar and accepted, although even now it would be possible, and might be helpful, to produce a numerical system for the rooms and spaces of Knossos.

A far more important contribution of that first season was their speedy assessment of the architectural and stratigraphical sequence of Knossos, which by 1905–6 had crystallised enough to produce the nine-fold Minoan sequence (Early, Middle and Late, divided into I, II and III phases) in Evans's brilliant short paper, *Essai de classification des époques de la civilisation minoenne.* The foundation of this system, which became the standard framework for the Cretan Bronze Age, was set in 1900. Helped by Mackenzie's knowledge of the sequence at Phylakopi, Evans quickly grasped the idea of two main periods of use of the Palace buildings, as we see in his first report. There was a 'Kamáres' (Old Palace period) phase, named for the Middle Minoan polychrome pottery from the Kamares Cave which Myres had already tied to the Middle Kingdom in Egypt, through identifying sherds of it that Flinders Petrie had found at Kahun. After that came a 'Mycenaean' (New Palace period) phase, following the terminology used before Late Minoan pottery had been distinguished from Late Helladic (or Mycenaean) pottery.

Evans also recognised that there had been a Neolithic settlement preceding the first phase. The concept of a post-Neolithic Early Minoan (Early Bronze Age) period as part of a tripartite (and 'Minoan') system did not emerge until 1903. As for re-use ('reoccupation') of parts of the building later in the Late Minoan (Late Bronze Age) period, there is no mention in Evans's first report. It must, however, have been in Mackenzie's mind as he wrote to Evans, shortly before the start of the second season in 1901, with the explicit suggestion of such a phase, which he had already adumbrated in his excavation notebooks for the 1900 season.

The speed of Evans and Mackenzie in starting to create scientific order at such a complicated site remains most impressive. It is interesting that the alternative to Evans's Minoan framework – namely, the four-part palatial system based on the building sequences of the palaces, and promoted notably by Nikolaos Platon – takes us back, in a sense, to their first observations before the Minoan sequence had evolved. The palatial system with its Prepalatial, Protopalatial (Old Palace), Neopalatial (New Palace) and Postpalatial periods is best seen as a parallel to the Minoan system, and not as an anti-system. It certainly reflects better the broad course of events in Bronze Age Crete but it does not have the refinement of Evans's nine-part Minoan system, let alone its subdivisions. Scholars tend to find nowadays that they use both systems concurrently.

Further seasons followed from 1901 to 1905. After a break in 1906 because of lack of funds, work resumed from 1907 to 1910 and the final pre-war season was in 1913. In 1901 Evans concentrated on the steeply sloping east side of the palace, with the 'dramatic' discovery – as Mackenzie wrote – of the Grand Staircase, and the many excavation problems that ensued (FIG. 17). Luckily, two of the workforce had been miners at Laurion in Attica and could advise on tunnelling and shoring up the tunnels. That same year the restoration of Knossos began in the Throne Room – a process that lasted until 1930 for Evans, to be resumed after the Second World War by Platon and subsequent ephors. It is now culminating in the Archaeological Service's major conservation scheme, with European Union regional funding, of the Palace site which attracts and has to endure over a million visitors a year.

This current conservation includes refurbishing Evans's 'reconstitutions', as he called them, for the excellent reason that they have become – like his Minoan historical system – an integral part of Knossos and equally of modern concepts of the Minoans and their culture. Everyone is dependent on the notebooks, plans and photographs and on the reconstitutions of Evans and his team for understanding how they observed and interpreted Knossos when it was still in its unreconstructed state. Without these documents, it is impossible to come close to seeing or reconstructing in the mind how the site was on discovery, which is a task that students of the Minoans must attempt repeatedly in the hope of understanding better the raw evidence from those early years for the complex realities of the Bronze Age Cretans.

In 1926 Evans recalled that a German colleague had told him that 'Knossos has passed through three "periods" of conservation – marked respectively by the use of wooden supports, of iron girders, and of ferro-concrete', which was Evans's pioneering contribution. In his reconstructions, which were so often necessary for the continuing progress of the excavation, he and his architects could follow the depictions of Minoan buildings on the fresco fragments which are among the greatest finds from Knossos. His architects – Theodore Fyfe, Christian Doll and, after the First World War, Piet de Jong – were a distinguished and observant group who tackled a horrendously difficult site with gusto. Doll also designed Evans's house at Knossos, the Villa Ariadne which is like a grand bungalow from British India transposed to Crete, where it was

FIG. 17 Christian Doll, in straw hat and dark waistcoat, supervising the restoration of the Grand Staircase. (Evans Archive)

built to industrial standards with factory-type ribbed vaulting (to help withstand earthquakes, which it has done most successfully) and adorned with relief double axes on the drain heads. A raised ground floor allowed for cool semi-basement bedrooms (FIG. 18).

In 1902 digging continued on the east side of the Palace. The following year produced several highlights: the snake goddesses and other finds in the Temple Repositories, the terraced Theatral Area and the so-called Royal Villa, the first of the grand houses outside the Palace to be excavated. 1904 saw the exploration of the Royal Road, with the first discovery of Linear B tablets outside the Palace in the building later known as the Armoury, and the excavation of the Zafer Papoura cemetery and the so-called Royal Tomb at Isopata, which must have been an imposing edifice (but was destroyed in the Second World War). A first-class publication of these tombs, *The Prehistoric Tombs of Knossos*, appeared in 1906. In the meantime work following the line of the Royal Road led in 1905 to finding 'The House of the Fetish Shrine', which later became the Little Palace. Another important – and enlightened – advance was starting a 'reference museum' for 'the baskets of minor fragments of pottery

FIG. 18 On the steps of the Villa Ariadne: Evans, Mackenzie and Doll (*in front*). (Ashmolean Museum Oxford)

taken from the various Palace rooms and from different metre-depths of the exploratory sections'. This is the genesis of the Stratigraphical Museum which houses prime evidence from Evans's and subsequent excavations at Knossos and remains an essential source for study and research. Evans would be pleased to know that there is still much to quarry in the Stratigraphical Museum, especially for modern scholars putting together comprehensive reports of different areas of the Palace and its surrounds – something that on the whole he did not manage to achieve.

After the 1905 season Evans ceased to write preliminary reports for the British School's *Annual*. The period from 1907 to 1910 saw a considerable amount of restoration plus excavation around the Palace, for instance in the Early Minoan houses below the south front of the Palace, the Little Palace (continuing from 1905) and the Tomb of the Double Axes at Isopata and nearby tombs in 1909–10, which Evans published just before the war. By that time he had succeeded in revealing the centre of a completely new early civilisation on the eastern frontiers of Europe, with an unexpected level of sophistication including the use of three different (and then all undecipherable) scripts. He had also combined the evidence from Knossos with that of other sites in Crete to produce a sequential framework for the progress of Bronze Age culture on the island which has, on the whole, stood up extremely well to plenty of testing from new theories and from applying it to new sites. Thanks to Evans, Bronze Age Crete was firmly on the map of world history and appreciation of classical Greece was enriched by the knowledge of a long-lived sophisticated culture centuries beforehand. No one could doubt that in some mysterious way the bull cults and confusing architecture of Knossos were the source of the later myths of Minos and the labyrinth; and it was easy for imagination or fantasy to essay many further connections about the new world of the Minoans.

In 1901 Hogarth took the British School team to far eastern Crete for the first of six seasons of work which soon ensured that this barely known territory was recognised as an integral part of the Minoan culture, as work in the second half of the twentieth century has confirmed. Hogarth excavated at Zakros which, with its fine natural harbour, had long been used as a safe haven and the last landfall for the sponge fishers from the Dodecanese before they crossed the Libyan Sea to Cyrenaica, as Captain T.A.B. Spratt had observed almost half a century earlier. Evans, who had visited Palaikastro in 1895 and Epano Zakros, where he had probably noticed its Late Minoan I country house, recommended the site. It was an unusual season, rich in the irony that time and chance provide in field archaeology. Although Hogarth found houses in the Minoan town as well as pottery of good quality and an important group of clay sealings, he missed by a metre or two the fine Minoan palace at the foot of the town, which Platon excavated starting in 1961. To compound his (mis)fortune, he also made a two days' trial at the site of Petras near Siteia – and missed its palace, which Metaxia Tsipopoulou has been excavating in recent years. But he did observe that 'the Mycenaean [i.e. Late Minoan] village at Petras belonged to the same age, and we can hardly doubt that it met the same fate, as Zakro, Palaikastro and Gournia'.

Hogarth looked for tombs of course but his foreman, Gregori Antoniou of Larnaca, 'one of the most experienced tomb-finders in the Levant', decided that the rock was too hard for cutting chamber tombs. Hogarth observes that this is correct since the one place to show any signs of cut rock is the quarry at Pelekita five kilometres to the north (which Hogarth was the first to identify), while the early burials he found at Zakros were in caves or rock shelters. 1901 is also known for the flash flood in May that roared through the gorge of Zakros, destroying houses and the mill and wrecking the olive trees, 'while' (next morning) 'stranded boulders and stones were strewn so thick on once fertile fields as to make all seem one broad river-bed'. What was Hogarth to do? 'If I could not recover their trees or put back their soil, I could still do what the Briton always does in such emergencies – write a cheque', he wrote. But 'the Headman . . . was evidently as much embarrassed as grateful'. The money was spent eventually on pipes to bring water down from a spring.

Hogarth's team included the young John Marshall, who agreed to study some of the pottery but had an attack of fever and had to leave early. Soon afterwards and at the age of twenty-six, he was appointed Director-General of the Archaeological Survey of India, when Lord Curzon was Viceroy. Later, he attributed any skill in exploring such sites as Harappa, Mohenjo-daro and Taxila to what he had learnt as a student of the British School. 'It fell to me to be . . . the first exponent' (of archaeology and scientific excavation in India), he wrote in 1936, 'and to train up a body of students whose work is still based on the traditions and methods developed on the soil of Greece'.

FIG. 19 The first excavators of Palaikastro: Dawkins, Bosanquet and ?Myres. Angathia 1903. (BSA Archive)

There were two other projects in eastern Crete in those early years. In 1901–2 R.C. Bosanquet, who succeeded Hogarth as Director of the School, worked at the long-lived inland site of Praisos and in 1902–6 led a distinguished group which included R.M. Dawkins and J. L. Myres (FIG. 19) in investigating the Minoan town of Palaikastro and its surrounds. It was a fruitful undertaking, both for recovering much of a prosperous town that recalls the wealthy merchants' democracy of wool towns in the Cotswolds or wine towns in France or Germany in which no one house predominates, and for the finds, including figurines of humans and animals from the peak sanctuary of Petsophas. The report of the third season of 1904 is the first to use the new terminology of Early, Middle and Late Minoan (FIGS. 20 and 21).

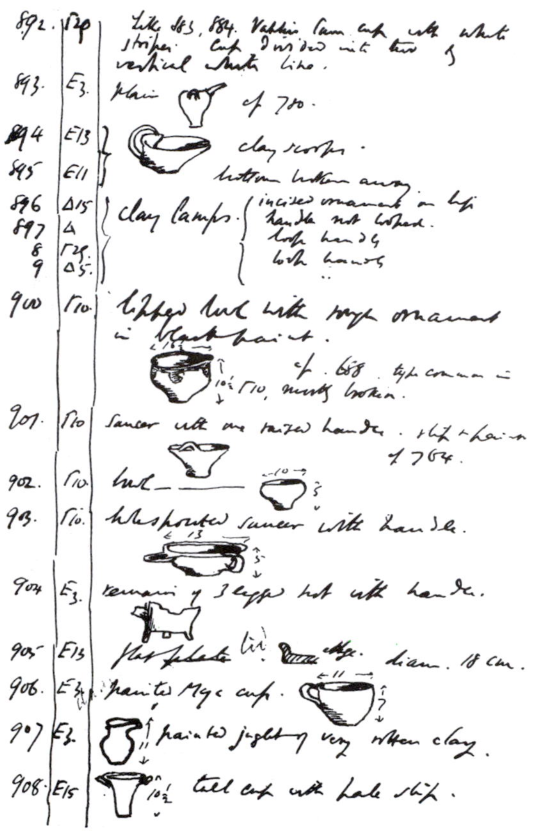

FIG. 20 A page from Bosanquet's notebook for Roussolakos, 1903. (BSA Archive)

That year, however, a new generation of students at the British School turned to Sparta and Laconia, which soon became a focus of British research in Greece – to such a degree that the Annual Meeting of the Subscribers of the School in October 1906 hoped 'that the School's long connexion with Crete will not be altogether broken'. Fortunately, that has been far from the case, not least at Palaikastro and Praisos where recent investigations have added much to our understanding of the eastern end of the island and relating its archaeology and history to the centre.

The period before the First World War saw two other small, but interesting excavations. In 1913 Dawkins and M.L.W. Laistner excavated at the Kamares cave, the sacred cave for Phaistos and Haghia Triadha high above the Mesara plain on a saddle of Psiloreiti, which an article by Myres in the 1890s had turned into the type-site for the best Middle Minoan pottery. They took with them Yannis Katsavalis from Palaikastro as mender/foreman and also Antoniou the old foreman from Cyprus, as he had worked with Hogarth at the Dictaean cave in 1900. 'His wide

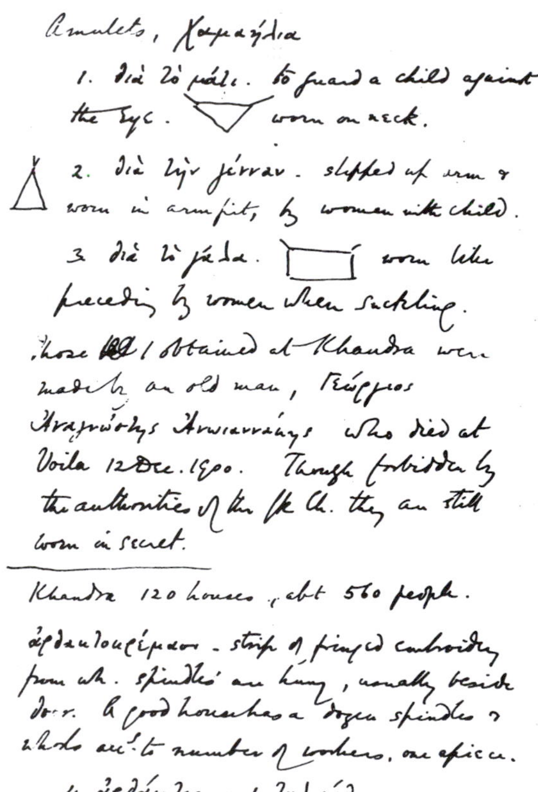

Amulets, Χαιμαλίδια

1. διὰ τὸ μάτι. to guard a child against the eye. worn on neck.

2. διὰ τὴν γέννα. slipped up arm & worn in armpit, by women with child.

3. διὰ τὸ γάλα. worn like preceding by women when suckling.

Those I obtained at Khandra were made by an old man, Γεώργιος Ἀναγνώστης Ἀντωνιαννάκης who died at Voila 12 Dec. 1900. Though forbidden by the authorities of the Gk Ch. they are still worn in secret.

Khandra 120 houses, abt 560 people.

ἀρδαλουσίμαρον – strip of fringed embroidery from wh. spindles are hung, usually beside door. A good house has a dozen spindles & whorls acc. to number of workers, one apiece.

4 ἀρδάλια = 1 ...

FIG. 21 A record of the use of amulets and embroideries made by Bosanquet while travelling in Crete. (BSA Archive)

experience . . . assured that nothing would be left undone to make the [Kamares] cave yield its secrets', they wrote. In April and May 1914, following a lead from Hazzidakis, Dawkins excavated part of a Late Minoan I, Late Minoan III and Archaic settlement, together with a *tholos* tomb, at Plati on the plain of Lasithi. It brought British excavating in Crete back to the area of one of the pioneering campaigns of 1900 – and was in turn to lead on to the exciting discoveries of John Pendlebury in the 1930s in Lasithi.

So the pattern was set, which has marked British work in Crete ever since, of attempting to study the whole of the island – and not just in its Minoan phases or just at Knossos where the British were fortunate to have the opportunity to work. This interaction in research between the centre and the regions has proved exceptionally fruitful in understanding both and their relationships, so as to produce a fuller picture of the archaeology and history of an island that is at the same time large enough to be it own (small) continent. The decade and a half of work that Evans and Hogarth started in 1900 remains an exciting and perhaps unparalleled achievement in establishing so much so quickly about Crete and the new world of its Bronze Age.

GERALD CADOGAN

J. Boardman, *The Cretan Collection in Oxford. The Dictaean Cave and Iron Age Crete* (Oxford, 1961).

R.C. Bosanquet et al., reports on Palaikastro, *BSA* 8 (1901–2) – 12 (1905–6).

R.C. Bosanquet et al., reports on Praisos, *BSA* 8 (1901–2), 11 (1904–5) and 12 (1905–6).

A. Brown, *Arthur Evans and the Palace of Minos* (Oxford, 1983).

R.M. Dawkins, report on Plati, *BSA* 20 (1913–4).

R.M. Dawkins and M.L.W. Laistner, report on the Kamares cave, *BSA* 19 (1912–3).

A.J. Evans, *The Palace of Minos at Knossos* i–iv with index volume (London, 1921–36). For further reports of the excavations, see also especially *BSA* 6 (1899–1900) – 11 (1904–5), and *Archaeologia* 59 (1906) and 65 (1914).

J. Evans, *Time and Chance: the Story of Arthur Evans and his Forebears* (London, 1943).

D.G. Hogarth, *Accidents of an Antiquary's Life* (London, 1910). See also reports on the Dictaean Cave in *BSA* 6 (1899–1900) and on Zakros and Petras in *BSA* 7 (1900–1).

S. Horowitz, *The Find of a Lifetime: Sir Arthur Evans and the Discovery of Knossos* (London, 1981).

N. Momigliano, *Duncan Mackenzie: a Cautious Canny Highlander and the Palace of Minos at Knossos* (London, 1999).

B. Rutkowski, *Petsophas. A Cretan Peak Sanctuary* (Warsaw, 1991).

L. V. Watrous, *The Cave Sanctuary of Zeus at Psychro. A Study of Extra-urban Sanctuaries in Minoan and Early Iron Age Crete* (*Aegeum* 15; Liège, 1996).

BETWEEN THE WARS

While the map of Europe had changed dramatically between 1914 and 1918, the archaeological map of Crete had scarcely changed at all, and the British contribution was still dominated by the figure of Sir Arthur Evans. He continued to excavate in the Palace of Minos throughout the 1920s, in the South-East and North-West areas, in the Corridor of the Procession, and in both the Central and West Courts. But his main efforts were now directed not so much to excavation as to publication. The first volume of *The Palace of Minos* appeared in 1921, and the fourth and last volume in 1935. This monumental work, both much more and much less than an excavation report, is a mirror image of its author – larger-than-life, self-confident, urbane, and most of all passionate about Minoan Crete and its people.

With the publication of the first volume in 1921, Evans clearly felt that his work at Knossos was entering its ultimate phase, and he took steps to ensure that when he was no longer able to continue exploration of the ancient city other British scholars would be able to finish the great task. In 1922 he offered his entire estate at Knossos, including the Palace and the Villa Ariadne, to the British School, a gift which was gratefully accepted, and legally recognised by decree in 1924. He also made provision for the salary of a Curator at Knossos, paving the way for both a permanent archaeological presence on the site and for on-going research on Minoan

FIG. 22 R. W. ('Squire') Hutchinson. (BSA Archive. MC 5–35)

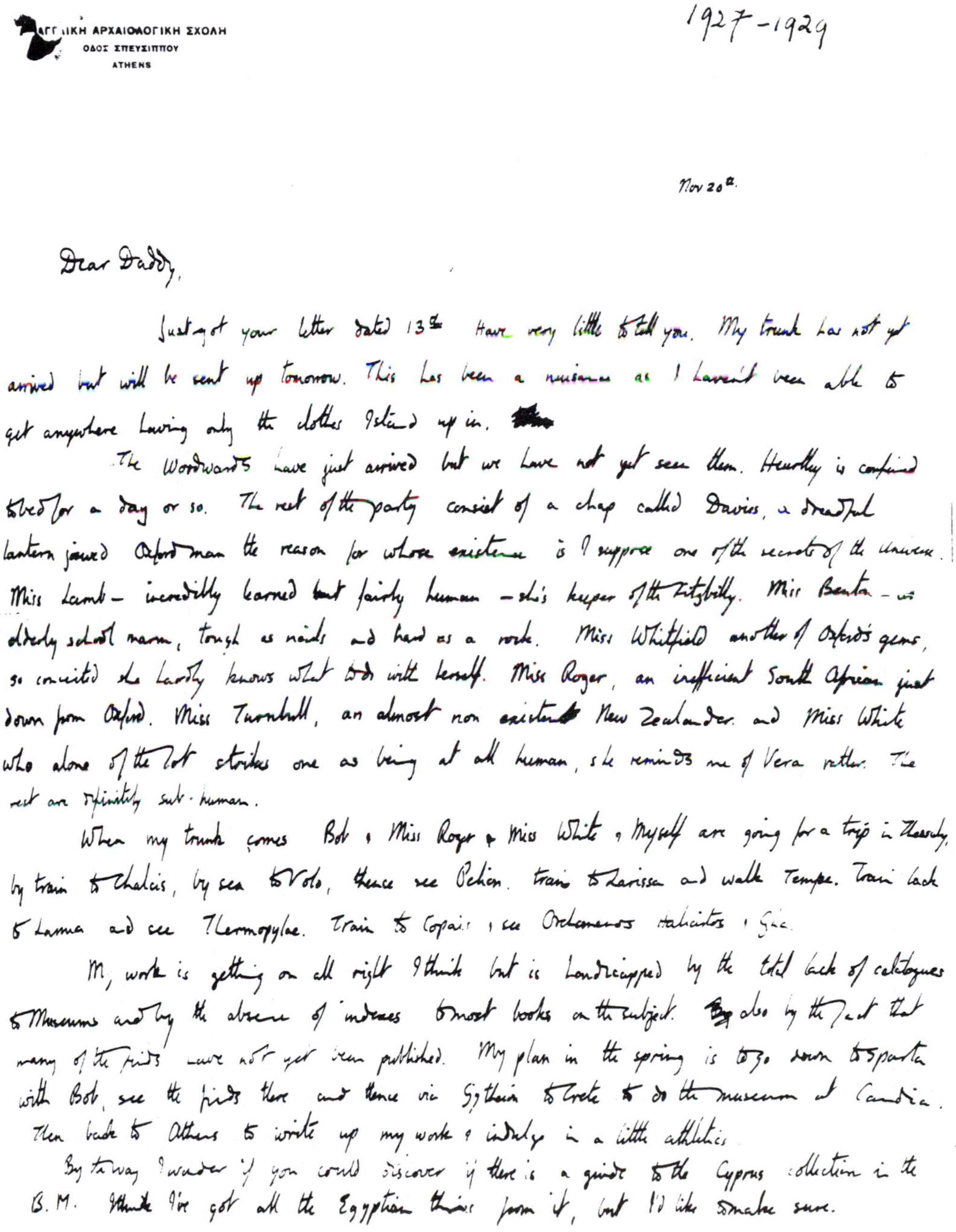

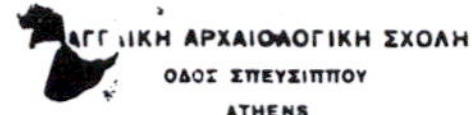
ΑΓΓΛΙΚΗ ΑΡΧΑΙΟΛΟΓΙΚΗ ΣΧΟΛΗ
ΟΔΟΣ ΣΠΕΥΣΙΠΠΟΥ
ATHENS

1927–1929

Nov 20th.

Dear Daddy,

Just got your letter dated 13th. Have very little to tell you. My trunk has not yet arrived but will be sent up tomorrow. This has been a nuisance as I haven't been able to get anywhere having only the clothes I stand up in.

The Woodwards have just arrived but we have not yet seen them. Heurtley is confined to bed for a day or so. The rest of the party consist of a chap called Davies, a dreadful lantern jawed Oxford man the reason for whose existence is I suppose one of the secrets of the universe. Miss Lamb – incredibly learned but fairly human – she's keeper of the Fitzbilly. Miss Benton – an elderly school marm, tough as nails and hard as a rock. Miss Whitfield another of Oxford's gems, so conceited she hardly knows what to do with herself. Miss Roger, an inefficient South African just down from Oxford. Miss Turnbull, an almost non existent New Zealander. and Miss White who alone of the lot strikes one as being at all human, she reminds me of Vera rather. The rest are infinitely sub-human.

When my trunk comes Bob & Miss Roger & Miss White & myself are going for a trip in Thessaly, by train to Chalcis, by sea to Volo, thence see Pelion. train to Larissa and walk Tempe. Train back to Lamia and see Thermopylae. Train to Copais, see Orchomenos Haliartos & Gla.

My work is getting on all right I think but is handicapped by the total lack of catalogues to Museums and by the absence of indexes to most books on the subject. Also by the fact that many of the finds have not yet been published. My plan in the spring is to go down to Sparta with Bob, see the finds there and thence via Gythium to Crete to do the museum at Candia. Then back to Athens to write up my work & indulge in a little athletics.

By the way I wonder if you could discover if there is a guide to the Cyprus collection in the B.M. I think I've got all the Egyptian things from it, but I'd like to make sure.

FIG. 23 On his arrival at the British School at Athens, Pendlebury writes a sharp description of the inmates to his father. He meets his future wife (Miss White), and plans a first visit to Crete. (BSA Archive. JP/L/268)

FIG. 24 Pendlebury exercising at the Villa Ariadne, 1934. (Seton Lloyd, *The Interval. A life in Near Eastern Archaeology* (Oxford, 1986), courtesy of Dr Dominique Collon)

Crete in general, and Knossos in particular, by successive generations of British archaeologists. Duncan Mackenzie was appointed the first Curator in 1926, to be followed by J. D. S. Pendlebury in 1929 and R. W. Hutchinson in 1934.

While Evans was completing his exploration of the Palace, others were adding to our knowledge of the environs of Knossos and particularly of its cemeteries. E. J. Forsdyke excavated the Middle to Late Minoan cemetery of chamber tombs at Mavrospelio in 1926–7, at the same time Humphry Payne was investigating Protogeometric to fifth century burials north of the Palace. In 1932–3 Payne and A. Blakeway explored the Protogeometric to Orientalizing cemetery at Fortetsa, and in 1938 Hutchinson (FIG. 22), assisted by Vincent Desborough and Vronwy Fisher excavated the important, though robbed, tholos on the Kephala ridge. Evans himself excavated the most impressive Minoan tomb discovered between the wars – the Temple Tomb – in 1931, in time for it to appear in the final volume of *The Palace of Minos*.

By then, however, although Evans remained the father-figure of Minoan archaeology another, younger giant, appeared. John Pendlebury had graduated from Cambridge in 1926, after a distinguished academic career exceeded only by his prowess as an athlete (FIGS. 23 and 24). He quickly became actively involved in the archaeology of both Greece and Egypt and in quick succession was appointed Curator at Knossos in 1929, succeeding Duncan Mackenzie, and Director of the Amarna excavations in 1930 (FIGS. 25 and 26). His archaeological double life created problems for the School, and it is clear from his letters that Pendlebury himself found some of his curatorial responsibilities, which included managing the estate, something of an impediment to his main interest in life, which was archaeology in the field. In 1934, he relinquished the Curatorship at Knossos.

If the move was intended to free him to undertake more extensive fieldwork and excavation, particularly beyond the bounds of Knossos, then it was eminently successful.

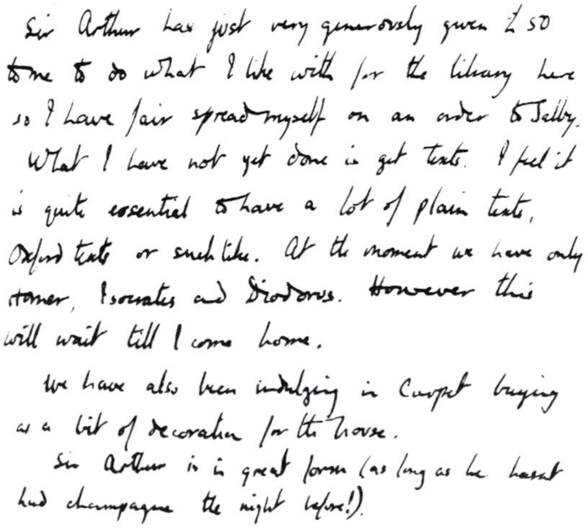

Sir Arthur has just very generously given £50
to me to do what I like with for the library here
so I have fair spread myself on an order to Jelly.
What I have not yet done is get texts. I feel it
is quite essential to have a lot of plain texts,
Oxford texts or such like. At the moment we have only
Homer, Isocrates and Diodorus. However this
will wait till I come home.

We have also been indulging in Carpet buying
as a bit of decoration for the house.
Sir Arthur is in great form (as long as he hasn't
had champagne the night before!).

FIG. 25 A glimpse of a visit by Sir Arthur Evans to Knossos, and Pendlebury's opportunities to improve The Taverna (the house converted for him) and its library. (BSA Archive. JP/L/427)

again it seems obvious to me that the present plans are useless for a guide. They are innacurate and complicated. I am therefore going to get de Jong next year to do a set of simple revised ones which shall be understandable. If you look at them I think you will see what I mean.

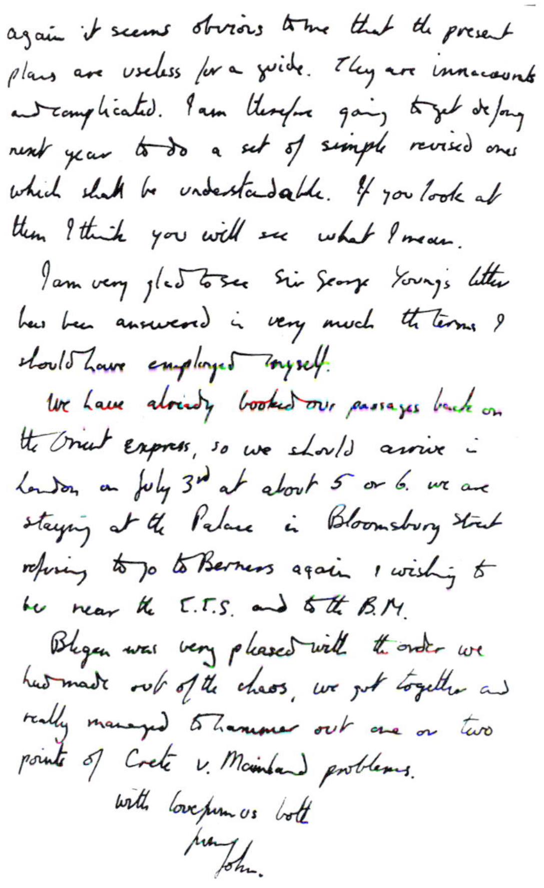

I am very glad to see Sir George Young's letter has been answered in very much the terms I should have employed myself.

We have already booked our passages back on the Orient express, so we should arrive in London on July 3rd at about 5 or 6. We are staying at the Palace in Bloomsbury Street refusing to go to Berners again & wishing to be near the E.T.S. and to the B.M.

Blegen was very pleased with the order we had made out of the chaos, we got together and really managed to hammer out one or two points of Crete v. Mainland problems.

With love from us both

from John.

FIG. 26 Pendlebury plans a Guide to the Palace at Knossos, refers to his reorganisation of the pottery, and to a hopeful meeting with Professor Carl Blegen. (BSA Archive. JP/L/467)

During his Curatorship Pendlebury had rightly spent much of his time dealing with the archaeology, as well as the day to day management, of Knossos. In his first year as Curator he had not only assisted Evans in the excavations in the West Court but had also begun to organise and catalogue the contents of the Stratigraphical Museum. This work had continued apace in the following years, while at the same time he and his wife Hilda had excavated and published the Middle Minoan IA houses in the West Court. By 1932, with the help of Mercy Money-Coutts (FIG. 27), he had begun the publication of the *Guide to the Stratigraphical Museum in the Palace of Knossos*, and the following year his *Handbook to the Palace of Minos, Knossos* was published, so that by the time he relinquished the Curatorship he had more than met his obligations to Knossos.

He now felt free to begin a programme of fieldwork and excavation elsewhere in Crete. Ever since his first visit to the island he had travelled far and wide, mostly on mule or on foot, enjoying the hospitality of the Cretans who

FIG. 27 Mercy Money-Coutts (later Seiradaki). (BSA Archive. MC 4 #67)

grew to know and love him, but also keeping notes on all the ancient sites he saw (FIG. 28). Some of his travels and his discoveries were described in papers published in the *Annual*, others would eventually appear in his book *The Archaeology of Crete*. Nothing could, or would, prevent him from his famous forays into the wilder areas of the island, but he nevertheless mustered enough self-discipline to focus his main efforts now on a single discrete part of the Cretan landscape – the upland plain of Lasithi.

FIG. 28 *Right,* John Pendlebury in Cretan dress, with Kronis Bardakis, a companion on many journeys. (Hilda Pendlebury)

Nowhere in his publications of his work there does he really explain why he chose this location, nor why he decided to undertake a study in landscape history rather than the study of a single site or a single period. But everything we know about John Pendlebury suggests he would have been attracted by the lofty, romantic remoteness of Lasithi and the wide chronological and spatial horizons of the subject. Certainly his programme of work in Lasithi was not as random as it might appear at first sight. Having compiled a catalogue of all the archaeological sites he could discover in Lasithi, he first selected for excavation (in 1936) the cave at Trapeza, the use of which was predominantly Neolithic and Early Bronze Age. This was followed in 1937 by both an extensive excavation at Kastellos, where occupation spanned the period from Early Minoan II to Middle Minoan III, and by six much less well-known soundings at other sites ranging in date from Neolithic to Hellenistic. These were carried out to 'ascertain the distribution of antiquities in this part of the district of Lasithi'. He then turned his attention to the site of Karphi, which at the time he believed to belong to the Late Minoan period, but which proved on excavation to be a 'refuge' settlement of Late Minoan IIIC. Once Karphi was finished he planned to move on to Papoura, a site of the Geometric period, but the outbreak of war put paid to this idea. Nevertheless, it is clear that Pendlebury was following what today we would call a strategic research design, involving a long-term commitment to a single area and a structured programme of fieldwork and excavation. His objective, it seems, was to trace the development of human settlement in Lasithi from Neolithic to early historic times. This approach, together with his interest in, and intimate acquaintance with, the landscape and topography in which he worked, shows Pendlebury to have been far ahead of his time.

The other striking feature of Pendlebury's work in Lasithi was the speed with which the fieldwork was conducted and its publication completed. Three substantial excavations and six soundings, in addition to field survey, were undertaken in just four years between 1936 and 1939. While by modern standards there is here a hint of indecent haste, there is no doubt that Pendlebury drove himself and those who worked with him very hard. Working at Karphi, in particular, can never have been easy and on occasion even he had to admit defeat: 'I am writing this on June 8th having just had to stop work and come down from the site owing to rain and intense cold'. Nevertheless the task was completed, and the report on Karphi, like those on Trapeza and Kastellos, was published in the *Annual* within a year of the excavations ending.

Amazingly, at the same time that he was working in Lasithi and writing-up three excavations, he was also putting the finishing touches to *The Archaeology of Crete*, which was published in 1939. Here he demonstrates just how much knowledge of ancient Crete he had accumulated in the space of ten years, just how much of its surface he had himself explored, and how much he had come to love and understand the island, its people and its history. In ten brief but hectic years between 1929 and 1939 Pendlebury set standards of fieldwork and publication which were to challenge and inspire the next generation of British archaeologists in Crete. He achieved so much, and promised so much more.

It would be easy to believe that Pendlebury's frenetic activity in Lasithi and his rush to publication were prompted by a premonition of what fate might have in store for him. Certainly by the time he was completing the report on Karphi in 1939 he must have been aware that plans for further work in Crete and Lasithi would have to be put on one side. In the introduction to the report he wrote, without further explanation: 'it has been decided to publish the present report without delay'. This was wise, and admirable, but there is no reason to think it was foresight; it was simply Pendlebury as enthusiastic and impatient as ever, clearing the decks and finishing the job in hand, in the sure knowledge that all archaeological work in Crete, Greece and the rest of Europe, was about to be interrupted by the outbreak of war.

KEITH BRANIGAN

J. K. Brock, *Fortetsa: Early Greek Tombs near Knossos* (BSA supp. vol. 2; Cambridge, 1957).

A. J. Evans, *The Palace of Minos* i–iv (London, 1921, 1928, 1930, 1935).

E. J. Forsdyke, 'The Mavro Spelio Cemetery at Knossos', *BSA* 28 (1927), 243–96.

R. W. Hutchinson, 'A Tholos Tomb on the Kephala', *BSA* 51 (1956), 74–80.

H. W. and J. D. S. Pendlebury, 'Two Protopalatial Houses at Knossos', *BSA* 32 (1930), 53–73.

H. W. and J. D. S. Pendlebury and M. Money-Coutts, 'Excavations in the Plain of Lasithi. I.', *BSA* 36 (1936), 5–131.

H. W. and J. D. S. Pendlebury and M. Money-Coutts, 'Excavations in the Plain of Lasithi. II.', *BSA* 38 (1940), 1–145.

J. D. S. Pendlebury et al., *Guide to the Stratigraphical Museum, in the Palace of Knossos* (London, 1933).

J. D. S. Pendlebury, *A Handbook to the Palace of Minos, Knossos* (London, 1933).

J. D. S. Pendlebury, *The Archaeology of Crete* (London, 1939).

J. D. S. Pendlebury, M. Money-Coutts and E. Eccles, 'Journeys in Crete, 1934', *BSA* 33 (1934), 80–100.

THE SECOND WORLD WAR

When the Prime Minister Neville Chamberlain declared war on Germany on 3 September 1939, the grave announcement had little discernible impact on Crete or on British archaeological activities in the island. By coincidence the intense period of British exploration, excavation and research which went on in the 1930s had already come to an end. After the reconstructions at Knossos were completed in 1930, Sir Arthur Evans paid his last visit to the site in the spring of 1935, and with the ceding of the land and the Villa Ariadne to the British School at Athens, clearance of the Minoan palace and its environs continued on a less ambitious and more limited scale. J. D. S. Pendlebury made an extensive survey of sites in the upland plain of Lasithi in the 1930s and finished his last season of digging at Karphi in January 1939. He had left Greece in July the same year, which also saw the appearance of his magisterial synthesis, *The Archaeology of Crete*. R. W. Hutchinson, was Curator at Knossos and in February 1940 was still able to continue excavating, opening a reused Minoan *tholos* and two other tombs of the early Iron Age at Khaniale Teke near Knossos, and in April cleared a Late Minoan II chamber tomb south of the Temple Tomb. As Dilys Powell notes, 'under the Hutchinson régime the Villa Ariadne had preserved during the first eighteen months of the war a vague scholarly calm'. All that changed with the prospect of a German invasion and the consequent departure of Hutchinson and his mother from Herakleion on 30 April 1941 for Alexandria in Egypt. He was to spend the rest of the war working in Cairo. In his absence the post of Curator was left vacant and the keys of the Villa Ariadne were handed over to the British Consul in Herakleion, Mr. Elliadi. Evans's former house was not to remain empty for long.

In May 1940 Pendlebury, having begun training with a cavalry regiment, was called to the War Office in London and sent back in June to Crete as British Vice-Consul in Herakleion. He was given this cover to enable him with immunity to help organise the Cretan resistance to German attack, and it was not until after Greece entered the war on 28 October 1940 that he came out in Captain's uniform as Liaison Officer between the British Military Mission subsequently sent to Crete and the Greek military authorities. His responsibilities left him little time for pursuing archaeological interests, though he maintained contact with Hutchinson and the staff at Knossos who were aware of his clandestine activities, but he did help to identify two scarabs from the funerary deposits at Khaniale Teke, and enquired in his letters home about publications and colleagues. His death at the hands of the German invasion forces on 22 May 1941 at Kaminia robbed British archaeology of one of its brightest stars (FIG. 29).

The circumstances of Pendlebury's execution by the Wehrmacht were investigated by his

FIG. 29 John Pendlebury's grave in the Allied Cemetery. (D. Huxley)

widow Hilda and Hutchinson, and by another outstanding academic, T. J. Dunbabin who contributed his account together with that of Nicholas Hammond to the volume *John Pendlebury in Crete*. Born in Tasmania, Australia, in 1911, Dunbabin went to school and began his university studies in the Classics in Sydney before going to Corpus Christi College, Oxford. He graduated with a First in Greats in 1933 and entered the British School at Athens as a student in 1935. The following year he became Assistant Director of the School and in the spring of 1937 led a small party to take part in Hutchinson's excavation of a large Roman villa accidentally discovered just north of the Villa Ariadne. In 1939 he was appointed Deputy Director of the British School, a position he held nominally until 1946. At the outbreak of war he returned to England, was commissioned as a Captain in the Intelligence Corps in 1940 and joined the Special Operations Executive the following year. After training in Egypt, he was landed clandestinely in occupied Crete in April 1942. He served in the island on and off until April 1945, working with the Cretan Resistance and supplying intelligence to the Allies on enemy movements and actions. Dunbabin eventually rose to the rank of Lieutenant Colonel but in Crete dressed as a mountaineer, rendering him almost indistinguishable from the local population but for the distinctive walk which not even he could master and which gave him away to the Cretans.

Dunbabin's disguise was good enough to fool the occupying German forces but not his colleagues from the Deutsches Archäologisches Institut in Athens. They, however, came to Crete not to take part in the military occupation but to carry out archaeological fieldwork at the instigation of the Commander of the 5th Mountain Division, General Julius Ringel, who took up residence in June 1941 in the Villa Ariadne, and the Commander of Fortress Crete in Khania, General Alexander Andrae. Apart from a short dig between 27 October and 12 December 1941 near the Little Palace at Knossos, the German archaeologists concentrated their work in the summer of 1942 in western Crete where they hoped to find a Minoan palace rivalling those uncovered by their British, French and Italian colleagues at Knossos, Mallia and Phaistos respectively. The significance of this undertaking lay in the fact that up till the invasion and occupation of Crete by the Wehrmacht, no German excavations had ever taken place in the island. Nor were they done with the approval of the Greek authorities. News of this archaeological activity, especially the 1942 fieldwork in the Amari Valley which Dunbabin frequented during his undercover military mission, reached Dunbabin from his own intelligence sources. One item which came to his attention this way was an article by Corporal Ulf Jantzen in the Wehrmacht's local

German language newspaper, *Veste Kreta*, of 18 February 1943, which he subsequently quoted in an article on 'Antiquities of Amari' in the *Annual* of the British School.

This study, based on Dunbabin's own observations during the three years he spent travelling the valley, which he and his British colleagues code-named 'Lotus-Land' because of its bountiful food and liquor supplies, was published 'as a small contribution to the archaeology of Crete, and as a token of gratitude to my hospitable Amari friends'. It must be assumed, though there is no documentary evidence known to have survived or even been kept, that these details were recorded by Dunbabin in note form, but his efforts to maintain his archaeological interests are clearly demonstrated by his acquisition during his time on Crete of part of a hoard of early Greek coins, nearly all minted in Aegina, which were accidentally discovered near Matala in 1943. It is not therefore surprising that following the end of his duties in Crete he was drafted by the Headquarters of the British Land Forces Greece in June 1945 into the Department of Fine Arts and Antiquities in the Monuments, Fine Arts and Archives Branch. There he carried out the research for and prepared the draft of the report issued by the British Committee on the Preservation and Restitution of Works of Art, Archives, and other Material in Enemy Hands, on *Works of Art in Greece, the Greek Islands and the Dodecanese. Losses and Survivals in the War*. This booklet was published by His Majesty's Stationery Office in London in 1946 but does not mention Dunbabin's name. Dunbabin also wrote a survey of 'Archaeology in Greece, 1939–45', which was published in *The Journal of Hellenic Studies* 64 (1944). He saw this as complementing the anonymous report he helped compile during his secondment to the Department of Fine Arts and Antiquities.

Despite the atrocities committed by the Wehrmacht against the Cretan civilian population during the war, the death of his own comrades, both Cretan and foreign, and the dangers to which he was himself exposed, Dunbabin remained both during and after the conflict a gentleman scholar in behaviour and outlook. Anecdotal evidence leaves no doubt that he was aware of and may even have accidentally encountered, when in disguise, the German archaeologists working in Crete whom he knew, but he never made any hostile move or disparaging comment against them, despite their connection with the occupying forces, and his reviews of their fieldwork, particularly the results published under Matz's editorship in *Forschungen auf Kreta 1942* in Berlin in 1951, show his respect for the professional way in which they conducted their excavations and treated their Cretan workmen. He resumed his academic contacts with Professor Ulf Jantzen after the war to their mutual benefit, but published nothing about his wartime experiences except indirectly, and dispassionately, in a review in *The Oxford Magazine* of 13 May 1954, of D. M. Davin, *Crete (Official History of New Zealand in the Second World War 1939–1945)* (Oxford, 1953). Symbolically it seems only appropriate that after the Wehrmacht evacuated Herakleion on 11 October 1944, Dunbabin, together with the physician and antiquary, Dr Giamalakis, and a party of some twenty-five Cretans, re-occupied the Villa Ariadne. According to A. R. Burn, 'as Dunbabin walked up the drive, Manolis, Sir Arthur's Cretan butler, opened the door to him!' The Allies entered the city later in October but it was not until over six months after that that the German forces capitulated, having held out in Khania in the meantime. And it was in the Villa Ariadne, by that time British military headquarters in the island, that on 9 May 1945 General Benthag

FIG. 30 The Allied Cemetery at the head of Souda Bay. (D. Huxley)

signed the unconditional surrender document on behalf of the Wehrmacht.

Another Classical scholar, T. B. Mitford, Lecturer in Humanity at the University of St Andrews in Scotland, was seconded from the Dorset Regiment, into which he was commissioned in 1939 as a Major, to the Special Air Services and sent to work with Pendlebury in Crete. He took part in the defence of Souda Bay during the German airborne invasion in May 1941 and escaped to Egypt after the Allies' defeat. In August 1944 he returned to Crete to assist the local Resistance in the western part of the island, carrying 'pistol in one pocket, squeeze paper in another', for Mitford was a professional epigraphist and could not resist the opportunity to record any ancient Greek inscriptions he saw. Though his diary contained notes and transcriptions of the texts he encountered, he published no work on his observations in Crete but devoted the rest of his academic career to Cyprus and Cilicia which provided him with the epigraphic material he used in a long and distinguished series of publications until his death in 1978.

With the liberation of Crete Hutchinson was keen to return to Knossos, of which he was still Curator, but war service at G.H.Q. in Cairo detained him until he was released and able to resume his duties in Crete in late 1945. As it was, he had to operate out of the Taverna, as the Villa Ariadne was occupied from April 1946 to September 1947 by the Liaison Officer to the British Military mission in Crete and other Army and Air Force officers. According the Dilys Powell, 'it was not long before his report on finds made during "agricultural operations in 1940" [i.e. the chamber tomb south of The Temple Tomb] bore witness to the tenacity of archaeological preoccupations'. Though his appointment was extended in the autumn of

1946 for another three years, Hutchinson resigned in 1947 and took up an academic position at Liverpool University. His book on *Prehistoric Crete*, published in 1962, was intended 'not so much as a revision of but rather as a supplement to Pendlebury's *The Archaeology of Crete* . . .'.

Dunbabin, after his assignment in Greece came to an end with his demobilisation from the army in December 1945, returned to England and to a Readership in Classical Archaeology at Oxford. There he devoted the next two years, until Easter 1948, revising an early version of his *magnum opus* on *The Western Greeks* which had been submitted to All Souls College in 1937 for examination for Fellowship by thesis. The volume, published in Oxford in 1948, gave no hint of the causes for the delay in completing this work, but Dunbabin continued to interest himself in Crete, as his bibliography shows, until his untimely death at the age of only forty-three in 1955. As Patrick Leigh Fermor said in his address at the memorial service held in Herakleion Cathedral for Dunbabin, 'we do not only remember him today as a brilliant scholar, but as our old friend and companion and counsellor during the long and bitter German occupation. It is no hard task to weave the encomium of so good a man'.

ROBERT MERRILLEES

A. Beevor, *Crete. The Battle and Resistance* (London, 1991).

T. J. Dunbabin, 'Archaeology in Greece, 1939–1945', *JHS* 64 (1944), 78–97.

T. J. Dunbabin, 'Antiquities of Amari', *BSA* 42 (1947), 184–93.

T. J. Dunbabin, Review of *Forschungen auf Kreta 1942,* in *Antiquity* 26 (1952), 165–6.

T. J. Dunbabin, *The Greeks and their Eastern Neighbours* (London, 1957).

J. Evans, *Time and Chance. The Story of Arthur Evans and his Forebears* (London, 1943).

J. Freifrau Hiller von Gaetringen, 'Deutsche Archäologische Unternehmungen im besetzten Griechenland 1941–1944', *AM* 110 (1995), 467–96.

R. R. Holloway, 'An Archaic Hoard from Crete and the Early Aeginetan Coinage', *The American Numismatic Society Museum Notes* 17 (1971), 1–23.

R. W. Hutchinson, *Prehistoric Crete* (London, 1962).

F. G. Maier, 'Terence Bruce Mitford 1905–1978', *The Proceedings of the British Academy* 67 (1981), 433–42.

F. Matz (ed.), *Forschungen auf Kreta 1942* (Berlin, 1951).

R. S. Merrillees, *Greece and the Australian Classical Connection* (Forthcoming).

John Pendlebury in Crete. (Printed for private circulation at the University Press, Cambridge, 1948).

D. Powell, *The Villa Ariadne* (London, 1973).

H. Waterhouse, *The British School at Athens. The First Hundred Years* (London, 1986).

Works of Art in Greece, the Greek Islands and the Dodecanese. Losses and Survivals in the War (London, 1946).

1945–1990

When archaeological activity resumed after the war, it fell to R. W. Hutchinson, whose Curatorship at Knossos continued until 1947, and Piet de Jong (Curator 1947–52) to oversee the restoration of the property and the other facilities which were Evans's legacy. Due to the heavy financial burden involved and the anomalous position where even the Palace of Minos remained the property of the British School, the formal transfer of the Palace, the Villa Ariadne and the Evans estate to the Greek government was arranged by the Managing Committee in 1952. But, sensibly, the Taverna and its surrounding land were kept for the School's use, along with other valuable privileges including residence in the Villa when needed (by arrangement with the Ephoreia), excavation rights without compensation inside the boundaries of the Evans estate, and a recognised interest in archaeological work in the wider Knossos area. These were the circumstances which formed the basis on the ground for an extraordinarily rich and varied sequence of Cretan studies emanating from the School during the past fifty years, both from excavation and other research. Knossos continued to be the prize site for British archaeological studies in Greece and is likely to remain so. It is still the only site at which the British School maintains a permanent research facility, to the great benefit of those who work there.

Setting the Agenda: The Directorship of Sinclair Hood, and his influence

A Turning Point in British Interest in Crete

At the beginning of this period the influence of the pioneer and creative work of Evans and of Pendlebury were still overwhelming. It was really only with the break-through decipherment of Linear B as Mycenaean Greek by Michael Ventris, with John Chadwick and others, again in the year 1952, that a whole new perspective began to open up, at least for the study of the all-important role of the Minoans in the wider Aegean world. Since British School scholars have been equally dedicated to Mycenaean studies, there was inevitably a continued tension and a fluctuation in their interest and in activity at the two centres, and this is reflected in the amount of energy and resources devoted to each, even though what Hutchinson referred to as 'the battle royal' between Evans and Wace was now long past. The decade of the 1950s was much devoted to Mycenae, where Wace's excavations were reported in the *Annual* most years, and its 1951 volume was dedicated to him. But the emphasis and direction of the School's students, especially in fieldwork, is much influenced by the successive Directors of the School, and six of the nine post-war Directors of the BSA, as well as at least ten of the sixteen Assistant Directors, have worked on excavations in Crete. In 1954

Sinclair Hood followed John Cook, whose interests had turned towards the eastern Aegean, and he shared those interests – as shown by his years of work on Chios. But as Director during a critical period of growth he refocused the centre of school fieldwork back on Knossos. Much of the value of subsequent work is due to his influence, enthusiasm and energy; many rising scholars and fieldworkers studied with him or worked on his excavations, including John Boardman, Gerald Cadogan, Mark Cameron, Nicolas Coldstream, Peter Fraser, George Huxley, John Ellis Jones, John Lazenby, Mervyn Popham, Hugh Sackett, Richard Tomlinson, Michael Ventris and Peter Warren, and most were trained by him as excavators. Many went on to serve the School at the highest level of management.

One measure of the School's growing interest in Crete lies in the number of papers published in the *Annual* of the British School over the years and devoted specifically to Crete. In the decade before 1957 the percentage of all papers on Crete was eight per cent; in the decade following 1957, when Sinclair Hood's enthusiasm and influence began to bear fruit in print, it more than quadrupled to thirty-four per cent; and remained substantial at thirty per cent in the second decade (1968–77), only slightly lessening in the subsequent twenty years, surely a tribute to a profound and lasting influence.

Meanwhile – to return to the Crete of the first post-war decade – Hutchinson brought to publication some of his pre-war excavations (the Teke tombs with John Boardman in *BSA* 1954, the Kephala Tholos and another Late Minoan tomb in *BSA* 1956) and handed some over to other scholars (the Villa Dionysos to Michael Gough); and his wide-ranging study *Prehistoric Crete* (1962) long remained perhaps the most useful and accessible compact survey available. Pendlebury's distillation of his knowledge of the island in *The Archaeology of Crete* (1939) was described by Hutchinson as 'easily the best general account of the Minoan Culture' and has still not been properly superseded. Pendlebury's distribution maps of the island's occupation recorded so much less information for west Crete than for central and east Crete that it was difficult to estimate how much of the discrepancy was due to the facts on the ground and how much to our lack of knowledge, whether caused by the wetter climate and thicker vegetation at the west, or simply by comparative inactivity by archaeologists. When T. J. Dunbabin contributed an update in a note on the Amari valley (*BSA* 1947), his comment was 'it is ill gleaning after Pendlebury'. However, the picture has changed radically with the new findings of recent decades.

Survey and the Widening Horizons of Research in Crete

It was left to Sinclair Hood, who added survey work to his activities as excavator, administrator and scholar, to extend significantly the boundaries of our geographical knowledge of Minoan settlement. Full details of the surrounding area of Knossos, as well as of the palace itself, were made available in the *Archaeological Survey of the Knossos Area* (1958), later revised and brought up to date with the co-operation of David Smyth (1981), and in the *Palace Plan* (1981), worked on with William Taylor. The results of wider research in field survey were published in the *BSA*, some with the help of Gerald Cadogan and Peter Warren, and include 'Travels in Crete, 1962', (1964), 'Minoan Sites in the Far West of Crete', (1965), 'Ancient Sites in the Province of Ayios Vasilios, Crete', (1966), and 'Some Ancient Sites in South-West Crete', (1967). These articles illustrate some of the facets of his work. One is his remarkable stamina, which has often challenged much younger colleagues and assistants (as when he led his Knossos excavation team on a twelve-hour climb from Anoyeia via the Cave of Zeus to the summit of Mt Ida – and back – one Sunday). Another is his success as a stimulating teacher (albeit one without a classroom), a success which might be measured by the record of those he guided. In the case of Cadogan and Warren this would include their outstanding contributions to Minoan archaeology in *new* areas including Debla (Early Minoan settlement in the west) and Myrtos (Early Minoan settlement and Late Minoan Villa in the south), as well as at Knossos itself. The two studies they contributed to *Knossos, A Labyrinth of History* (in Sinclair Hood's honour), one relating early Knossos to surrounding sites and to those further south, the other a discussion of Minoan roads, are surely an avowal of his influence in this particular area.

Survey work by others followed, further expanding our knowledge of Crete and, latterly, bringing in modern methods of survey along with a competence in the theory and practice of statistics and sampling. Work took place in the south (David Blackman and Keith Branigan on the Ayiopharango Valley, 1975–7, 1982), in the west (Alan Peatfield on Peak Sanctuaries, especially Atsipadhes, 1983, 1989–, and in the Ayios Vasilios Valley, 1992–), and in the east (Alexander MacGillivray and Hugh Sackett at Palaikastro, 1983; James Whitley at Praisos, 1992–; Keith Branigan at Ziros, 1993–).

These take their place among a series of regional and increasingly *intensive* local surface surveys by Greek teams and members of other foreign Archaeological Schools. Notable is the work of Paul Faure all over Crete, particularly in cave researches, of the American School in east and south Crete, especially in the Gournia and Kavousi areas, and that of I. Tzedakis with S. Chryssoulaki and others on the Minoan road systems. With a much wider horizon Kristof Nowicki is extending our knowledge of refuge sites in mountainous regions, many never previously visited, let alone studied. Following Pendlebury's researches at Karphi and the publication of the pottery by Mercy Seiradaki in 1960, this site had become probably the best recorded major refuge settlement site in Crete. The increased interest in this field today is recorded in Paul Rehak and John Younger's survey of current knowledge and new excavations (*AJA* 1998). But Nowicki's own feats of mountaineering and endurance are largely responsible for his success in extending our knowledge island-wide and over many periods. He is one among many scholars and fieldworkers who have been able to use and benefit from the facilities (both hostel and library) of the British School at Knossos.

The British School has also made contributions to other areas of survey, such as underwater research (John Leatham and Hood in *BSA* 1958–9) and a study of the quarries of East Crete (M. K. Durkin and C. J. Lister in *BSA* 1983).

Meanwhile at Knossos itself research into the post-Minoan periods was bringing important results: in his volume *Fortetsa, early Greek Tombs near Knossos* (1957), J. K. Brock published the ceramic finds from earlier excavations of Humfry Payne and Alan Blakeway, in what has remained a standard textbook for the typology and chronology of the four centuries following the Minoan era. On a related theme, the rich finds with imported gold jewellery, from the Teke Tomb at Knossos, first published in 1954 by Hutchinson and Boardman, were reconsidered by the latter a decade later (*BSA* 1967). He then made the original proposal that the tomb's first Iron Age occupant was an immigrant jeweller from the Near East (a proposition still further discussed recently by Gail Hoffman *Imports and Immigrants*, Michigan 1997).

Minoans and Mycenaeans: the Linear B Controversy

Among Sinclair Hood's early publications were those on tombs at Knossos, especially his *Late Minoan Warrior Graves*, starting in collaboration with Piet de Jong in 1952, and continuing in 1956 and later, partly in co-operation with George Huxley and Nancy Sandars. They fitted the pattern of a late period (LM II–IIIA) militarism noted by Evans (*PM* iv. 785). But they ran counter to a generalized picture of Minoan society as peaceful, lacking in the arts of war, free from the need for great fortifications like those of the mainland, one where sophisticated arts flourished, along with a certain emphasis on the female principle, as seen in the representations of the divinity. Such a picture of the Minoans in their heyday was outlined by Jacquetta Hawkes (a visitor to Hood's Knossos excavations in 1960) in her *Dawn of the Gods* (1968), a picture she contrasted with that of the warlike Mycenaeans. But in the 1950s although Mycenaean parallels were recognised for these Warrior Burials, their significance could not be fully appreciated. This became possible only later, in the light of the decipherment of Linear B, which was not immediately accepted, indeed Hood was one of those scholars who were the most sceptical of the decipherment. Later the pattern of Warrior Burials was to be dramatically confirmed by Mervyn Popham's rich finds in a collapsed chamber tomb at Sellopoulo near Knossos (*BSA* 1974) (FIG. 31). There, whether or not the burials were of actual Mycenaeans, a possibility discussed in the publication, the Mycenaean connection was inescapable, being shown by weapons, pottery, the assemblage of bronzes and other finds. In addition one of the best synchronisms of the period, linking early Late Minoan III and early Late Helladic III with Egypt was provided by a scarab with the cartouche of Amenophis III (late 15th to early 14th century BC).

FIG. 31 Sellopoulo Tomb 4 (1968). (a) The chamber tomb collapsed, but unrobbed

Continued progress in the study of Linear B was made possible after the death of Ventris by the work of John Chadwick who, with John Killen published (e.g. in *BSA* 1958 and 1962) the body of fragmentary Linear B tablets from Knossos which had not been included by, or available to, J. L. Myres earlier (*Scripta Minoa*, Oxford 1952).

The decipherment of Linear B as an early form of Greek, an achievement in which members of the British School played a leading part, but which from the start had become a co-operative enterprise with an unusually international flavour, was an extremely influential

FIG. 31(b) Mervyn Popham, Petros Petrakis and Spiros Vasilakis clean bronzes

factor in determining the direction of subsequent research. It had made probable the presence of a Mycenaean ruling élite at Knossos at a time when the administrative organisation was still intact, in what is now termed the 'Final Palatial Period'. Evans's Creto-centric positions came under attack, with some reason, especially for the later periods, but, as often happens, the revisionism was pressed too far, so that even personal attacks were made, the 'battle royal' was renewed and scholars were almost forced to take a stance 'for' or 'against'. A major part of the controversy, set going by Professor L. R. Palmer on philological grounds, was the chronological one regarding the date of the Knossos Linear B tablets. Could they really be some two hundred years earlier than the Pylos archive (generally accepted as Late Helladic IIIB/C) as Evans's dating implied (i.e. Late Minoan II)? Palmer's frontal attack in the Sunday newspaper *The Observer*, accusing Evans of deliberately falsifying his excavation records, arrived at Knossos during Hood's excavations in July 1960. In fact one of the hopes of the Royal Road excavations then in progress was to locate a Linear B archive, in the vicinity of Evans's armoury tablets, and to recover and record its stratigraphical and ceramic date without any shadow of a doubt. So the current work was right in the centre of the controversy. It had

FIG. 31(c) LM IIIA stirrup jar

FIG. 31(d) Faience jewellery and scarab

FIG. 31(e) The scarab (Amenophis III)

FIG. 31(f) Gold ring with 'epiphany scene'

become clear that searching for new evidence in the notebooks of Evans and his assistants, to support either side in the controversy, could never be as conclusive as the discovery of a new archive in a contemporary excavation and a controlled context. Indeed any of the major excavations of the succeeding years at Knossos,

FIG. 31(g) Gold ring with enamel cloisonné decoration

FIG. 31 (h) Sealstone with bull, and gold bead wristlet

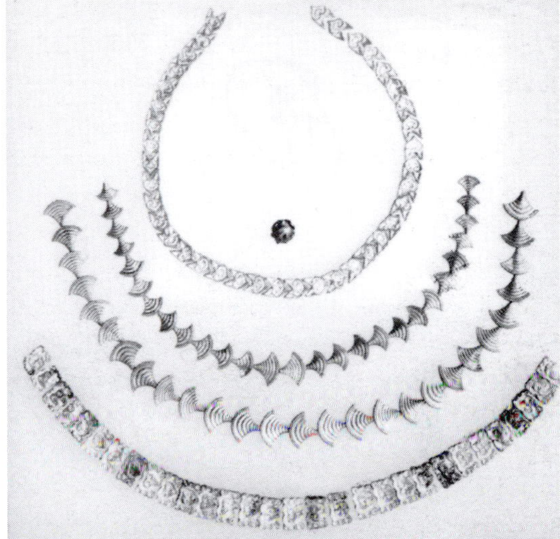

FIG. 31(j) Gold jewellery

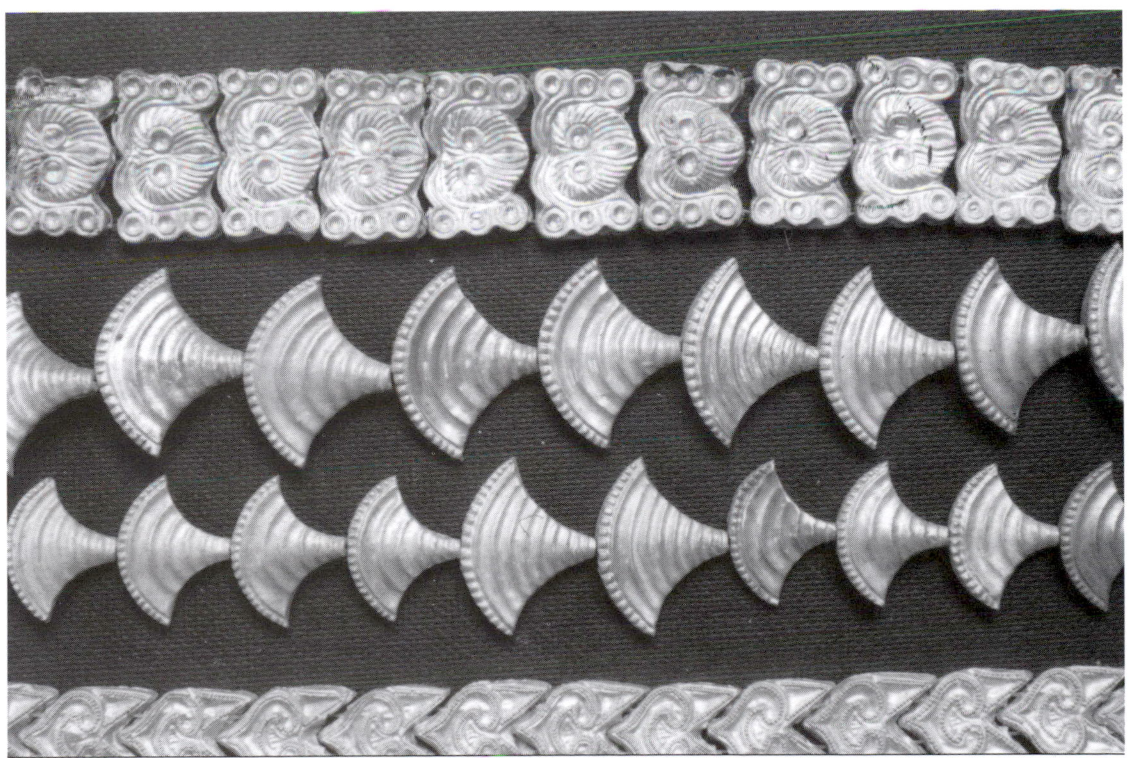

FIG. 31(k) Gold jewellery. (Photos L. H. Sackett)

whether directed by Popham, Warren or Colin Macdonald, would doubtless regard such a result as desirable, even if not a declared aim. But an archive is not easy to come by. Those Linear B documents which have been found (in particular an inscribed stirrup jar at the Unexplored Mansion) appear to extend the use of the script into the later period (into Palmer territory) for Knossos, and more certainly three tablets found by Erik Hallager at Khania do this. But the controversy itself has rumbled on, rather than petered out. Rehak and Younger give an up to date assessment of current opinion in *AJA* 1998, emphasizing the complication that the Knossos archive was never a unity, nor a one period phenomenon.

One of the positive results of this very public controversy (even the Prime Minister, Harold Macmillan, was questioned on the subject in the House of Commons) was a vigorous and broadly based programme of scholarly research, scrutinizing Evans's conclusions and his use of evidence. The re-examination and full publication of his material of all periods was undertaken, and new excavations were scheduled.

The Oxford University Press put the archaeologist's and the philologist's analysis of the situation by Boardman and Palmer on the record under one cover in *On the Knossos Tablets* (1963). Popham undertook a review of the Late Minoan periods, which involved publishing Evans' stored material and a re-assessment of the chronology and nature of the destruction(s), putting him in the eye of the storm. He quickly made his revised analysis of the pottery sequence readily available in his 'Late Minoan Pottery, A Summary', (*BSA* 1967). Possibly his most influential publication came in 1970 with the full study of the contexts of the relevant major destruction (*The Destruction of the Palace at Knossos: pottery of the LM IIIA period*). Part of the work involved a complete re-organisation of Evans' sherd material and its disposal in the new Stratigraphical Museum at Knossos; a major task which has immensely benefited other scholars ever since.

In this general and progressive review of Evans's findings, most other periods were covered by scholars from the British School. John Evans, who conducted new excavations in the Neolithic strata beneath the Central Court and elsewhere in the palace area, made a major re-assessment of the long Neolithic period, vastly extending its chronological horizons by taking advantage of the new Carbon 14 dating techniques. His reports began in *BSA* 1964 and a recent summary was given in 1994 in the Festschrift for Sinclair Hood, *Knossos: A Labyrinth of History*. Reports by other scholars, whose research covers the succeeding periods, are given in the same volume: David Wilson summarizes his continuing re-assessment of the Early Minoan periods; MacGillivray, who is publishing his study of the Old Palace periods in the new *BSA Studies* series, reviews the chronological framework and the architectural history of this era (MM I–II); and Popham, whose refinements of the sequence of Late Minoan pottery styles with his assessment of their stratigraphical contexts have appeared over the years, reviews the position at the time of the destruction of the New Palace, taking his study on to the end of the Bronze Age.

It is significant that an important contribution to this volume comes from Wolf-Dietrich Niemeier, already an acknowledged authority, who discusses the New Palace periods (MM III–LM IB), in a sense the high point. The decipherment of Linear B, and the resulting controversy with its far-reaching implications for the study of Aegean prehistory in its wider context, had drawn into the arena scholars from many countries. Naturally enough they were interested in undertaking research at Knossos itself.

The site, along with its material now available for study in the Stratigraphical Museum, was opened up in a way that would not have been possible during Evans's lifetime. Niemeier, Jacques Raison, Jean-Pierre Olivier and Jan Driessen are among those who have made major contributions to specifically Knossian studies.

Although consideration of the decipherment of Linear B and its importance have taken us beyond the years of Sinclair Hood's Directorship, acknowledgement of his influence is made by all these scholars. And there is more. The re-assessment of successive periods of Cretan history extended to later periods. In the same volume, 'Dark Age' and Archaic to Roman periods are treated by Nicolas Coldstream, George Huxley, Peter Callaghan and Sara Paton. The two former had worked with Hood on his excavations, one notable product being the publication of *Knossos, the Sanctuary of Demeter* (1973) by Nicolas Coldstream, who also published numerous studies of Geometric and earlier finds from these and other excavations at Knossos. In her study of Roman Crete, Sara Paton followed Ian Sanders, whose pioneering survey had been published posthumously in 1982. He had acknowledged Hood as a source of his inspiration, as well as Hector Catling, then at the Ashmolean, and Warren in his rôle as director of excavations at Myrtos.

Sinclair Hood's own work has continued throughout the subsequent decades, not only in the extended task of preparing his excavations for publication, but also in various special studies. Among other things he collaborated with Mark Cameron in producing the revised *Knossos Fresco Atlas* (1967), while Cameron's own study of the House of Frescoes followed in *BSA* 1968. Hood is assembling a corpus of all Minoan masons' marks. And in 1987 he lent his experience in the field to Doniert Evely, Colin Macdonald, Peatfield, Vasso Fotou and Nicoletta Momigliano in their test excavations at the Palace of Minos (*BSA* 1994).

The Following Decade: The Directorships of Peter Megaw and Peter Fraser

Although far from simple, British research in Crete in the twenty or so years following the Second World War had been such that it could be related to the strong influence of one or two individuals, and to a major breakthrough like the decipherment of Linear B. The situation in the succeeding two or three decades is not the same. Vance Watrous, in the third of a very useful series of reviews of Aegean Prehistory in *AJA* (1994), well describes the trend as 'an explosion of specialized studies on many aspects of Minoan civilization'. He mentions a bibliography of 443 articles and books for just the years 1965–77, with topics including 'administration, architecture, chronology, cult, economy, fresco painting, funerary customs, iconography, international connections, ivories, metalwork, palaeobotany and palaeozoology, physical anthropology, politics, sculpture, seals, society, stone vases, tools, toponomy, trade, vase painting, and writing'. Another important development is the exchange of information at international congresses and in their publications. Added to the Cretological conferences have been those at Thera, at the Swedish and French Schools, and the *Aegaeum* series. Expanded Greek resources have also enabled the Ephoreias to initiate much wider and richer programmes of excavation and research. All this is reflected in the yearly reports of successive BSA Directors in *Archaeological Reports*.

Examples of such specialised studies contributed by members of the BSA are those on sealings and sealstones (John Betts, Margaret Gill and Popham, in continued search for greater certainty on the contexts of the Linear B archive at Knossos, and Judith Weingarten); on the Vaulted Tombs of the Messara, and other Early Minoan topics (Keith Branigan), Late Minoan IB marine style pottery (Penelope Mountjoy); on Minoan crafts, manufacturing processes and tools (Doniert Evely); and on Minoan stone vases (Peter Warren). Many others are referred to below, but the inevitable selectivity in what follows can make it possible to cover only the British School's excavations and other fieldwork, and just to touch on the main areas of other research.

During the Directorships of Megaw and Fraser (1962–71) the opportunity for extended seasons of fieldwork was granted to Popham, whose outstanding contributions to the archaeology of Euboea as well as Crete were recently acknowledged by his colleagues, friends and students in *Minotaur and Centaur* (BAR 1996). One of his early contributions, deriving from renewed excavation at Palaikastro which had been initiated with the strong support of Hood, was part of the re-assessment of the ceramic sequences set up at the beginning of the century. Perhaps the most important new development there was the discovery of a LM IIIC refuge site on Kastri (*BSA* 1965 and 1970). But in addition the earlier LM sequences were reconfirmed, and a new LM IB destruction deposit from Block N was fully published. The village at Angathia and the environment at Roussolakkos had changed little from the early years of the century, but the archaeological site had suffered from decades of neglect and depredations including quarrying for cut masonry. Those parts of Blocks Beta, Gamma and Delta which had been left open were rediscovered from among bushes and rubble, with the help of John Hayes, one of the team's many future scholars, who included Cadogan, John Graham, David Hardy, Helen Hughes-Brock, Martin Price and Warren. An interesting link with the early excavations came in a personal letter of greeting from Marcus Tod, Assistant Director of the School in 1902–5, to Hugh Sackett, who as Assistant Director of the School led the excavation team with Popham. In copper plate script it gave a graphic account of the early work, describing for instance a lightning visit to Petsophas by J. L. Myres, which produced the first publication of the peak sanctuary there. The 1962–3 work was overseen by the Knossos foreman, Manolis Markogiannakis, who with his wife Ourania made the long journey to this Cretan 'outback', on all dirt roads beyond Ayios Nikolaos. Twenty years were to pass before the British School returned to the site in a systematic way, years during which Kostis Davaras, in his role as Ephor of East Crete filled the gap with rescue excavation, as well as with strong protective authority to counter the encroaching modern development which has affected so much of north Crete. Meanwhile throughout the 1960s, at another early British School site nearby, Nikolaos Platon was making one of the outstanding discoveries of the half century in his excavations at the palace at Zakros. His new perspective on the development of Minoan culture, re-analysing it into four periods (Prepalatial – Protopalatial – Neopalatial – Postpalatial) became accepted usage, especially from the *architectural* point of view, though Evans's tripartite scheme of Early Minoan (EM) – Middle Minoan (MM) – Late Minoan (LM), with all its refinements into subdivisions, remains essential to the world of ceramic development, on which ultimately our understanding of both local development and interconnections depends.

In the years 1967–8 Warren conducted an excavation in South Crete at Myrtos. The site, on the hill at the sea's edge called Phournou Koryphi, was one of those visited by Hood, Warren and Cadogan on survey in 1962.

Although the slopes were mostly denuded, the crest of the hill seemed to have sufficient depth to contain the remains of a settlement and to warrant investigation. Surface sherds had indicated an Early Minoan II date. The excavation was successful in fully uncovering this basically one period village, and then by studying and publishing its contents promptly as *Myrtos: An Early Bronze Age Settlement in Crete* (1972). The well stratified destruction deposit, the interesting architecture (in a kind of cellular agglutination), the remarkable terracotta goddess with water jug (now the pride of the Ayios Nikolaos museum), and the resulting study of the economic, social and environmental aspects of a *complete* village, made this a model up-to-date excavation. Here was an important contribution to our understanding of the EM II period in Crete, a period which was concurrently getting similar treatment in the Cyclades by Colin Renfrew. Summary accounts of it are readily accessible in Warren's *Aegean Civilisations* (1975 and 1989), and in *The Aerial Atlas of Ancient Crete* (J. W. and E. E. Myers and G. Cadogan (eds.), 1992), itself a monumental and brilliantly illustrated compendium of Cretan sites, based on many days of adventurous, not to say hair-raising, experiences with balloons in the vagaries of Aegean winds. Since the ideas and principles of the New Archaeology were influential and becoming common currency in the 1970s, one might, in retrospect, credit Warren's good sense and humanity with protecting us from their excesses, and so introducing into Minoan Studies the substance of their advances without the jargon.

The 1967–73 excavation at the 'Unexplored Mansion', adjacent to the Little Palace, was the first major undertaking to follow Hood's work at Knossos, and among the first to take advantage of the new facilities at the Stratigraphical Museum. The Taverna Annexe was transformed from *apotheke* and workroom to residential rooms, sherds were no longer washed and spread for study under the pine trees in the small yard there (now a garden), but planned space became available in the workrooms and the spacious courtyard at the Museum itself. Few excavations can have had such facilities so close; it was even possible to run a power line to the excavation for such novelties as an industrial vacuum cleaner, so useful (in skilful hands) for the cleaning of extensive floor deposits.

Popham's full involvement in the review of Evans's chronology, and in the controversies discussed above, as well as his expertise in Late Minoan ceramics, had spurred his interest in excavating an important building at Knossos where a good sequence of Late Minoan periods might be preserved. The site was well chosen. Indeed, its fine ashlar masonry had been noticed by Evans, whose minor tests were not productive and who was deterred by the major overlay of historic periods. For Popham relief from the burden of removing this came when the British School invited Sackett to undertake the first major deeply stratified post-Minoan excavation here in 1967. A large team was assembled, with the assistance in the first year of Cadogan (then Macmillan Student) and of Ellis Jones later. Fundamental was the vital work of Kenneth McFadzean in recording the complex series of superimposed layers, brought to final publishable state by David Smyth. A large team of Knossian workers, most of them trained by Hood, was managed by Antonis Zidianakis, whose first year as foreman in 1967 led to many years of responsible leadership and caretaking both at Knossos and in other parts of Greece. The value of his work was publicly recognised when Popham dedicated the first volume of the 'Unexplored Mansion' report in his honour. Although this site had not been chosen for the quality of the Roman and other late remains, these were substantial (and had even drawn the attention of the German military in 1942, bravely stopped by Platon). They were published by the British School in 1992 as *Knossos, from Greek City to Roman Colony,* edited by Sackett. A large number of British School scholars took part in the study and publication of what turned out to be an important sequence of periods from the Dark Ages onwards. The publication was comparatively full, since an overriding circumstance of the work was that everything be removed in order to make the Minoan 'Mansion' available for subsequent excavation. Architecturally speaking, therefore, the publication is the only record of the finds – except for wall frescoes which were removed to the Stratigraphical Museum. When mosaic floors of a kind never even hinted at in the excavation turned up during machine work in the neighbouring field, the reaction was not envy but a sense of relief.

Relief, however, was by no means felt when Dark Age pits were found to have penetrated all the way down to the original floor level in parts of the northern half of the Minoan building. Nonetheless, during the first season of excavation by Popham in 1968, using the same experienced team of Knossians, an interesting sequence of Late Minoan III re-occupation deposits was found in most of the north part of what had earlier been a very fine building. Evans's term 'squatter occupation' might well be used to describe the later phases. If the progression of life here could be taken to reflect that at Knossos generally, including at the Palace, this could bring some support to Evans's characterisation , which had recently come into question, because it could hardly suggest an important administrative centre. These results from the north half of the building complemented and contrasted with the later finds from the southern half, both chronologically and stratigraphically. In the south were found the extremely rich and undisturbed LM II burnt destruction deposits which form the highlight of the publication *The Minoan Unexplored Mansion at Knossos* (1984–5) by Popham and others (FIG. 32). This provided the fullest yet known, indeed the defining, deposit of the LM II period, the very time which had been associated by Evans with the major destruction of the Palace and the Linear B archives, but which would now fit into the new interpretation of the sequence being proposed by Popham and others. An important part of this publication was that of Hector Catling, acknowledged authority on Aegean bronzes and by now Director of the School, in which he proposed that the substantial collection of evidence for bronze working found in the LM II contexts, including metal waste and crucible fragments, showed a Mycenaean activity at Knossos equivalent to beating ploughshares into swords.

This had been a major excavation in terms of both the work-load and the results. Some 2,500 cubic metres of soil and debris had been removed, and a five to six metre high baulk moved back from the west side of the Little Palace to that of the 'Unexplored Mansion'. There followed almost twenty years of study and preparation for publication. And the results were valuable both for the Late Minoan sequences, outstanding for the LM II period, and for the hitherto undervalued Dark Age and historic, principally Roman, periods. It was left for Kenneth Wardle to undertake a major excavation of specifically Roman character in the last decade of the century. Hood's legacy, especially in terms of method, was handed on to another generation of BSA fieldworkers, and full advantage was taken not only of his team of trained workmen, but of the remarkable expertise of Petros Petrakis as vase-mender and conservator. Future scholars who worked on the site and the finds include, in addition to those already

FIG. 32 The Unexplored Mansion Excavation 1967–73.
(a) Mervyn Popham examines the site before excavation (March 1967). (Photos H. Sackett)

mentioned, Mark Cameron, Jill Carington Smith, Paul Cartledge, Oliver Dickinson, Doniert Evely, Reynold Higgins, Roger Howell, Penelope Mountjoy, Cressida Ridley, Ian Sanders, Elizabeth Schofield, Andrew Stewart, Stuart Thorne, Elisabeth and Geoffrey Waywell, Dyfri Williams and John Younger.

The Directorship of Hector Catling (1971–89)

There were many developments during the years of the Unexplored Mansion excavation, which had been interrupted for two years due to the call for further work in Euboea at Lefkandi by its directors. Hector Catling had taken over the Directorship in Athens in 1971, and Warren had succeeded Popham as Assistant Director in 1970. Popham had put much effort into supervising the building and arrangement of the new Stratigraphical Museum, whose facilities raised the standards of work conditions, and increased immeasurably the accessibility of material, but also made it possible to increase the scope of fieldwork. This eventually put the School in a position to help the Archaeological Service face the intolerable pressures of city development. For while on the one hand the explosion of archaeological activity described by Watrous (and quoted above) only increased, on the other it was fed – or 'force-fed' – by rescue work following tourist development and other building activity through an extended period of unprecedented prosperity in Crete. Herakleion changed from being a provincial centre best reached by boats of varying comfort, to a cosmopolitan city with perhaps the highest average personal income of any in Greece, from which it was possible even for an academic to *commute* by air to Athens.

Several of the major developments during Catling's directorship enabled the British School to contribute in other new and significant ways to archaeology in Greece. The Fitch Laboratory pioneered in making scientific techniques more readily available, the new wing of the BSA library expanded its offerings, and the creation of more courses for British students and teachers was matched by expanded scholarships and bursaries available to Greeks for study in Britain. These were general advances which also contributed to specifically Cretan studies. Catling himself, while devoting his time and the School's excavation programme to Sparta, also from the beginning took a personal interest in work in Crete. His important contributions to *both* publications of the Unexplored Mansion is witness to this; they involved him and Elizabeth Catling in many long hours of study in the Stratigraphical Museum, for which he had now become responsible.

Excavations

Warren and Cadogan were among the first to take full advantage of the new facilities at Knossos. Warren directed a series of excavations

FIG. 32(b) Kenneth McFadzean resetting the upper courses of the west façade

FIG. 32(c) The excavation completed

at Knossos during the years 1971–2, and Cadogan excavated at Myrtos (Pyrgos) in South Crete during the years 1970–3, 1975–6, 1981 and 1982, following Warren in that part of the island.

Warren's excavations at Knossos were centred on the area to the south of the Royal Road, and met with stratigraphical complexities similar to those of Hood's earlier tests nearby. Principal among the finds were a new branch of the early (MM II) road system, running south, and a large LM I building, perhaps a 'grand-stand', associated with it in a later period of its use. New was the discovery of a unique, but rough, building of the Arab occupation near the Kairatos river, dated to the ninth and tenth centuries AD. However, these results were overshadowed by those of his later excavations behind the Stratigraphical Museum (discussed below).

At the same time Cadogan uncovered the hilltop settlement of Myrtos (Pyrgos), with its fine central building or 'Country House'. While the settlement had an extended history all through the Bronze Age (EM II–LM IB), and notable characteristics included an early two-storey communal tomb, MM tower and water cisterns, a street system and rich ceramic deposits, its principal monument is the country house. Its well-appointed architecture can be termed palatial, having an ashlar façade, gypsum-lined bench and stairway, and a front court paved with coloured schist paving and balconies overlooking the sea (FIG. 71). The

FIG. 32(d) Kenneth McFadzean, *left*, and Ellis Jones inspect the Roman road (1967)

FIG. 32(e) A local resident in the 2nd century AD; plaster portrait

finds too suggest local administration, since they include Linear A tablets, clay sealings and the equipment of a shrine. The LM IB destruction deposits, with their equipment and stored foodstuffs (barley, vetch and olive oil) brought the period of final occupation vividly to life. The excavation was an important, even defining, example of a site type of such interest that the 1992 Swedish Colloquium was specially devoted to it (*The Function of the 'Minoan Villa'*, R. Hägg (ed.) 1997). Sensibly, the excavations took place after the summer heat and the distractions of seasonal tourism. Golden vine-leaves, the smell of wood smoke and the commanding view of mountains, river basin and southern sea, enhanced the excavators' sense of the past environment known to the Minoans, the study of which has become an important aim of archaeological research. One indispensible colleague in this excavation and the study of its ceramics was the late Vronwy Hankey, whose active role in Cretan archaeology goes back to the days of Pendlebury. Her long and eventful life made her one of the most interesting and enjoyable of all the people mentioned in these pages. Among her rôles were the *materfamilias* (her rendering of the village style *yiayia* cry could have brought in a whole family from far-flung fields!), the world traveller and diplomat (with experience in places as widespread as the

FIG. 32(f) The major foundations of the Unexplored Mansion appear, with Elisabeth Waywell, Mervyn Popham, Mark Cameron, Susan Bird and Geoffrey Waywell

Lebanon and Panama) and the fieldworker and research scholar (starting with her important publication of the Mycenaean tombs of Chalkis). Her knowledge of Egypt and the Levant made her especially qualified to collaborate with Warren in producing their *Aegean Bronze Age Chronology* (1989), today an influential guide to a complex and difficult, but fundamental, subject.

British School property and interests at Knossos were watched over with care and hospitality by Antonis and Aspasia Zidianakis, to whom all visiting scholars owed so much, until the appointment of Roger Howell as Knossos Fellow in 1977, followed by Jill Carington Smith (1977–80). The development of Herakleion in these years involved extensive work, for instance in upgrading electricity, telephone and water services and the widening of roads, and since Knossos lay right on the minor road, but main route, linking Herakleion with its hinterland, a permanently resident and qualified archaeologist became necessary.

Carington Smith records some thirty-three rescue operations during her tenure at Knossos, many of which required long hours following a bulldozer through the fields, digging a new

FIG. 32(g) A rich LM II floor deposit in the South Corridor

FIG. 32(h) LM III stirrup jar with Linear B sign

pipeline or the like. She published two of these in *BSA* 1982 (a Roman tomb with good Roman glass) and *BSA* 1994 (a Hellenistic winepress). But the principal challenge came with the decision to build the new University of Crete Medical Faculty adjacent to the Venizeleion Hospital on the site of known ancient cemeteries at the northern boundary of Knossos. The rich early Iron Age tombs at Teke lay at the north side of this area and the early Christian Basilica, excavated by William Frend between 1955 and 1960 towards the south. Carington Smith was involved full time at this site, with the indispensable help of Smyth as surveyor, while Catling also devoted much of his time to the work. Some three hundred interments were cleared over the years 1977–9. The

FIG. 32(j) A selection of LM II vases

Stratigraphical Museum was filled to capacity with baskets, bags and boxes labelled *KMF*. The sometimes excruciatingly difficult circumstances of excavation have been referred to in the series of preliminary reports. But the richly documented final publication in four volumes *Knossos The North Cemetery: Early Greek Tombs* by Nicolas Coldstream, Hector Catling and others (1998) makes it all worthwhile and more than justifies the effort. The main burden of the criticism offered by the *AJA* reviewer, appropriately an active member of the British School's new generation of fieldworkers in Crete, was to 'ask for more', and perhaps it will be up to scholars such as himself to provide this, once the mass of new information has been digested.

Other rescue work at Knossos included that of Peter Callaghan, whose excavation of the 'Shrine of Glaukos' in the upper village, and its publication (*BSA* 1978), added to our knowledge of the Classical and Hellenistic periods. Particularly important among the results of his other studies which followed (in *BSA* 1981, 1985 and elsewhere) was his identification of Hadra Ware as a Knossian product. With the co-operation of Richard Jones and the Fitch Laboratory, spectographic analysis, combined with his ability to trace the local stylistic development of this ware at Knossos, made a convincing case. A fuller picture of Knossos in the Early Hellenic and the Roman periods was gradually built up through excavation reports and pottery studies by Coldstream (twenty-one relevant articles by him are listed in *Klados*, the 1995 volume of essays written in his honour), and by Wardle and Hayes (especially the Villa Dionysos pottery in *BSA* 1983). This increased interest in the post-Minoan periods culminated in Wardle's new series of excavations near the Villa Dionysos and in the organisation by Michael Curtis of colloquia devoted to Post-Minoan Crete (the first held in November 1995 and published as the second *BSA Studies* volume in 1998).

Contemporary with the rescue excavations at the north boundary of Knossos, and partly arising from their circumstances, were those of Warren at the Stratigraphical Museum, aimed at making a now much needed western extension of that building possible. In a sense he was faced with a 'no win' situation in that if the finds were of no value the building could be justified, but if important enough to become permanent monuments, building permission might never be granted. That the latter would be the case became apparent not only from his discovery of a well stratified series of Late Minoan buildings, including circular structures interpreted as dancing floor and bandstand (with adumbrations of Ariadne), and other finds including unusual frescoes, but from the publicity attending on the discovery of children's bones in contexts which provoked discussion of possible cannibalism. This only compounded the stir of publicity already affecting Minoan archaeology as a result of the dramatic discovery by Iannis Sakellarakis of the temple at Anemospilia on the north slopes of Mount Juktas, with its scene of human sacrifice, caught and preserved intact by the fallen debris of the very earthquake they were perhaps trying to avert.

This was only one of the many ways in which the work of Sakellarakis had an impact on that at Knossos. As director of the Herakleion Museum and Ephor of Central Crete during a period of strong left-of-centre nationalism in Greece when foreign activity and influence (including that of the British at Knossos) came into question, he was overseeing the entire area. His extraordinarily productive work at Archanes, the richest close neighbour to Minoan Knossos, recently published with Efi Sakellaraki in two volumes as *Archanes* (1997) and his excavations in the Cave of Mt Ida with its millennia of votives, and at Zominthos the interesting Minoan establishment nearby, all surely come within the purview of the Minoan 'capital' city and enrich discussion of its culture.

It should be said here that those working at Knossos were also privileged over the many years covered in this chapter to be able to collaborate with other Greek scholars of the highest calibre, men and women who for all their own busy agendas nonetheless found time to take an active personal interest in developments at Knossos. They all visited, advised, discussed, brought a new perspective or broadened our horizons. Among these were Marinatos, Platon, Alexiou, Lebessis, Tzedakis, Kritsas and Karetsou, whose own excavations, in their remarkable variety, changed our views of the agricultural (Vathypetro), the Palatial (Zakros, Khania), of harbours (Amnisos), tombs (e.g. Katsamba, Armenoi), peak sanctuaries (Kato Symi and Juktas), and most spectacularly of Minoan life, art, external connections, chronology and final disaster (Thera). Work at the latter site has continued under the direction of another particular friend of the BSA in Christos Doumas.

In view of increasing responsibilities, the position of Curator at Knossos was renewed in 1980 and awarded to Alexander MacGillivray (1980–4), succeeeded by Alan Peatfield (1984–90). MacGillivray had gained local experience on Warren's recent excavations. Since there were fewer calls for local rescue excavations, MacGillivray turned his interest to east Crete and, with Sackett and Driessen, conducted a survey of the Roussolakkos area (1983) before beginning a new series of excavation and study seasons there from 1986 to the present. With the help of the Institute for Aegean Prehistory land was purchased in the area of Block M and further north and, while the administrative centre of the town has not yet been found, seven Neopalatial buildings were excavated, and full preliminary reports published in the *BSA*. Perhaps the most dramatic find, associated with Building 5, was the chryselephantine *kouros* (FIG. 70) which takes its place among the masterpieces of Minoan glyptic, and to which the first volume of final studies is devoted (FIG. 33). The renewal of activity at the site has been helpful in stemming the increasing pressures for development in the area.

The quality of excavation work during these years owed much to the School's foreman Nikos Daskalakis and his assistant Andreas Klinis. Their long years of experience in both Crete and other parts of Greece (especially perhaps at Lefkandi) made them invaluable observers of stratigraphy, expert conservationists, and influential advisers to the archaeologists with whom they worked.

Scientific and other research

Catling had been involved in new techniques of research into specific problems of Minoan archaeology long before his Directorship began. Already in 1963 he contributed a paper which pioneered scientific analysis in the identification of ceramic provenance, 'Minoan and Mycenaean pottery: composition and provenance' in *Archaeometry* 6. There followed a series of publications in *Archaeometry, BSA* and elsewhere which developed this and related themes, continuing his fruitful collaboration with the Oxford laboratory, and later with the Fitch Laboratory at the School in Athens. These are listed in *PHILOLAKON*, the volume of papers published in his honour in 1992, along with many others, including studies of metalwork and excavation reports, which show that in addition to his major commitment to Sparta he made time to continue research into the archaeology of Crete. Apart from the Sellopoulo, Unexplored

FIG. 33 At Palaikastro the excavators celebrate with a Minoan ritual gesture the discovery of the ivory statuette; *left to right,* Hugh Sackett, Stuart Thorne, Nicolas Coldstream (then Chairman of the British School), and Alexander MacGillivray. (S. Thorne)

Mansion and especially the North Cemetery reports already mentioned, regular articles in *BSA* (1968, 1976, 1977, 1979, 1980, 1981, 1982 and 1983) relate to Crete. One might single out the research (*BSA* 1980–1) which identified Khania as the probable source of a series of large LM IIIB stirrup jars inscribed in Linear B and indicating a widespread export of olive oil from this west Cretan centre. In addition the increasingly full summaries in *Archaeological Reports* provide the most accessible overview of work in Crete, as well as elsewhere in Greece. The increase in subject matter to be covered by the latter publication during the long and productive Directorship of Catling was commented on by Cavanagh, who pointed out in *PHILOLAKON* that the 29 pages of the Director's first report in 1971 had increased to 113 pages by 1989. Freedom, in retirement, from this burden and the publication of the North Cemetery at Knossos, will no doubt at last give him the full time needed for the Sparta publication.

The Later Years

While Catling served as Director for eighteen years, the following decade, for various reasons, saw four new directors of the School. Elizabeth

French, who has a lifelong interest in Mycenae, took up the post in 1989 and gave her full support to the active work in Crete. The fact that the old controversy between Wace and Evans now appeared irrelevant is as much a commentary on the progress of scholarship as on personalities; indeed most of Wace's positions have long since been vindicated.

Excavation at the peak sanctuary of Atsipadhes was conducted in 1989 by Peatfield, and was followed in 1994–5 by survey in the neighbouring area of the Ayios Vasilios valley in the search for a related settlement site. This work, done in *synergasia* with the ephoria of West Crete, made it possible to reconstruct in outline the settlement pattern in this area both during the Bronze Age and later. Study seasons in the intervening years, which still continue, took place at Rethymnon, where the finely appointed new Museum, the increased archaeological activity, and its modern outlook, reflect the influence of the comparatively new University and its work there over the past two decades.

In 1991 a British survey team under James Whitley returned to the Eteocretan site of Praisos in east Crete for the first time since Bosanquet's excavations at the beginning of the century. New plans were made and the surface remains described, both Archaic to Hellenistic and Minoan, including previously unrecorded LM IIIB/C structures. Extensive remains of this period (probably a major refuge site) among others were found in the wider survey conducted around and in the hill country above Praisos in 1994–5 by the same team.

Excavation at Palaikastro continued with the uncovering in 1994 and 1996 of a major building (Building 6) with Knossian style architecture and an uncharacteristically early final destruction, in LM IA. Elizabeth French visited the site in 1995 for the opening of the newly restored olive press building of Moni Toplou, as an excavation and study facility.

In recent years excavation at Knossos has been directed by Wardle and others, including Macdonald who held the Curatorship from 1990 to 1999. This is discussed in his account of the contemporary position there. It must be said that under his direction there has been a kind of renaissance at the Taverna, and at the Stratigraphical Museum (for which a legacy to the School by Piet de Jong was used), with the assistance over the years of Steven Townsend on the domestic side and with the garden. This is now more than ever, an active centre, where research and scholarly interchange take place in the library, over the sherd tables and in a programme of lectures, all of which draw the interest of those working in Crete, not least our Greek colleagues, in a way fitting for the ancient 'capital' of Minoan culture.

HUGH SACKETT

KNOSSOS PRESENT AND FUTURE

In the last decade of the century in which Sir Arthur Evans started excavating the Palace of Minos, the School's research at Knossos has taken new paths. In and around the Palace there have been several excavations of varying scale, partly in response to the needs of conservation of the site, and partly to elucidate specific questions about the history of the buildings. Outside the Palace a growing sense of the long span of human use of the Knossos valley, of which the Minoan era is only a part, has led to the excavation of a section of the Roman city and a renewed interest in survey and in assembling the evidence of the various settlements and their hinterlands since Neolithic times.

The first project of the new century will be an intensive survey of the valley to be called the Knossos Urban Survey, and a new edition in Greek and English of Sinclair Hood and David Smyth's valuable *Archaeological Survey of the Knossos Area* (1981). Both these projects will be undertaken in collaboration with the Herakleion Ephoreia of the Archaeological Service. Both aim to provide a far larger database with which to address questions of the development of settlement, including contemporary planning issues, in the Knossos valley. Aware of the importance of conserving and presenting the ancient remains, the School is supporting the Service's schemes for the valley, and has undertaken a major joint venture with it and the University of Cyprus for saving and restoring the second century AD mosaics in the grand town house, known as the Villa Dionysos, which are among the most important of that period in the whole Roman Empire.

Excavation

Questions still remain, of course, about the Palace itself; with this in mind Marina Panagiotaki, assisted by Doniert Evely, undertook tests in the Central Shrine area in 1995. They helped to confirm one of the conclusions of excavations behind the Throne Room (*BSA* 89 (1994), 101–2) namely that the arrangement of the east side of the West Wing is essentially a neopalatial one, probably belonging to Evans's period of 'Great Rebuilding' at the very beginning of the Late Bronze Age (*AR* 1995–6, 39).

So little is really known about the layout of prepalatial Knossos, (was there, or was there not, a palatial precursor to the Old Palace?), that every fragment of evidence concerning the first civilised society of Europe is of great potential value. In 1960 Sinclair Hood and Gerald Cadogan had investigated the so-called 'Early Houses' and 'Early Paving' outside the south front of the Palace, but questions still remained, particularly after David Wilson's work on Early Minoan pottery deposits, Nicoletta Momigliano's study of EM III–MM I pottery, and Alexander MacGillivray's re-examination of Old Palace pottery groups. Consequently 1992 and

1993 saw two small-scale excavations in the immediate vicinity of the Palace. The results of these have now been published showing that the Early Houses belong to several different Early Minoan phases culminating in the construction of the substantial South Front House in EM III, while the Early Paving is laid on material of the first phase (MM IB) of the Old Palace Period, and a contemporary ramp may have run south to north over the east side of the house towards the Old Palace (*BSA* 91 (1996), 1–58).

Immediately to the west, restoration work by the Archaeological Service on the South House (much reconstituted by Evans) necessitated a certain amount of excavation by the Service with the Knossos Curator, Colin Macdonald, in early 1993. Important Early Neolithic levels were uncovered next to a trench excavated during John Evans's campaigns showing that proper occupation existed at this early date even on the very southern edge of the Kephala hill, a fact which has a great bearing on estimates of the size of the Neolithic settlement at Knossos, which was previously thought to have been confined to the centre of the hill.

A little further to the north west, where in the 1980s Vasso Fotou had studied the so-called 'South-West House' and 'House North-West of the South House' (henceforward 'Area of the South-West Houses'), Colin Macdonald carried out tests and excavations in two seasons. Here were two of seven independent houses in the immediate vicinity of the Palace, the seventh of which lay to the west, unexcavated apart from its east façade. The results clarified the development of settlement on the slopes around the Palace during both the Old and New Palace periods (*AR* 1992–3, 68; *AR* 1993–4, 75). It was discovered that the two Neopalatial houses excavated by Hogarth (House North-West of the South House) and Evans (South-West House) were in fact a single, probably Late Minoan I, structure built on two successive terraces, making this the largest known independent building at Knossos apart from the Little Palace. In addition parts of houses of the Old Palace period, probably about half the size of their Neopalatial successors, were found beneath on terraces, indicating that the later builders had adapted the earlier terrace system to create larger structures. One Middle Minoan IIA deposit yielded a fragment of a Linear A tablet (FIG. 34), the earliest so far in Crete,

FIG. 34 Fragment of Linear A tablet and impressions on its reverse of the reeds on which it had been placed (much enlarged). MM IIA deposit north of SW House. (I. Papadakis)

FIG. 35 Clay sealing showing the palm of a human hand, from the same deposit as FIG. 34. (Courtesy of I. Pini for *CMS* V). (C. Macdonald)

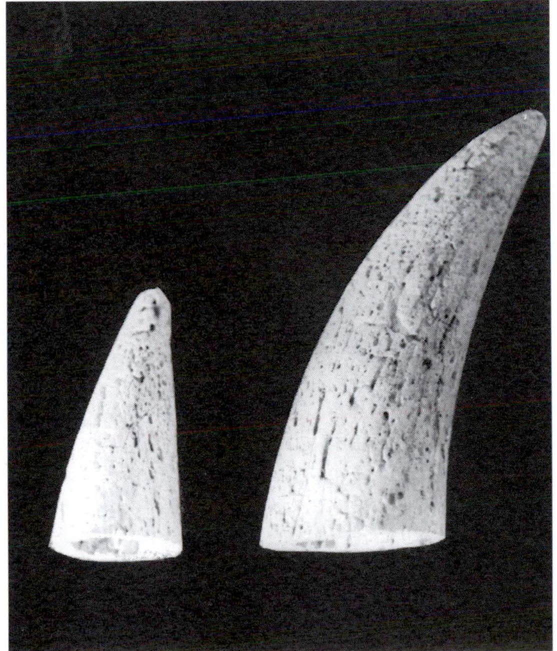

FIG. 36 Bovid horncores, carefully cut; MM IIA, from the same deposit as FIGS. 34 and 35. (C. Macdonald)

among debris from workshops connected with sealstones and horns (FIGS. 35 and 36).

To the west the seventh independent Neopalatial house proved to be a later construction (LM II) built above a LM I predecessor with much re-use in the thirteenth, tenth, and seventh centuries BC (*BSA* 92 (1997), 191–245). Of earlier remains only some scanty Early Minoan walls and part of a house destroyed in MM IIA illustrated how the major Old Palace period terracing in this area had obliterated almost all evidence of Early Bronze Age structures (FIGS. 37 and 38). The latest feature here was a fine fifth century BC cobbled road which swept across this house and the South-West House towards the Minoan South-West Propylaeum, where Evans located a 'Sanctuary of Rhea'.

1992 and 1993 also saw a series of rescue excavations. The Curator was asked to follow the digging of a trench for a new sewage system which had begun at the Venizeleion hospital and ran as far as the bridge over the Vlychia in the south, and along most streets of Bougada Metochi to the west. Glimpses were caught of almost every period from that of the Old Palace

FIG. 37 MM IB Bridge-spouted jar with 'swastikas' (SVII 5, P.771). (C. Macdonald)

FIG. 38 MM IIA Bridge-spouted jar with 'targets' (SVII 8, P.348). (C. Macdonald)

to Roman, but the most notable discovery was a long stretch of roughly cobbled road running north-south along the line of the modern road from the first coffee shop of the village up to the School's Taverna in the direction of the heart of the Roman colony.

Another excavation took place where previously the School had discovered two Hellenistic kilns (*BSA* 45 (1950), 165–92). Here in December 1993, five tests on two terraces revealed much about the Minoan and Hellenistic history of the extreme periphery of Knossian habitation, some 800 metres south west of the Palace. Occupation went back as far as the last phase of the Old Palace period (MM IIB) and may have been connected with bee-keeping. The main phases of Minoan occupation, however, coincided with the transition to the Late Bronze Age with debris from the great earthquake destruction in which was found a Linear A inscribed jar (FIG. 39). Later levels were of mature LM IA, with part of a typical lily fresco, and LM II. This material nicely complements that found by Hector Catling nearby (*BSA* 74 (1979), 1–80). The Hellenistic remains proved even more interesting with the discovery of a ceramic production area, and the intact furnace chamber of a square kiln. The area holds great promise for future excavation jointly with the Ephoreia.

Survey

In 1991 and 1992, attention began to be turned towards the large unexcavated field on the Evans Estate which lies between the Roman Villa Dionysos and the Edwardian Villa Ariadne. Colin Shell conducted a geophysical survey aimed at identifying remains lying beneath the surface using a magnetometer and radar (*AR* 1991–2, 59–60; 1992–3, 68). The field was clearly going to reveal chiefly Roman remains in view of the existence of the Villa Dionysos and the unexcavated centre of the Roman city to the north; in addition, 'Roman Concrete Ruins' were visible in several parts of the field. The survey was not as successful as had been hoped in the light of two campaigns of excavation undertaken by Kenneth Wardle, which were able to confirm some results and reject others (*AR* 1993–4, 75–6; 1995–6, 41–2). These

FIG. 39 Linear A inscription on MM IIIB jug from deposit in the Hellenistic Kiln Area. (C. Macdonald)

seasons of investigation marked a renewed interest in the history, as opposed to prehistory, of the Knossos valley.

Two new complementary projects, already mentioned, which are in preparation jointly with the Service, will together provide more detailed information on the Knossos valley than for almost any other archaeological zone in Greece. One stems directly from the pioneering work which produced the second edition of the *Archaeological Survey of the Knossos Area* in 1981. That volume is a distillation of almost eighty years of formal and informal scrutiny of the valley. The result is an impressive array of information about sites and chance finds, many of which are now destroyed or lost. This information and that compiled since 1978 by the School and the Archaeological Service are being combined to produce a bilingual third edition, as well as a formal computer database into which all future information can be fed to form the first comprehensive and active archaeological archive in Crete.

The main new project, called the Knossos Urban Survey, under the direction of Alexandra Karetsou, the Ephor in Herakleion, and Todd Whitelaw, will make use of, and add to, the existing archive, but will survey the valley more intensively and systematically with organised field walking to pinpoint sites and collect sherds. Our dating of Knossian pottery can now be extremely precise. There will be detailed mapping of old and new discoveries, and selective magnetometer surveying to assess the extent of ancient remains. Apart from the data generated, the two survey projects will greatly assist management of the archaeological zone.

Conservation and Presentation of Sites

It has long been apparent that the archaeologist has preferred to spend his budget on discovery as opposed to study, conservation and consolidation. This has led to rapidly produced preliminary reports of spectacular finds, delays in publishing the final report and neglect of the site itself. Happily, this is changing and there is greater pressure to complete the final study with speed and to take care of the remains which were excavated in the first place. Several of the projects begun at Knossos in the last decade are closely concerned with conservation and presentation. More generally there is within the School a great emphasis on the prompt publication of new material and fuller publication of the old.

In the 1990s the Ephoreia has had both to conserve the Palace and present it to more than one million visitors a year. Much remains to be done, and that which has been achieved owes much to European Union regional funding through the generous support of the Cretan Regional Authority (Periphereia Kritis).

An archaeological park

The idea of an archaeological park for Knossos was proposed by the then Curator in 1995. Since then, the School has been able to finance a pilot study for discussion with the Archaeological Service. A large part of the land bought by Sir Arthur Evans lay north west of the Palace, where, in 1906, he was to build the Villa Ariadne and plant its Edwardian garden. Today, the southernmost corner is taken up by the Little Palace and the Unexplored Mansion, while its northern tip is the Villa Dionysos. These two sites provide an appropriate beginning and end for an archaeological tour, as they represent two of the most important elements of the history of Knossos: Neopalatial Minoan grandeur and Roman town splendour. In between, other aspects of the history of the valley both ancient and recent can be visited, notably part of the Minoan town behind the Stratigraphical Museum, and the Villa Ariadne of Sir Arthur, presently being restored by the Service. This last is of interest not only as a unique English house and garden in Crete but also as the residence of the German High Command in the Second World War and the place where the final surrender of the German forces took place two days after VE day (9 May 1945). The Curator commissioned a study of the Edwardian garden including a full plan, an *index plantarum* and an *index antiquorum* (courtesy of Sara Paton). If a park proceeds, let it be an organic creation to show how archaeology works on the ground.

The Stratigraphical Museum Extension Site

Excavated between 1978 and 1982, the site (part of the Minoan town) was investigated for the last time in 1997 with a view to preparing it for roofing (*AR* 1980–1, 73–92; 1982–3, 63–87; 1984–5, 124–9; 1987–8, 86–104; 1997–8, 114–5). It is to be hoped that it will include access to the important elements of the site: the LM IIIA 'Dancing Circles', the LM IB kiln, the street system, which includes the westward extension of the Royal Road, and the LM IB North House where children's bones were discovered in a cult context (*BSA* 81 (1986), 333–88).

The Villa Dionysos

Under the direction of Sara Paton, a full programme of roofing and conservation, jointly with the Service and the University of Cyprus, is now underway. The work began in 1997 with a preliminary study and first-aid conservation of the fine second-century AD mosaics. European regional funding has been secured to erect shelters above the three sides of the Villa which have mosaic floors. Despite the discovery of another mosaic in September 1998 on a terrace immediately west of the Villa, the roofing, designed by architects Nikos Skoutelis and Flavio Zanon, is being erected. The proposal for the *in situ* conservation of the mosaics is a truly European effort of Italian, Cypriot, Greek and British teams. The final result will not only leave the mosaics in a superb state of repair but also allow their maintenance by Greek specialists who will have followed the process of conservation from the very start.

Storage, Conservation and Study

The Strategraphical Museum is the central working area of the British School at Knossos. Despite concerted attempts to address the universal problem of storage, including full excavation to the west of the building, no satisfactory solution has been found which can take into account all the important factors within the archaeological zone: adequate space for the next hundred years, proximity to the site and to the present museum, financial feasibility, and respect for the environment. Our ability to conserve and store materials such as metals, ivory, bone, glass and fresco is severely limited by the lack of an area to devote to them within the museum.

Much material from Knossos remains unpublished in both the Stratigraphical and the Herakleion Museums. The 1990s has seen a drive to clear some of this backlog, and this will continue well into the next decade. The task has been approached from two directions. The first entails the study and publication of key pottery deposits which can refine our ceramic and, therefore, chronological divisions, as well as informing us about developments in ceramic technology and Minoan trade, both within Crete and beyond its shores. Here detailed work has been carried out by David Wilson and Peter

Day, who have combined modified traditional pottery studies with petrographic analysis (microscopical examination of fired clay matrices) to examine Early Minoan pottery deposits in Central Crete, chiefly at Knossos. The School's ceramic studies of Early and Middle Minoan pottery groups were brought together in a workshop in 1992 (*BSA* 88 (1993), 21–8), followed by the publication of Alexander MacGillivray's study of pottery groups from the Old Palace period (BSA Studies 5, 1998). Substantial new Middle Minoan deposits will be published soon.

The second approach is to publish as fully as possible those excavations which, by modern standards, have been presented inadequately in the past. Most of Sir Arthur's excavations fall into this category. However monumental and wide-ranging *The Palace of Minos* is seen to be, it is not an excavation report. Thus, various scholars have taken on parts of the Palace or other monuments in an attempt to give them the detailed attention they deserve. Marina Panagiotaki is publishing a full report on the Central Palace Shrine, including all the objects from the Temple Repositories. As with all such work, great use is made of the original notes made by Evans and particularly those by Duncan Mackenzie. The new Curator, Eleni Hatzaki, has not only completed her publication of the Little Palace but she also supervised conservation operations for the Service, during which much new evidence was revealed to date architectural phasing. (Both these works are in press at the time of writing). In the meantime she has begun work on the full publication of the so-called Temple Tomb. There are many other such clearly defined units which can be fully examined by scholars in the future. This approach will help to present the Palace of Minos and other ancient sites in the valley in a scientific and comprehensive manner.

Summary

The last decade of field research into pre-Roman Knossos ranges widely. The Neolithic settlement on the Kephala hill, although no doubt centred in the area of the Central Court, proved very much larger in the Early Neolithic period than previously thought, extending as far as the area of the later South House. Close by, Early Minoan building, notably the EM III South Front House, shows a solid kind of construction on the same orientation as the later Palace, but lacking the formal terracing first introduced in the Old Palace period and clearly revealed in the area of the South-West Houses. This more organised approach to urban construction may be a reflection of one aspect of central palatial control. In the New Palace period ostentatious architectural design is added to palatial urban planning in the form of the independent houses in the vicinity of the Palace. The surprising dearth of Linear A tablets at Knossos has ended with the important discovery of the earliest datable inscribed fragment (MM IIA), possibly indicating what many had assumed, namely that written records in Crete are likely to have been used first at Knossos. By MM IIB, settlement can be found as far away as 800 metres from the Palace, although it seems highly unlikely that the entire ground between was covered with houses.

The transition to the Late Bronze Age was marked by an earthquake followed by rebuilding and new building. The South-West Houses appear to belong to this stage and were damaged, at least one of them severely so, towards the end of Late Minoan IA. Both this area and that of the Hellenistic kilns have demonstrated an occupation gap in the succeeding LM IB period followed by an entirely new building phase in LM II (the Mycenaean period), although Minoan architectural features such as the pier-and-door partition are still part of the repertoire. Destructions have been found in LM II, LM IIIA2 and LM IIIB. No new structures demonstrating Minoan features are to be found after LM II and doorways tend to be either narrowed or entirely blocked up. There appears to be a gap in occupation in the immediate vicinity of the Palace, as in the Palace itself, from the twelfth until the tenth century BC, although we know the main town to the west was densely occupied. For the first time, substantial settlement remains and a pottery kiln of the seventh century have been found, followed by the now convincing gap in Knossian history between 630 and 525 BC. Around 450 BC a well-built road was constructed above all the earlier remains, running in the direction of Evans' Sanctuary of Rhea, the earliest finds from which may be broadly contemporary. The area of the Hellenistic kilns may be seen as a traditional ceramic production area from the sixth century until the onset of Roman colonisation.

The Way Forward

The 1990s have seen the School at work in excavation, conservation, survey and study. Close co-operation with our Greek colleagues has never before been so important and active. The great work of conservation will be the Roman Villa Dionysos, but the greater progress will be a more universal awareness of the need for conservation. The Knossos Urban Survey will help us understand better how settlement developed in the valley over 9000 years. The School's stated aim in the area of Minoan excavation at Knossos is to investigate more of the town of Knossos, the largest and most important prehistoric settlement in Crete. After one hundred years, we know little of its layout, not even the urban context of the Little Palace and the Unexplored Mansion. Further excavation to the north of these buildings would reveal much, as would excavation to the west of the Stratigraphical Museum. Linear B tablets and sealings may eventually be found in datable deposits. Knossos, however, is unlikely to be able to assist greatly in another pressing matter, the absolute date of the eruption of Thera, the most impressive natural event of the second millennium BC. But no one knows. Archaeology in Crete can have specific stated aims and methodologies, but the discoveries of tomorrow can never be predicted.

COLIN MACDONALD

A CENTURY OF ACHIEVEMENT

TOPOGRAPHICAL AND ENVIRONMENTAL STUDIES

The aim of this contribution is to outline the development of British topographical and environmental studies in Crete since 1900. It is not intended as an evaluation of these studies. Nor does it seek to compare British efforts against those of other nationalities, which have been considerable. The organising principle is a basic distinction between exploration and survey. The earliest British topographical and environmental research in Crete was carried out by people exploring the island, noting archaeological sites when they saw or heard about them and collecting information about the environment almost incidentally. They were succeeded in the 1960s and 1970s by the project-orientated researchers with their more formal methods of collecting and synthesising information. By the 1980s the scientific approach had become virtually standard (FIGS. 40 and 41). Site survey almost always included an environmental element.

Exploration

British topographical and environmental studies in Crete can be tenuously linked to William Lithgow, who visited the island at the beginning of the seventeenth century, but they really began with the young academic, Robert Pashley. He toured the island in 1834, asking local people for information about ancient remains and noting their locations, when these could be verified. Charting the Aegean Sea and the coasts of Crete during the early 1850s, led the naval officer, Captain T. A. B. Spratt, to travel extensively in the interior of Crete. He not only completed the triangulation needed for his professional surveys and collected the coastal detail necessary to the Admiralty Pilot and his magnificent two-sheet chart of Crete, but he also noted much information about the flora, fauna and geology of the island which he subsequently published as *Travels and Researches in Crete* (1869). Amongst other subjects, appendices were specifically devoted to a systematic account of the island's geology in relation to neighbouring areas, a list of birds observed by Colonel H. M. Drummond-Hay and a study of the land snails. The text gave special prominence to the archaeological remains which Spratt saw on his travels, and their sites were plotted on the Admiralty charts, whilst the two-sheet map of the island which accompanied *Travels and Researches* coloured in the main geological formations, as then known.

Evans's excavations at Knossos were preceded by exploratory travels in Crete in the 1890s. During the spring of 1894 he looked simply for the source of the picture writing found on the seal stones from Crete which so intrigued him. In April 1895 he and the young J. L. Myres searched specifically in central and eastern Crete for evidence (including pottery scatters) which would indicate the existence of archaeological sites. In the spring of 1899,

FIG. 40 Praisos. Students undertaking site survey and site sampling of a Middle Minoan II ritual site (site 46). (J. Whitley)

FIG. 41 A student with a Sokkisha EDM used in topographical planning. In the background is the First Acropolis of Praisos. (J. Whitley)

Evans was back in eastern Crete once again. This time he was accompanied by the Director of the School, D. G. Hogarth, who went on to excavate in the cave above Psychro, 'a village of the inner Lassithi plain', as he put it. Two years later, Hogarth was camped on the beach at Zakros, where he had begun excavations, when the area was hit by a tremendous storm. It produced enough rain in a few hours to turn the stream into a raging torrent which changed its course and reconfigured the beach. This cataclysmic event aside, and reports of the odd earthquake, Evans and Hogarth said relatively little about the environment. The deficiency was made good to some extent by A. Trevor-Battye's *Camping in Crete*. This contains appendices on mammals, birds, flora, the physical characteristics of Crete, its harbours and anchorages, husbandry and industries and the people, as well as an account of the caves of Crete. The latter was contributed by Dorothea Bate who had investigated the ossiferous deposits of twelve caves in the island during 1904 and found the remains of pygmy elephant and hippopotamus, along with those of 'normal' antelope, deer and rodents.

Although R. W. Hutchinson acquired an extensive knowledge of the island, by all accounts John Pendlebury (1904–41) was the greatest explorer of Crete, certainly in his generation, and his knowledge of the island was unrivalled. This is apparent in his book *The Archaeology of Crete* (1939). The introductory chapter outlines the island's topography and makes reference to deforestation, erosion, rivers and springs. However, more than half of the chapter is devoted to routes, the timings on which were mostly his own, and he was able to relate them to the location of ancient sites. Pendlebury also published an account of four expeditions which he made from Knossos in 1934, the year in which he relinquished the curatorship. Thirty-five new archaeological sites were found, but he does not reveal how he and his companions discovered them, other than to attribute the degree of success in the Malevizi area to the Knossos foreman, Emm. Akoumianos, who had an unrivalled nose for antiquities! Pendlebury's excavations in the plain of Lasithi (1936–9) were preceded by some exploration in the area. Doubtless this shaped his clear topographical description of the plain and its surroundings, though it is in part deprived from Spratt and Hogarth. R. M. Dawkins too had already noted how the great depth of soil in the plain may have buried a number of sites and how the location of modern villages above the plain was related to its liability to flood, whilst their precise siting seemed to be related to springs and the 'mountain paths which connect Lassithi with the outer world'. Pendlebury's Lasithi project was pioneering, nonetheless. He emphasised the importance of routes, described the flora of the area, and drew upon Miss Bate's work on cave deposits.

Survey

The studies organised and carried out by Sinclair Hood in the early 1960s mark the transition from exploration to intensive site survey in Crete and prepared the way for the first specifically environmental research carried out there by the British. They began in July and August 1962. Three areas were explored – the coastal plain east of Rethymnon and its hinterland; the Amari Valley and its approaches; and the south coastal area between Viannos and Ierapetra. As with Pendlebury, who set out to check sites noted by Evans, the declared intention of Hood's work was simply to visit known sites, this time in order to revise the lists produced by Pendlebury. However, the discovery of new sites was inevitable. Subsequently,

Hood synthesised already published information and more fieldwork for five areas west of Mt. Ida, then for 'the province of Ayios Vasilios' in the south-centre of the island and finally for two areas on the south-west coast of the island (one west of Palaiokhora and the other between Sphakia and Frangokastelli). Most reported sites were recorded, including medieval churches, but the emphasis throughout was on the prehistoric period. This allowed Hood to demonstrate that the districts visited had been occupied earlier than had previously been thought and also to show that 'the whole of Crete had been occupied during every phase of the Minoan Bronze Age, if not earlier in the Neolithic times'. Hood's reports, however, were not concerned with revealing the methodology of site discovery. To that extent, they are in the tradition of exploration. On the other hand, they arose from an overt effort to explore territory in a systematic fashion and thus mark the beginnings of intensive survey in Crete.

The 1962 survey on the south coast discovered the Minoan sites near Myrtos, subsequently excavated by Peter Warren and Gerald Cadogan. Warren's researches at Phournou Koryphi in 1967 and 1968 were influenced by the 'New Archaeology' emanating from Cambridge. In that spirit they were accompanied by systematic studies of the physical geography of the area (Malcolm Wagstaff), its vegetation (Oliver Rackham), plant remains (Jane Renfrew), fauna (M. R. Jarman) and shells (N. J. Shackleton). These were published as appendices to the main archaeological account (1972), but informed Warren's discussion of his findings. Rackham's work was perhaps particularly important because his findings at Myrtos led him to question conventional ideas about a climax woodland forming the 'natural' vegetation in southern Greece.

Although environmental questions had been tackled in a few other research projects in Greece, notably in Messenia (published 1972), those linked to Myrtos marked a significant development not only in the archaeological study of Crete, but in the history of archaeological research in Greece as a whole. Few archaeological projects today lack an environmental dimension and such research is an integral part of the survey programmes which, as noted in *Archaeological Reports,* became particularly numerous in the late 1980s and 1990s.

The first of a new style of study, fully integrating site survey with topographical and environmental studies, covered the Ayiopharango valley on the seaward side of the Asterousia Mountains which fringe the Mesara plain. From the first David Blackman and Keith Branigan intended that their survey in 1971 and 1972 should cover 'the entire human occupation of the lower catchment from the earliest times to the present day, and that the natural environment of this occupation should be as fully established as possible. . . . In so far as it was possible, the survey team covered the entire area of the lower catchment from the river bed to the watershed, in order that the total pattern of human settlement in the area might be recorded'. In the subsequent report, A. R. Doe and D. C. Holmes discussed the physical environment of the catchment, including its geology, exploitable resources, hydrology, water availability and, importantly, its post-Palaeolithic evolution. They also joined the debate, then current, over the origins of the sediments originally characterised by C. Vita-Finzi as 'Younger Fill'. One of the chief protagonists for a climatic origin to the fill, John Bintliff, confined himself to the pedology and land use of the area, but employed the geographical notions of land use potential and carrying capacity to allow the interpretation of the archaeological data in environmental form. These studies allowed Blackman and Branigan, on the one hand, to link the distribution of sites and the development of settlement patterns to changing physical conditions and, on the other hand, to produce realistic estimates for local population levels.

Much of the environmental work carried out in Crete since last century has been summarised in the remarkable and delightful book written by Oliver Rackham and Jennifer Moody, *The Making of the Cretan Landscape,* while a useful survey of the island's geology and the setting of particular sites has been provided by Michael and Reynold Higgins in *A Geological Companion to Greece and the Aegean*. In several ways *The Aerial Atlas of Ancient Crete* is the culmination of British topographical and environmental studies in Crete, though its realisation was the result of Anglo-American co-operation. The earliest aerial photographs date from 1976, but the majority were specially taken for the project during the 1980s. The *Atlas* covers forty-nine major archaeological sites in a standard and comparative way. In addition to the aerial photography taken from a tethered balloon and an interpretative plan, ten items of information are presented covering the occupation history, the geographical situation of the site and its geomorphology.

Excavation of the Palace of Knossos has been the focus of British archaeological activity in Crete since 1900, but over the first fifty years much information also accumulated about occupation in the vicinity of the site, especially during Minoan to Roman times. This included chance finds, trial sondages, and new excavations. In the autumn of 1952 Sinclair Hood took the obvious step of pulling all the then available information together and plotting it on a map. The area covered is a strip up to 6 kilometres wide and extending for some 14 kilometres inland from the coast. More information accumulated over the next twenty years, increasingly from rescue excavations, as well as further field investigation, and Hood took steps to revise and expand his original synthesis. The results were published in 1981.

The revision of the Knossos survey provided the opportunity for environmental research on the catchment. It was initiated by Neil Roberts. He summarised the available information on the geology and soils of the area, as well as its climate and 'natural' vegetation. Roberts's main contribution, however, was his study of the geomorphological evidence for environmental change and he was fortunate enough to find secure dating evidence in the form of an Arab copper coin of 232–247 H (AD 847–61) lying above sherds of Greco-Roman type. His work has been extended by Nicola Harrison's doctoral research on the soils of the area.

Related Studies

British topographical and environmental studies in Crete have been accompanied by a number of other studies related to archaeology. These have been in the fields of anthropology, historical cartography and climatic change.

Anthropological studies go back almost as far as the excavations at Knossos and were supported by the same Cretan Committee of the British Association for the Advancement of Science. It started with W. L. H. Duckworth's 1903 study of human remains from Palaikastro, but was extended to the examination of modern Cretans, including 'the whole of the police force of Candia', a number of workmen on the Italian excavation at Haghia Triadha, policemen from Vori and Pyrgos, and villagers from Angathi and Adrovisti near Palaikastro. C. H. Hawes took the studies even further and examined skulls preserved at the monasteries of Arkadhi and Ayia Triadha (in Akrotiri), as well as the heads of considerable numbers of living Cretans. By the time the project ended in 1910 over 3000 modern Cretans (including school children from Vori and Angathi) had been measured and 'contoured' in an attempt to isolate 'the ancient stratum among the modern people' by eliminating the alien elements introduced in recent times, especially Venetian and Turkish.

After 1912, British interest moved away from physical to social anthropology. Among more recent British contributions here Sonia Greger's study of the people of the Lasithi village of Magoulas, especially the women, is of particular importance. Not only is it set in an area where considerable British archaeological work has been carried out, but it looks at a community where, she claims, meaning was once defined by honour, reciprocity and the seasonal round of agricultural work, but which is now adjusting to the modern world represented by tourists, as well as European Union regulations and subsidies.

Climatic change, particularly change over the past few centuries, is under-researched in Greece compared with other parts of Europe. The absence of appropriate source material is partly to blame. However, Jean Grove has sought to use the short-term weather observations of travellers such as Olivier and Raulin to tackle the problem for Crete, but she has also found a particularly useful resource in the observations of the Venetian administrators, chiefly for the period 1548 to 1648. The administrators often noted exceptional weather in their reports to the central authorities, especially as it related to the agriculture and food supply of the island. Collating this material and comparing it with modern climatic means has allowed Grove to make realistic statements about the climate of Crete in the late sixteenth and early seventeenth centuries.

Maps of the sixteenth and seventeenth centuries provide an entrée into how Venetian officials perceived the topography of Crete and evaluated it for purposes such as defence. Elizabeth Clutton revealed the potential of these sources with her study of Francesco Basilicata's maps of Crete, 1612 and 1629. Sadly, her research has not been followed up and at least 250 maps remain in the Venetian archives largely unstudied, at least from the stance of historical geography.

Studies in historical cartography and other subjects related to the archaeology of Crete in the larger sense are similar to the British contribution to topographical and environmental research on the island. They are incomplete in spatial and temporal coverage. Much British topographical and environmental research in Crete has been small-scale. It has rarely consisted of completely free-standing projects (an exception would be a geographical survey of the Selinon region), but the research has often been associated with, or preparatory to, conventional archaeological research, centred primarily on excavation. Nonetheless, the British contributions to topographical and environmental research can be seen as original in conception and innovative in their methodology. They have certainly given British archaeological research in Crete a distinctive flavour.

MALCOLM WAGSTAFF

'Archaeological and ethnographical researches in Crete', *Report of the British Association for the Advancement of Science* (1908), 344–50.

D. M. A. Bate, 'Four and a half months in Crete in search of Pleistocene mammalian remains', *Geological Magazine,* Decade V, Vol.2 (1905), 193–202.

D. J. Blackman and K. Branigan, *Ayiopharango* (1975), 17–36.

E. Clutton, 'Political conflict and military strategy: the case of Crete as exemplified by Basilicata's

Relatione of 1630', *Transactions of the Institute of British Geographers,* N.S. 3 (1978), 274–84.

E. Clutton, 'Some seventeenth century images of Crete: a comparative analysis of the manuscript maps of Francesco Basilicata and the printed maps of Marco Boschini', *Imago Mundi* 3 (1982), 48–65.

W. L. H. Duckworth, 'Report on anthropological work in Athens and Crete', *Report of the British Association for the Advancement of Science* (1903), 404–11.

W. L. H. Duckworth, 'Archaeological and ethnological researches in Crete', *Report of the British Association for the Advancement of Science* (1912), 224–68.

S. Greger, *Village of the Plateau* (PhD Thesis, University of Manchester, 1985).

J. Grove, 'Climatic reconstruction in the eastern Mediterranean with particular reference to Crete', *Petromarula* 6 (1992), 16–20.

J. M. Grove and A. Conterio, 'The climate of Crete in the sixteenth and seventeenth centuries', *Climatic Change* 30 (1995), 223–47.

N. M. Harrison, *The Soil Resources and Landscape Evolution of Knossos, Crete* (PhD Thesis, University of Birmingham, 1997).

C. H. Hawes, 'Archaeological and ethnological researches in Crete', *Report of the British Association for the Advancement of Science* (1909), 287–91.

C. H. Hawes, 'A report on Cretan anthropometry', *Report of the British Association for the Advancement of Science* (1910), 228–50.

M. and R. Higgins, *A Geological Companion to Greece and the Aegean* (London, 1996).

D. G. Hogarth, *Accidents of an Antiquary's Life* (London, 1910).

M. S. F. Hood, *Archaeological Survey of the Knossos Area,* (London, 1958).

M. S. F. Hood, P. Warren and G. Cadogan, 'Travels in Crete, 1962', *BSA* 59 (1964), 50–99.

M. S. F. Hood, 'Minoan sites in the far west of Crete', *BSA* 60 (1965), 99–113.

M. S. F. Hood and P. Warren, 'Ancient sites in the province of Ayios Vasilios, Crete', *BSA* 61 (1966), 163–91.

M. S. F. Hood, 'Some ancient sites in south-west Crete', *BSA* 62 (1967), 47–56.

M. S. F. Hood (with D. Smyth), *An Archaeological Survey of the Knossos Area,* 2nd ed., revised and expanded (BSA supp. vol. 14; London, 1981).

J. W. Myers, E. E. Myers and G. Cadogan (eds.), *The Aerial Atlas of Crete* (London, 1992).

J. D. S. Pendlebury, E. Eccles and M. B. Money-Coutts, 'Journeys in Crete, 1934', *BSA* 33 (1932–33), 80–100.

H. W. and J. D. S. Pendlebury and M. B. Money-Coutts, 'Excavations in the Plain of Lassithi', *BSA* 36 (1935–36), 5–131.

O. Rackham and J. Moody, *The Making of the Cretan Landscape* (Manchester, 1996).

N. Roberts, 'The location and environment of Knossos', *BSA* 74 (1979), 231–42.

D. M. Smith (ed.), *The Selinon Region of South-West Crete,* (School of Geography, University of Manchester, 1966).

A. Trevor-Battye, *Camping in Crete* (London, 1913).

A. J. B. Wace, 'John Devitt Stringfellow Pendlebury', *BSA* 41 (1940–45), 5–7.

P. Warren, *Myrtos: Early Bronze Age Settlement* (BSA supp. vol. 7; London 1972).

THE NEOLITHIC PERIOD

Then it was in the first year of the excavations at Knossos came a discovery of the greatest importance in this connection: that of the Neolithic People of Crete. The far-reaching consequences that follow from this discovery cannot easily be overestimated.

Duncan Mackenzie, *BSA* 12 (1906), 224.

For Neolithic studies, the early years of the twentieth century were quite literally epoch-making, with Arthur Evans's early discoveries at Knossos being paralleled on the Greek mainland in the work of C. Tsountas, A. J. B. Wace and M. S. Thompson. Yet, while these scholars on the mainland were able to devote their full attention to the Neolithic, Evans's energies would always be absorbed understandably by the later Bronze Age Minoan civilisation. However, that said, Evans's contribution was considerable. He not only 'created the discipline', but also provided the ideas and set the questions for the next generation of scholars. It is also thanks largely to Evans that one might legitimately talk about a special British involvement in the study of Crete's Neolithic, which springs not just from Evans's scholarship, but also the subsequent long-standing British connection with the site, which was his other legacy. Despite over a century of archaeological exploration, Knossos remains the earliest inhabited and most deeply stratified Neolithic site on the island, making it for many phases of the Neolithic *the* site by which others are judged. And so it has been upon the efforts of a small number of British scholars, who have worked to identify, define and clarify Neolithic Knossos, that much of what we understand about the Neolithic period – still one of the darkest in the island's history – is based.

The history of research into Neolithic Crete may be understood in two phases. Firstly, in what might be called the 'pioneer' phase (1897–1945) the Neolithic was first identified and the first steps were taken in its definition both at Knossos and at other sites around the island. In the following phase (1945–present day) a new generation of scholars has re-examined and clarified this early work, through study and re-study of previously excavated material, through new excavations and through the application of new ideas and new analytical techniques.

The 'Pioneer' Phase: Discovery and Classification

The Neolithic deposits receive their first treatment in the very first report in the *Annual* of the British School on the excavations at Knossos (Evans *et al.* 1900). Hand-made pottery, 'celts', 'perforated maces', obsidian knives and cores, bone implements, and figurines all receive mention. The pottery was immediately recognised as stylistically earlier than anything previously known. F. B. Welch noted its general resemblance to Neolithic pottery from other sites in south-east Europe and gave a brief first discussion of now familiar diagnostic features, such as pierced lugs and handles 'shaped like the wishbone of a fowl'. In the same year a test to bedrock revealed the great depth (*c.*7.5 metres) of Neolithic deposit and Hogarth's tests to the west and south west of the Palace gave early indications of the extent of the Neolithic settlement. In subsequent seasons Evans continued to test the underlying Neolithic settlement.

Already in his early reports Evans sought to place Neolithic Knossos in its correct cultural and chronological context. Implicit in his thinking was the idea that the first settlers had originated in the east and introduced their culture to the island. In much of this he must have been influenced by his observation, stated explicitly in *The Palace of Minos* i. (1921), that the earliest levels at Knossos did not represent the earliest stage of that culture. Evans points particularly to the technological accomplishment inherent in the earliest ground stone and ceramics. In *The Palace of Minos* ii. (1928) Evans argued for the existence of an 'Anatolo-Cretan Neolithic' quite different from that of the Greek mainland. In support of this he suggested Anatolian comparanda for Cretan Neolithic figurines and maceheads and noted that Crete's geological history had given it a flora and fauna distinct from that of Greece and more akin to that of western Asia. He also used obsidian to demonstrate the existence of a 'commercial connection with Melos'. This theory of Anatolian origins remained the dominant hypothesis for cultural origins, despite a later study of the Knossos pottery by V. G. Childe, which attempted to argue for technological links with Greece and the Balkans (Childe 1937).

For his chronology Evans was heavily reliant on his typology of Aegean figurines (FIG. 42). The Knossian examples were considered to be close to those of Anatolia and ancestral to those known from Early Bronze Age Crete and the Cyclades. In the first volume of *The Palace of Minos* in what turned out to be a remarkably accurate estimate, Evans suggested a beginning at *c.*8000 BC and an end *c.*3400 BC. Evans also seems to have been aware of the possibility that crucial strata transitional between the Neolithic and the Bronze Age were missing, however his frequently contradictory statements suggest that he never quite made up his mind.

In 1903 Duncan Mackenzie produced a special study of the Neolithic pottery from Evans's pits and introduced the first tripartite division of the Cretan Neolithic, although the terms Early, Middle and Late Neolithic were applied only in the following year by Evans. The rarity of incised wares in the lowest levels was noted for the first time, the full development of incised wares and the first appearance of rippled wares were seen to be phenomena of the middle levels (FIGS. 43 and 44), while an overlap between Neolithic forms and painted wares was held to characterise the upper levels. It should, however, be noted that much of what constitutes Mackenzie's third phase would now be dated to the Early Minoan period.

Evans's model for cultural development on Crete appears to envisage an initial settlement of Crete from Anatolia, a long period of isolation, followed by a much shorter period where overseas contacts gradually increase. In *The Palace of Minos* ii. Evans described the end of the Neolithic as the 'latest stage reached by the insular culture on *purely indigenous lines*' [my italics]. Change during this period of isolation was seen in terms of gradual evolution. As Mackenzie wrote:

> The uniform character of the stratification, allowing for the *gradual processes of development*, as illustrated by the *gradual progress in ceramic evolution*, is in itself evidence that we have here to do with one *practically unmixed* race-stratum from beginning to end. [my italics]
>
> Mackenzie, *BSA* 12 (1906), 226.

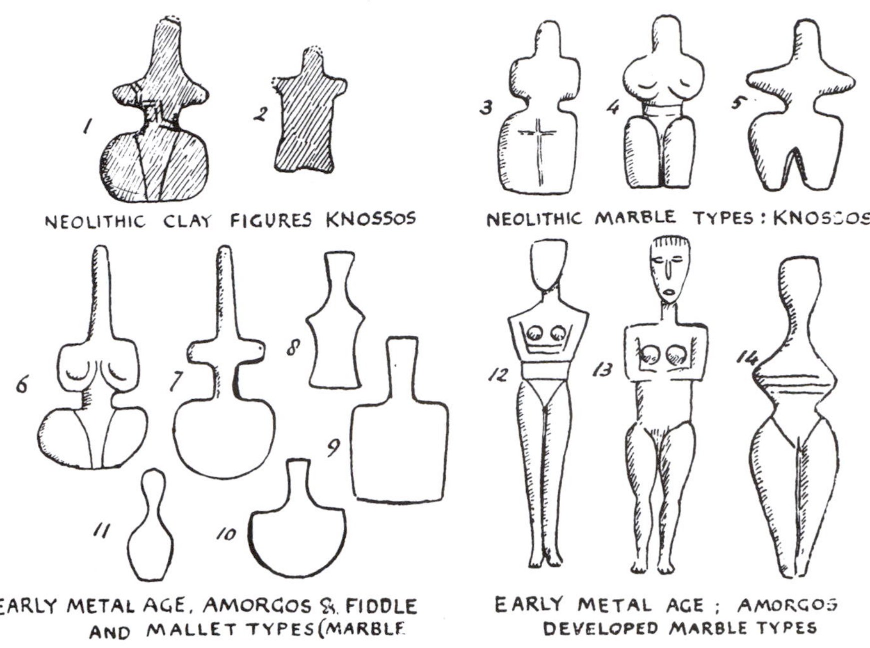

FIG. 42 Evans's typology of early Aegean figurines, published in *Man* 1 (1901)

FIG. 43 Early Neolithic incised sherds from Knossos. (Evans Collection, Ashmolean Museum Oxford)

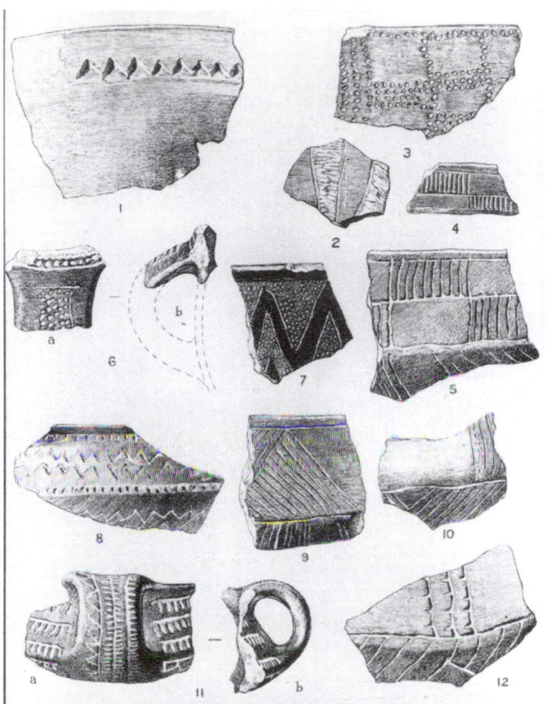

FIG. 44 Incised sherds from Evans and Mackenzie's Middle Neolithic Phase at Knossos. (*The Palace of Minos* i. (1921), 41 fig. 8.)

Discoveries in the Late Neolithic houses excavated in the Central Court, convinced Evans that in the last phases of the Neolithic new 'influences' from Anatolia could be detected: changes are noted in the ceramic repertoire and unusual individual artifacts, such as a flake of Yiali obsidian and a copper axe, were taken as indications of new connections to the east and south (*PM* ii. 16–17). For Evans, new contacts with the Nile were the main 'impulse' which 'lifted' Crete into the 'higher' Minoan stage of civilisation.

Elsewhere on Crete, other Neolithic sites began to be identified, many by members of the British School. In the east in 1902 R. C. Bosanquet found Neolithic in his excavation of the Skales cave, near Praisos, while two years later R. M. Dawkins excavated a Neolithic rock-shelter and a 'but-and-ben' dwelling near the village of Magasa. In the 1930s J. D. S. and H. W. Pendlebury and M. B. Money-Coutts excavated several caves which produced Late or Final Neolithic material, including the Trapeza burial cave on the Lasithi plateau, where 'Trapeza Ware' was first identified. Trapeza ware was also found in their excavations at Kastellos Pediados. In addition to excavation the Pendleburys and Money-Coutts rearranged and listed the Neolithic pottery from Evans's tests. In 1906 Neolithic was found below the Palace of Phaistos by L. Pernier and A. Mosso of the Italian School and identified by the French School at Mallia in the 1920s. Mention should also be made of the exemplary excavation in 1897 of the Miamou cave by A. Taramelli, who, although hampered at the time by a lack of comparanda, correctly identified the material discovered as Neolithic and thus ushered in the study of Neolithic Crete. In west Crete S. Marinatos explored several Neolithic burial caves.

It should be emphasised that the work of Evans and Mackenzie played a primary role in shaping early concepts of the Cretan Neolithic. Furthermore this conceptualisation had a profound influence on the ways their successors thought about the Neolithic: chronology, typology, Anatolian origins, the model of gradual growth over time, the idea of an essentially isolated Crete, are all research questions which begin with Evans and Mackenzie (FIGS. 45 and 46).

Post-War Research: New Techniques and New Data

In the post-war period by far the most important work was that done at Knossos, where much detail and definition was lent to the

FIG. 45 Neolithic stone axes from Knossos. (Evans Collection, Ashmolean Museum Oxford)

FIG. 46 Neolithic clay figurines from Knossos. (Evans Collection, Ashmolean Museum Oxford)

earlier work of Evans and Mackenzie. Special mention should also be made of D. Levi's extensive excavations at Phaistos and at other Mesara sites and the subsequent studies and publications of Lucia Vagnetti, which have done so much to define the last elusive phase of the Cretan Neolithic (Vagnetti 1975). In addition many Neolithic sites around the island have been brought to light through the efforts of the Archaeological Service, the most important being S. Alexiou's Neolithic houses at Katsambas, now re-dated by Katya Manteli to the Early Neolithic; Y. Tzedhakis's rescue excavation of the Gerani cave, C. Davaras's work at Pelekita and the important Final Neolithic well deposit at Phourni, excavated in 1959 and published by Manteli in 1992. Many new sites have been discovered through field survey, a process which began with the researches of Sinclair Hood, Peter Warren and Gerald Cadogan and continues to the present day through the work of David Blackman and Keith Branigan in the Ayiopharango valley, Vance Watrous in Lasithi and the west Mesara, and Jennifer Moody around Khania. Once combined, these new excavation and survey data have tended to show that sites proliferate across the island only in the later Neolithic, underlining still further the special value of Knossos.

At Knossos Audrey Furness studied Neolithic ceramic material from all of Evans's test pits, including much previously unstudied material, and produced the first formal classification of Neolithic pottery, defining shape types, decorative techniques and wares (Furness 1953). Since all Evans's tests had been dug in arbitrary levels, Furness was limited by the resolution of her data, and changes from one ceramic phase to another could only be demonstrated through frequency seriation. Thus, although she attempted wherever possible to distinguish Mackenzie's three separate Neolithic phases, in practice the transitions between phases were blurred and significant modifications inevitable. Most important was the introduction of a second Early Neolithic phase. Since, according to Evans and Mackenzie, Middle Neolithic was *the* age of rippled decoration, Furness apportioned those levels where rippling predominated to the Middle period. Hence the phase before this peak, and after Early Neolithic I, where incision predominated over rippling and which originally had been part of Mackenzie's middle phase, became under Furness Early Neolithic II.

The long-standing need for improved stratigraphical and chronological definition, suggested by Furness's detailed study, was addressed by a new series of excavations conducted by the British School (1957–60; 1969–70), headed in the first year by Hood and subsequently by John Evans (Evans 1964; Warren *et al.* 1968; Evans 1971). The significance of these excavations for subsequent understanding of the Cretan Neolithic cannot be overemphasised. Not only were new data generated in response to long-standing research questions, such as cultural origins, chronology, stratigraphy and artifact typology, but also previously ignored areas were explored such as economy and subsistence.

Trenches A and C, excavated to bedrock in the Central Court, produced a new stratigraphic sequence of ten strata, representing five phases of the Neolithic, and including the first tenuous evidence of a previously unsuspected earlier 'aceramic' phase, later to be found in greater quantity in tests X and ZE. A series of radiocarbon samples for the first time provided some relatively secure absolute dating of the Neolithic. Most surprising were the early dates for the Aceramic and EN I levels, which made the Cretan Neolithic more or less contemporary with that of mainland Greece. Interestingly Evans was able to note that even the earliest pottery immediately above the Aceramic level showed signs of 'development'. This led Saul Weinberg to question Evans's observation of a 'continuity of development' between strata X and VIII and to propose a hiatus in occupation between strata X and IX (Weinberg 1965). Evans, however, was able to point to the absence of an actual break in the stratigraphy, the spread of radiocarbon dates and the strong cultural continuity between the two strata as strong indications in favour of continuity (Evans 1970).

At the other end of the sequence, the latest radiocarbon dates provided support for the existence of a stratigraphical gap between Late Neolithic and Early Minoan strata, caused by later Bronze Age re-modelling of the mound. Stratum I, the last thinly-preserved LN occupation level, must begin before 4000 BC (Warren 1976) leaving a considerable gap before the beginning of Early Minoan. Interestingly at Phaistos, where the latest phases of the Neolithic are much better attested, the important work of Lucia Vagnetti and Paolo Belli has led to the definition of a Final Neolithic phase at Phaistos and at many sites around the island (Vagnetti and Belli 1978). During the 1969–70 excavations, John Evans attempted to locate these elusive strata in a series of soundings in the West Court (Evans 1971). Although a full stratigraphy could not be identified, a deposit of pottery was excavated in area FF, just below an Early Minoan II fill, which for the first time could be related to Final Neolithic Phaistos. However, although initially confident that a new phase had been found, Evans now believes the isolation of the deposit to be misleading, pointing to the presence of many traits characteristic of FN Phaistos already in Late Neolithic levels (Evans 1994). The issue remains unresolved partly because stratum I is still poorly understood. However a further advance was provided by the publication of stratum I material from recent excavations below the Throne Room (K. Manteli and D. Evely 1995).

In John Evans's detailed summary of the 1957–60 excavations the composition and contents of each of the ten strata were fully discussed and all catalogued objects were listed (Evans 1964). Study of the pottery in the first season was conducted by Furness and it was her classification that was subsequently followed by Evans in his publication; the new excavations, in Evans's opinion, confirming 'to a remarkable degree' the results of Furness's study. In the course of the excavations several houses or parts of houses were exposed, which still represent our best source for Cretan Neolithic building techniques. A new discovery was the existence of an earlier mud-brick architectural phase, which preceded the more familiar *pisé*, stone and *kouskouras* method.

Specialist studies were also conducted on some of the artifacts (Evans 1964; Warrren *et al.* 1968). The obsidian was analysed by J. R. Cann and Colin Renfrew and provenanced to Melos; molluscan remains were studied by N. J. Shackleton; stone axes and maceheads were examined by Warren, who proposed a new typology based on the geology of the raw material used. Figurines were studied by Peter Ucko, who argued that no strong parallels existed between Cretan figurines and those of surrounding Neolithic cultures (Ucko 1968).

In their analysis of the faunal remains M. R. and H. N. Jarman, argued for the presence of domesticated sheep, goats, pigs, cattle and dog at Knossos from the earliest levels. Furthermore, the absence of any wild equivalents amongst the island endemics suggested the introduction, with the first settlers, of animals previously domesticated elsewhere. This along with the presence of bread wheat, emmer, einkorn, barley and lentil in a grain sample from the Aceramic level and the occurrence of querns and rubbers throughout the deposit was taken as evidence that a 'fully developed mixed farming' economy was introduced and practised throughout the Neolithic (Evans 1968). Thomas Strasser's recent analysis of soils and settlement has confirmed that the presence of soils appropriate for mixed farming remained a significant factor in site choice during the Neolithic (Strasser 1996). In their report Jarman and Jarman also claimed, through their study of age-related kill-off patterns, to be able to detect diachronic changes in animal management strategies; however the validity of this has recently been called into question (Winder 1991).

More recently Elliott Lax and Strasser have argued that habitat destruction and resource competition caused by human land clearance and the introduction of domesticated animals were the principal factors in the extinction of several species of island endemic, such as deer, elephant and hippopotamus (Lax and Strasser 1992). However, while endemic deer appear to have survived the last glaciation, the Cretan hippopotamus and elephant are now dated to well before the Holocene (D. Reese, G. Belluomini and M. Ikeya 1996). Furthermore there is still no archaeological evidence for interaction between human beings and Pleistocene fauna (Y. Hamilakis 1996).

The new data generated by the excavations encouraged John Evans to address the old question of the origins of the Knossos culture. The 'developed' nature of the pottery and the presence of a 'developed' mixed farming economy continued to suggest origins overseas. The closest ceramic parallels available to Evans came from coastal Western Anatolia and the islands of the East Aegean. Although these were clearly millennia later than the Knossos material, Evans ingeniously proposed the existence of a missing coastal Anatolian 'parent' culture contemporary with Haçilar (Evans 1970), the first traces of which are only now beginning to emerge. In addition, the apparent absence of breadwheat from Greek Neolithic contexts and its presence at Çatal Hüyük were also considered signs of eastern origins. A more recent restatement of the 'Anatolo-Cretan Neolithic' hypothesis has been put forward by Cyprian Broodbank and Strasser (1991). Their modelling of the colonization process underlines that such an expedition, far from being accidental and passive, must have been planned and deliberate, indicating considerable maritime skill.

One of the most innovative aspects of John Evans's excavations was the series of tests designed to establish the area of the site for each phase of the Neolithic (Evans 1971). In addition to the Central Court and West Court soundings, a number of peripheral soundings were excavated, which when combined with the data from Arthur Evans's tests, allowed the reconstruction of the approximate shape of the original hill and the subsequent limits of expansion for each period of settlement. According to Evans the settlement expanded gradually from Aceramic through to the end of the long EN period, only quickening in its rate of expansion from MN, after which data on site size become difficult to interpret.

This model for cultural development is similar to that of Arthur Evans: both models envisage settlement from Anatolia, a long period of gradual development in relative isolation, followed by a period where links outside Crete gradually increase, with the actual point of transition to a 'more highly organized society' coming only after the Neolithic in Early Minoan. While for Arthur Evans LN was the crucial period where overseas contacts gradually increase, for John Evans this phase begins late in EN II and MN where 'marked changes' in the ceramic repertoire and a gradual increase in overseas contacts bear witness to 'a quickening intercourse with the Aegean' (Evans 1971).

Recently these models have been challenged by Broodbank, who has tried to argue that a period of rapid growth and sudden cultural change, reflective of a rapid transformation of social structure, occurs before the Bronze Age during the EN II and MN phases (Broodbank 1992). A variety of different strands of data, considered reflectors of social change, is examined, such as changes in site size, ceramic style and figurine frequency. However Todd Whitelaw has argued that in many cases the sample size is too small and the taphonomic and recovery biases too great to demonstrate the existence of 'real' changes in material culture (Whitelaw 1992).

Nevertheless, despite these problems, Broodbank's study serves as a reminder both of the greater range of questions which archaeologists now ask of their data and of the need for further detailed study of the material from Knossos and from other sites around the island. From the above discussion, it should be clear by now that the majority of our ideas about the Cretan Neolithic go back to the very beginnings of Neolithic scholarship. Since then, however, there have been many changes in the way wider scholarship has approached the 'Neolithic phenomenon': as a chronology, a technology, a culture, an economy, a population, a social structure and most recently as a conceptual system (A. Whittle 1996). Some of these developments find expression in previous work on Neolithic Crete, others do not. While there is no denying that giant steps have been taken in the last century of exploration, arguably there is a need to challenge the old ideas and assumptions and to formulate new questions – to rethink the Cretan Neolithic. This may be achieved only through further detailed study, whether re-study of old material, archaeological prospection or further well-targeted excavation. The British School, therefore, with its continuing presence at Knossos should have a significant role to play in the future of Cretan Neolithic studies.

PETER TOMKINS

C. Broodbank, 'The Neolithic Labyrinth: social change at Knossos before the Bronze Age', *Journal of Mediterranean Archaeology* 5 (1992), 39–75.

C. Broodbank and T. F. Strasser, 'Migrant farmers and the Neolithic colonization of Crete', *Antiquity* 58 (1991), 33–8.

V. G. Childe, 'Neolithic Black Ware in Greece and on the Danube', *BSA* 37 (1936–7), 26–35.

A. J. Evans, 'The Neolithic Settlement at Knossos and its Place in the History of Early Aegean Culture', *Man* 1 (1901–2), 184–6.

A. J. Evans, 'The Neolithic Stage in Crete', *PM* i. (1921), 32–55.

A. J. Evans, 'Discovery of Late Neolithic Houses beneath Central Court: Traditional affinities with Mainland East', *PM* ii. (1928), 1–21.

A. J. Evans, D. G. Hogarth, F. B. Welch and J. C. Lawson, 'Knossos: Summary Report of Excavations in 1900', *BSA* 6 (1899–1900), 3–93.

J. D. Evans, 'Excavations in the Neolithic settlement at Knossos, 1957–60', *BSA* 59 (1964), 132–240.

J. D. Evans, 'Knossos Neolithic, Part II, Summary and Conclusions', *BSA* 63 (1968), 267–76.

J. D. Evans, 'The significance of the Knossos E.N.I. Culture for Aegean Prehistory', J. Filip (ed.) *Actes du VIIe Congrès International des Sciences Préhistoriques et Protohistoriques (Prague 1966)*, (Prague, 1970), 381–4.

J. D. Evans, 'Neolithic Knossos: the growth of a settlement', *PPS* 37 (1971), 95–117.

J. D. Evans, 'The Early Millennia: Continuity and Change in a Farming Settlement', in *Labyrinth* (1994), 1–20.

A. Furness, 'The Neolithic pottery of Knossos', *BSA* 48 (1953), 94–134.

Y. Hamilakis, 'Cretan Pleistocene Fauna and Archaeological Remains: The Evidence from the Sentoni Cave (Zoniana, Rethymnon)',in *Fauna and first Settlers* (1996), 231–41.

E. Lax and T. F. Strasser, 'Early Holocene extinctions on Crete: the search for a cause', *Journal of Mediterranean Studies* 5 (1992), 203–24.

D. Mackenzie, 'The Pottery of Knossos', *JHS* 23 (1903), 157–205.

K. Manteli, 'The Neolithic well at Kastelli Phournis in eastern Crete', *BSA* 87 (1992), 103–20.

K. Manteli and D. Evely, 'The Neolithic Levels from the Throne Room System, Knossos', *BSA* 90 (1995), 1–16.

D. S. Reese, G. Belluomini and M. Ikeya, 'Absolute Dates for the Pleistocene Fauna of Crete', in *Fauna and first Settlers* (1996), 47–51.

T. F. Strasser, 'Soils and Settlement on Neolithic Crete', in *Fauna and first Settlers* (1996), 317–36.

P. J. Ucko, *Anthropomorphic Figurines of Predynastic Egypt and Neolithic Crete with Comparative Material from the Prehistoric Near East and Mainland Greece.* (London, 1968).

L. Vagnetti and P. Belli, 'Characters and problems of the final Neolithic in Crete', *SMEA* 19 (1978), 125–63.

L. Vagnetti, 'L'insediamento neolitico di Festós', *ASA* N.S. 34–35 (1972–3), 7–138.

P. M. Warren, 'Radiocarbon Dating and Calibration and the Absolute Chronology of Late Neolithic and Early Minoan Crete', *SMEA* 17 (1976), 205–17.

P. M. Warren, M.N. Jarman, H. N. Jarman, N. Shackleton and J. D. Evans 'Knossos Neolithic, part II: summary and conclusions', *BSA* 63 (1968), 267–76.

S. Weinberg, 'The Stone Age in the Aegean', *CAH* i. (Cambridge, 1965), 51–61.

T. M. Whitelaw, 'Lost in the Labyrinth? Comments on Broodbank's "Social change at Knossos before the Bronze Age"', *Journal of Mediterranean Studies* 5 (1992), 225–38.

A. Whittle, *Europe in the Neolithic* (Cambridge, 1996).

N. Winder, 'Interpreting a site: the case for a reassessment of the Knossos Neolithic', *Archaeological Review from Cambridge* 10.1 (1991), 37–52.

THE EARLY BRONZE AGE

I

During the third millennium BC the people of Crete achieved much. While the Kephala hill at Knossos had been the site of a built settlement since the early seventh millennium it was not until the fourth that others, such as Phaistos, appeared on open ground, as a development beyond the long-used caves and rock shelters. In Final Neolithic-Early Minoan I there were about three times as many new sites as the number continuing from Neolithic. Much of the evidence for expansion in these centuries around 3000 BC is, however, indirect, coming in Early Minoan I in the form of built circular tombs as at Lebena (Gerokampos), or cave burials as at Kanli Kastelli and Pyrgos in north central Crete, or in the unique and very large cemetery of rock-cut tombs at Ayia Photia east of Siteia. While such a population increase could on its own be explained by internal growth over about a thousand years (roughly 4000–3000 BC) the fact that it was accompanied by many external ceramic links suggests rather that arrivals from abroad were a major explanatory factor, namely some movement of people into the island from the north-east Aegean and western, especially north-western Anatolia, intermingling with the older Neolithic population, which was itself of Anatolian origin. Many of the new ceramic forms of EM I have close parallels in that region, especially with pre-Troy I and Troy I forms, as does the circular form of the Final Neolithic house at Phaistos with those in the oldest phase at Poliochni. The final establishment by M. Korfmann (*Studia Troica* 3) of the date of the beginning of Troy I in the late thirtieth century BC has provided a definitive chronological point.

The expansion of settlement brought about changes to the landscape. Pollen cores at Ayia Galene, at Tersana on the Akrotiri in west Crete, and from the seabed south and east of Crete, together with recent American and Canadian work in the western Mesara, have shown how a decline in natural oak forest was coincident with Final Neolithic and Early Minoan primary use of long established palaeosols; the earliest supervening alluvial deposits contained sherds, which suggests anthropogenic slope and soil erosion. These processes, which will have included forest clearance for usable timber, continued apace in the palace period, though plenty of cypress remained until Venetian times. Although the climate may have been more moist, and there were many more perennial rivers and streams, the evidence of crops grown – cereals, olives, vines and pulses – and of wild plants revealed in the pollen cores, such as *Cistaceae*, shows that it must have been close to that of today. Depictions of palms in the palace period recall the still quite widely distributed endemic palm, *Phoenix theophrasti*, and are further proof that the climate has changed little.

From the expanding settlement base and land use in the Final Neolithic and Early Minoan I periods in the late fourth millennium many villages or small towns are built all over the island, particularly in eastern Crete, through the third millennium. In early EM–EM II there were over twice as many new sites as the number continuing from FN–EM I. The increase in this case, over some five hundred years (roughly 3000–2500 BC, from within EM I to within EM II), appears to have been internal, given the strong continuance of material culture and use of cemetery sites from EM I to EM II. Even before the recent abundance of intensive surveys, over 250 sites from EM as a whole were known.

Pottery was exchanged between these communities, especially from the workshops of south central Crete (Asterousia mountains and the Mesara). Many places had links, direct or indirect, outside the island, as the widespread distribution of Melian obsidian, Cycladic metals, marble bowls and figurines and local forms of them demonstrates. Recent American investigations at Chrysokamino show extensive working of imported copper, perhaps from Kythnos. Nearby Mochlos was a port town with Near Eastern links, while those of Knossos and, at the end of the millennium, of Lebena extended to Egypt.

While occupation on many sites continued into the Middle Minoan or Protopalatial Period, as the sites themselves or their continuously used cemeteries such as those of Koumasa, Platanos or the remarkably rich Archanes (Phourne) show, there was also some disruption at the end of Early Minoan II, around 2200 BC. This is seen mainly in eastern Crete, as at the Myrtos sites and Vasilike, though even in that region the overall continuity of development in material culture is clear. Elsewhere large new settlements could be founded, as at Khamalevri on the north coast of west central Crete in EM III.

What then of political and social structures, and of beliefs, the major objectives of research set within a framework of history, that is of understanding long and medium term historical processes and short term events, and the linkages between all three? The history of agriculture or of resource exploitation, the rise, *floruit* and fall of states, the impact of a natural disaster or an invasion are examples of each process or event.

The history of settlement was briefly summarized above, with its strongly incremental trajectory of both site numbers and size at least to the end of Early Minoan II. Throughout this long period, however, there is no evidence for any political structure or unit beyond the village or small town, with its dependent agricultural territory and different degrees of exchange inside and outside the island. Places naturally varied in size, importance and character; Knossos was probably always the largest site, at 0.125 hectares. Myrtos (Phournou Koryphi) (FIG. 47) and the even smaller village excavated at Trypete may have been below average. For all sites local communal organization and decision-making is implied; the continuous outer defensive wall with protected entrances at Myrtos, conscious village layout with wide central road even at very small Trypete, the paved west court at Vasilike, could not have come into being without collective agreement, though what precise form of village political organization this took is unknown. Neither in architecture nor in the collective communal burials is there much emphasis on individual or family power, although differential social or family status could well lie behind differences of size and contents in the tombs of Mochlos.

After EM II, in the later third millennium, political and social changes may be discerned, as

FIG. 47 The Early Minoan settlement of Myrtos (Phournou Koryphi) from the south west. (P. M. Warren)

too in religious organization. Political change surely lies behind the construction, with a free-standing defensive wall, of the monumental building with its thirty-seven rooms and small central court at Ayia Photia on the coast just east of Siteia in MM IA. Whatever its purpose – centralized collection and processing of agricultural produce is a strong possibility – the building plan is new in Crete and may well reflect Near Eastern palatial forms; it implies an authority with some regional influence. So too must the Chrysokamino metalworking centre, this site also raising the most interesting question of how early its regional reference may have begun. The earliest building at Chamaizi, west of Siteia, preceding the well known MM IA 'oval' building, could have been the residence of a powerful family at a prominent physical location. At Palaikastro there was already a large building within EM II. At Knossos the earliest monumental constructions at the north-west corner of the later palace date back to EM III–MM IA.

Emergent powerful families and the concept of regional influence, probably with expansion of agricultural territory, seem an appropriate model for explanation of more powerful monumental constructions in the nineteenth century BC. The most notable of these is the southern unit at Phaistos, with its magnificent orthostat facade and stepped entrance, similar to buildings at Ebla in Syria, and facing a paved western court. This block is the first phase of the first 'palace' at the site. Differential control of metal or other resources external to the island may have been exercised by such families, but, despite metal artifact links with the Near East, evidence to support the hypothesis is lacking.

Finally, religious belief. Minoan ritual action, like that of many early religions, articulated and communicated hopes and fears for all aspects of the natural world to powers or forces believed to exist beyond the purely human sphere, powers conceived in both aniconic and anthropomorphic forms. The likely purpose was to promote a successful outcome, increase in crops, animal and human populations, maintenance of health, and, by apotropaic action, to prevent decrease through disease or pests.

There are several indications that major elements of Minoan religious practices and beliefs richly documented in the palatial period existed already in the third millennium, at both village and, eventually, at larger territorial levels. The Kamares cave began its life as a cult place in later prepalatial times, certainly in MM I and probably in EM III. So too did the other great natural locations for sanctuaries, the mountain peaks. Juktas was first used well before the end of the millennium, as too was Atsipadhes (Korakias) in the west and Petsophas above Palaikastro, with its female figurines richly painted in the EM III style. Given their wide distribution, these peak sanctuaries, as Alan Peatfield has remarked, are most unlikely to have been the only ones in the prepalatial period. Their mountain locations, as too that of the Kamares cave, indicate that they will have served not only adjacent villages or towns, such as Palaikastro, but wider regions. This is the spiritual basis of the formation of regions or territories beyond single village level. Keith Branigan has also argued for prepalatial local open air sanctuaries.

Within the built environment the shrine at EM IIB Myrtos (Phournou Koryphi) with its female terracotta figure (FIG. 48) on a raised stand, pots placed around on the floor and filling the adjacent small room in a manner reminiscent of the Late Minoan shrine treasuries, and the probable aniconic stone or baetyl at EM III Vasilike, the earliest known of its kind in Crete, exemplify the immediate focus of rituals. The paved forecourts of Early Minoan round tombs and that before tombs IV–VI on the cliff cemetery at Mochlos must have been used for funerary rituals and may have been a focus for non-funerary cult or secular gatherings.

FIG. 48 The Goddess of Myrtos, cult figure from Phournou Koryphi. Ht. 21.1 cms. (P. M. Warren)

II

The discoveries and interpretations of researchers from many countries, notably Greece itself with a long line of distinguished Cretan scholars, enable summaries such as the above to be written. Within this large company what has been the contribution of British scholars and others working through the British School towards knowledge of the third millennium Cretan Early Bronze Age? Proceeding from material discovery through to interpretation we may analyse the contribution over at least seven areas.

Survey

Although archaeological survey, with environmental and landscape history as core concepts, is of relatively recent application in Crete, we should recall that Evans's pioneering travels in 1894 and the following years and Pendlebury's extensive coverage of the island provided the essential foundations for later increments to knowledge of settlement distribution. The fieldwork of Sinclair Hood in the 1960s, assisted by Gerald Cadogan and Peter Warren, would now be called extensive survey. Its purposes were to re-examine sites on Pendlebury's lists and many others noted chiefly by Nikolaos Platon in his detailed annual accounts in *Kretika Chronika* of archaeological activity in Crete. In these studies during the 1960s of the coastal zones of west Crete, the coastal and inland west central zone and the Viannos-Ierapetra zone local information on new sites was often provided and these

FIG. 49 The Early Minoan settlement, with Elizabeth Warren indicating wall lines, at Megaloi Skhinoi, Ayiopharango. (P. M. Warren)

too were investigated. For the Early Minoan period Myrtos (Phournou Koryphi) and Myrtos (Pyrgos) were new settlement discoveries in the east, Galatas (Psathi) and Sellia (Kastellos) in the west. In the 1970s came a more detailed and intensive survey of a smaller area, rich in Early Minoan antiquities, by David Blackman and Keith Branigan, namely the Ayiopharango valley on the south coast, from Kaloi Limiones (Fair Havens) up to Moni Odhegetria (FIG. 49), with John Bintliff contributing site catchment and carrying capacity analyses. Such extensive looting of Early Minoan round tombs had occurred in this region (FIG. 50) and the adjacent Asterousia mountains in the 1960s that the Ayiopharango team's salvage and publication of many pottery fragments from the Ayia Kyriaki tomb was a notable service and addition to knowledge.

Through the 1980s intensive surveys of specific areas by several national groups was a natural development concomitant with similar

FIG. 50 Early Minoan round tomb (EM IIIB) at Megaloi Skhinoi, with Alekos Papadakis. (P. M. Warren)

field projects in many parts of mainland Greece and the Cyclades. In Crete, among no fewer than sixteen such surveys in recent years, Alan Peatfield and Christine Morris co-directed work with Greek colleagues in the Ayios Vasilios valley, Oliver Rackham and Simon Price shared in the unspeakably rugged Sphakia Survey with Canadian Lucia Nixon and Jennifer Moody from the United States, while Rackham again contributed environmental, ecological and botanical knowledge to the Vrokastro Survey under another American, Barbara Hayden, and Moody. At Kommos in 1978–9 and more recently at Pseira, Richard Hope Simpson directed intensive archaeological examination of the hinterland and territory of these important Minoan settlements, excavated by American teams. Occupation began in Early Minoan, if not Final Neolithic times. In east Crete James Whitley has recently surveyed the Praisos region and Branigan upland basins near Ziros, while the British School's investigations at Palaikastro began with an intensive survey of the wider site area by Alexander MacGillivray, Hugh Sackett, David Smyth, and Jan Driessen from Belgium.

Cretan environmental and ecological history from before the first human settlement through to the present time has been described by Rackham and Moody in their recent book (1996), based on wonderfully rich and diverse stores of knowledge acquired in their years of fieldwork across the island.

Sites and Excavations

Site investigations by British scholars have contributed substantially to knowledge of this period. Evans began with his well illustrated and remarkably prescient publication in 1895 of the finds (EM I–MM I) from the Ayios Onouphrios round tomb near Phaistos. At Knossos he and Duncan Mackenzie explored a complex Early Minoan sequence below the West Court, an area where much later John Evans revealed part of an EM II A house. The pottery from this building was published by D. E. Wilson, from Canada, in exemplary detail in *BSA* 80 (1985).

The excavations of the earliest settlement levels and of ossuary tombs at Palaikastro by R. C. Bosanquet and R. M. Dawkins, by M. Tod in the nearby EM I rock-shelter of Ayios Nikolaos and by J. L. Myres in the peak sanctuary of Petsophas at the beginning of the century were between them significant for knowledge of the whole EM period in the far east of the island. The Kamares cave, high on the southern face of Mt Ida, was excavated by the British School in 1913 and the work promptly published by Dawkins and M. L. W. Laistner. It is of course well known as a sacred cave in MM II, when many of the delicate, polychrome bridge-spouted jars and other vases were deposited. There are however stylistically earlier vases of MM I and possibly EM III date, so that cult use clearly started in prepalatial times. In Lasithi Pendlebury and his colleagues excavated the Neolithic and EM burial caves at Trapeza and Skaphidhia and began work at the EM and MM settlement at Tzermiadhon (Kastellos).

Twenty years later, in 1957–61, Hood resumed excavation, primarily stratigraphical, at Knossos. His excavation of an EM I well below the palace in the north-east area and of early levels, EM II and onwards, below the South Front of the building (from where Evans had published an excellent series of EM II pots and where Nicoletta Momigliano and D. E. Wilson were to continue recently for the School) provided further knowledge of the prepalatial settlement. John Evans' subsequent excavation of part of a substantial EM II A building below the West Court and Warren's of EM IIA constructions on the south side of the later

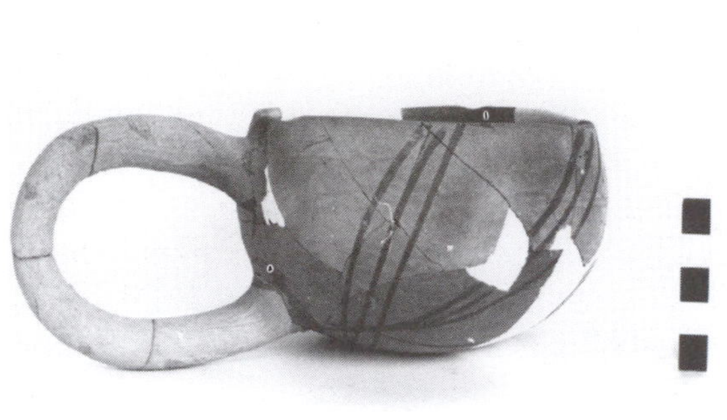

FIG. 51 Early Minoan IIA cup from the Royal Road excavations, Knossos. (P. M. Warren)

Royal Road (1971–3), with a small obsidian working area, an olive oil separator or wine press, fragments of imported Early Helladic II sauceboats, dark burnished and decorated EM IIA pottery (FIG. 51) and a tiny piece of a precious obsidian vase, almost certainly Egyptian Early Dynastic, added to the picture. It cannot be known whether settlement was continuous, but EM buildings are now known at Knossos over distances more than 200 metres apart.

In 1967–8 Warren excavated the EM IIA–B village of Myrtos (Phournou Koryphi), published in 1972. This small site, 0.125 hectares, was densely packed with about a

FIG. 52 Myrtos (Phournou Koryphi). South-east Magazine 54 at the moment of discovery. (P. M. Warren)

FIG. 53 The Early Minoan settlement at Debla in the White Mountains. View of Early Minoan I Triangular Building from the north east. (P. M. Warren)

hundred small rooms, passages and open areas, surrounded by a defensive wall with protected entrances (FIG. 47). Subsequent analysis by Todd Whitelaw indicated division into half a dozen units or houses, with living, working, cooking and storage areas (FIG. 52). The communal shrine lay at the south-west corner. On the basis of estimated oil storage capacities and consumption the population may be put within the range of 27–55 (more probably nearer the lower figure), composed of families, or one extended family, in the houses just referred to. The adjacent site of Myrtos (Pyrgos) excavated by Cadogan, also began in EM II and then continued on a larger scale to LM IB in the later fifteenth century BC.

Phournou Koryphi, through the work of Rackham and Jane Renfrew, contributed to knowledge of prepalatial agriculture. Many of the analysed charcoals were olive wood, some pruned, and an olive stone was recovered in the excavation, as some had also been in the EM I well at Knossos and at EM Lebena. The Tersana pollen core already mentioned, showed substantial quantities of olive pollen in the Final Neolithic and EM periods, suggesting olive cultivation in that area of western Crete at that time. Phournou Koryphi also produced evidence for vines and grapes, the latter as probable wine lees, wheat and barley. Debla, a very small EM I–II site in the northern foothills of the White Mountains overlooking the great plain west of Khania, was excavated by Y. Tzedhakis and Warren in 1971 (FIG. 53). J. R. A. Greig demonstrated from grain impressions in pottery from the site that oats were to be added to the EM spectrum of crop husbandry.

The evidence for EM oil and wine production has been thoroughly reviewed by Y. Hamilakis (1996), who has rejected Moody's interpretation of the high levels of olive pollen in the FN–EM period in the Tersana core as suggesting olive cultivation, preferring a climatic hypothesis of a hot, dry phase which would favour wild olive and *Cistaceae* (the latter present with *olea* in the core) against moisture-requiring trees. The arboreal decline, however, may well have been anthropogenic, coinciding as it did with the first substantial spread of settlement in the island in FN, while the presence of olive and vine pollen in all cores is entirely coincident with the other EM palaeo-botanical evidence; the archaeological evidence of EM clay tubs (olive oil separators or wine presses or both), together with their directly associated jugs and pithoi for pouring and receiving liquids, supports this picture of prepalatial agriculture, though naturally there is plenty of scope for additional evidence.

The work of Blackman and Branigan in the Ayia Kyriaki round tomb was cited above. Recent excavations by Warren on the Stratigraphical Museum site at Knossos, 350 metres west of the palace, indicate that the earliest levels, on the natural surface, may well extend back to EM II. The Atsipadhes (Korakias) peak sanctuary was excavated by Alan Peatfield and Christine Morris in 1989. It appears to have begun as early as EM I–II, on the evidence of cups deposited upside down on virgin soil. The use of figurines may have begun later, as apparently at Juktas.

The magnificent aerial record of Minoan sites, with scholarly apparatus, by Cadogan and his American colleagues, J. Wilson Myers and Eleanor Myers (1992) includes about ten places with visible Early Minoan use.

Finally, it is appropriate to refer to the excavations on Kythera by Nicolas Coldstream, George Huxley, with Richard Hope Simpson and John Lazenby in 1963–5, published in 1972, since the earliest Minoan occupation of the Kastri site was EM II–III, succeeding EH I–II on the adjacent Kastraki hill. This earliest Minoan settlement outside Crete was to have a continuous history down to Late Minoan I B.

Foreign Relations

Among numerous studies of Crete's external relations in this period, besides the Kytherean connexion just mentioned, we may notice those of Evans in *Cretan Pictographs and Prae-Phoenician Script* (1895) and in *The Palace of Minos* i–ii (1921, 1928), Pendlebury in *Aegyptiaca* (1930), Branigan in his monographs on metallurgy (1968, 1974), Colin Renfrew (1972), MacGillivray and Warren on Cycladic connexions, Cadogan, Hector Catling and MacGillivray on Cypriot, and J. D. Evans, Hood and Warren on north-western Anatolian and the latter on Egyptian.

Technology

Studies of raw materials, workshops and manufacturing processes comprising Early Minoan technology have a distinct place in British scholarship, through the work of Doniert Evely in his comprehensive study; Peter Day, Momigliano, Warren (with particular reference to the EM IIA potter's workshop at Phournou Koryphi) (FIG. 54), Whitelaw and Wilson on pottery; Branigan, Noel Gale and Sophie Stos-Gale in all categories of metalwork (FIG. 55) and metallurgical analyses; Olga Krzyszkowska on ivory, establishing that most of what was used for prepalatial seals was from hippopotamus, of which she identified and published a piece of an imported tusk from the EM IIA West Court house at Knossos; Mark Cameron on plaster; Helen Hughes-Brock on beads; Warren on stone vessels, of which the earliest of this remarkable Minoan industry was a group of EM IIA incised pieces in green chlorite or chlorite schist, with parallels in the contemporary Cyclades; and Robin Torrence and currently Tristan Carter with their respective work on obsidian, its production technology and Cycladic connexions.

Scientific Applications

In addition to faunal work by Jarman at Neolithic Knossos and at Phournou Koryphi, the palaeobotanical work by J. Renfrew and Rackham at the latter site, and by Greig on material from Debla, all three providing important information for understanding the components of prepalatial agriculture and stockraising, other scientific applications have included radiocarbon and thermoluminescent dating by V. R. Switsur and S. Fleming respectively, lipid residue chromatography analysis by D. Bowyer, ceramic technology studies by N. F. Astbury and P. Barron and metal composition determination by E. A. Slater, all on material from Phournou Koryphi, together with a wide range of metal artifact analyses in the work of Branigan and that of Gale and Stos-Gale. Recent applications of ceramic petrography by Day in collaboration with Wilson's ceramic studies at Knossos, and by Day, Whitelaw and Kyriatzi for the pottery of Phournou Koryphi

FIG. 54 Early Minoan IIA potter's wheels from Myrtos (Phournou Koryphi), showing upper surfaces. Diameters 23.0 and 20.6 cms. (P. M. Warren)

FIG. 55 Early Minoan IIA copper dagger from Myrtos (Phournou Koryphi). Length 11.6 cms. (P. M. Warren)

look set to transform knowledge of ceramic exchanges between Early Minoan communities. Two areas where expert knowledge in British universities can almost certainly produce unexpected and highly interesting new information are ceramic residue analyses, at levels of accuracy and identification far beyond what was possible at Phournou Koryphi in the late 1960s, to determine the contents of pots, and investigation of ancient DNA in human bones from EM tombs, to investigate genetic relationships, if any, between those buried therein. Proposals in each area are being formulated.

Chronology

The most accurate and detailed knowledge of sequential development is an essential requirement for political, social and historical reconstruction. The chronological aspect of Early Minoan study, in both its stratigraphical or relative and its absolute aspects, has been one focus of British work. Thus Evans's and Mackenzie's investigation of EM stratigraphy below the West Court at Knossos was followed by Hood's stratigraphical excavations (1957–61), including EM levels, by John Evans's isolation of the EM IIA building below the West Court and by Warren's determination of an EM IIA phase on the south side of the Royal Road (1971–3). The distinction of EM I levels at Debla and of EM IIA and IIB phases at Myrtos (Phournou Koryphi) was crucial for understanding these sites, while the latter confirmed the American Richard Seager's excellent stratigraphical discoveries and interpretations at Vasilike in 1904 and 1906. At Palaikastro the excavations of Mervyn Popham and Hugh Sackett in 1962–3 were published as stratigraphical tests, including EM levels.

The absolute chronology of the period has been set out by Warren and Vronwy Hankey (1989) and by S. Manning (submitted 1989, published 1995), the radiocarbon dates from Myrtos being fundamental for the reconstruction.

Interpretation

The summary of third millennium BC, prepalatial Crete given above offers brief interpretative consideration of political, social, economic and religious activities based on the sequential development of settlement in, or other use of, many kinds of site. The contribution of British scholars or of other nationals based in Britain or working through the British School to interpretative and explanatory study has been substantial. Pendlebury (1939), Hutchinson (1962), Branigan (1970a; 1970b), Renfrew (1972), Warren (1983, submitted 1976), Whitelaw (1983), Cherry (1983; 1984; 1986) and Peatfield (1987; 1992) have published discussions of the period as a whole, as distinct from particular aspects such as artifact categories or chronology. These discussions and research currently in progress promote a series of issues for investigation, such as the following selection.

1. Political structure. To what extent did the people of third millennium Crete have conceptions of territories, that is of territoriality, larger than the village or town unit with its hinterland of agricultural and other resources? We emphasize that there can be distinct kinds of territory, political, economic, religious, which have no requirements to be co-terminous. Such concepts appear to have been developed in the later third millennium (EM III–MM I A, perhaps even in later EM II). In his papers in the 1980s on the origin of state formation in Crete, John Cherry argued for relatively rapid and sudden change at the beginning of Middle Minoan, on the model of punctuated equilibria, and against previous explanations based on incremental growth. It will be apparent that discussions in the present contribution with developmental and chronological implications – highly developed ceramic technology in its range of shapes and decoration already in EM I, well before 3000 BC, recent evidence for EM I metallurgy at Poros and possibly Chrysokamino, settlement growth through much of the third millennium, complexity and scale of ceramic and other exchanges already by EM IIA, religious antecedents for palace-period shrines and their equipment well back in EM times, a well developed EM agricultural base – essentially support the incremental model, while agreeing that significant social thresholds are being crossed around 2100–1900 BC, visible in the first appearance of architectural monumentality.

2. What was the extent of intra- and extra-island exchange or trade? How large was any intermediary rôle, for example of Knossos or other north Cretan centres, controlling the flow of Melian obsidian from workshops all along the north coast to southern centres, or likewise of Cycladic marble figurines? The combined evidence of south Cretan EM II pottery at Knossos in some quantity (Day and Wilson – surely such petrographic analyses should be much promoted?) and the recent Archaeological Service (Serpetsidhaki) excavation of Cycladic figurines at the Kyparissi rock shelter, a site along an old route from north central to south central Crete, may be thought closely relevant to the question. On a different issue, what were the economic, political and even territorial correlates of the remarkable metallurgical discoveries at Chrysokamino, based on imported copper?

3. What were the content, form and locations of religious activity? Relevant evidence was discussed above, while more is needed. In 1978 the writer argued for a group of female cult figures, variations in their morphology being suggestive of polytheistic conceptions. The notion of the provision of liquid, milk or other, or of its close relationship to the figure, as an offering or libation, in fact serves to connect most of these figures and could well be an argument for a single great female divinity, with different aspects, as Evans believed for palatial Crete.

4. What did pots contain? Answers to such a simple question would in fact provide economic, environmental and dietary data of a quality almost entirely lacking to date. Ceramic residue analysis for identifiable organic traces is now possible, as noted, at highly sophisticated levels.

5. Were those buried in EM collective tombs related? Genetic studies of kinship structures is an area not yet explored for Minoan Crete, although there are plans, as noted. The potential for information on kinship and social structure is considerable.

There are certainly other research questions which may be formulated. They may be investigated in a very positive spirit. The reasons for this are not only that the necessary generous support for investigations has been forthcoming, but chiefly because the discoveries by researchers into the Minoan Early Bronze Age from all countries, notably those of our Greek hosts and colleagues at sites all over the island, have been so substantial even during the last two decades only, and carry so much potential information which the techniques now available from the physical sciences can unlock at much more detailed and richer levels.

PETER WARREN

D. Blackman and K. Branigan, *Ayiopharango* (1977), 13–84.

K. Branigan, *Copper and Bronze Working in Early Bronze Age Crete* (Lund, 1968).

K. Branigan, *The Tombs of Mesara: A Study of Funerary Architecture and Ritual in Southern Crete* (London, 1970).

K. Branigan, *The Foundations of Palatial Crete. A Survey of Crete in the Early Bronze Age* (London, 1970).

K. Branigan, *Aegean Metalwork of the Early and Middle Bronze Age* (Oxford, 1974).

K. Branigan (ed.), *Cemetery and Society in the Aegean Bronze Age* (Sheffield, 1998).

J. Cherry, 'Evolution, revolution, and the origins of complex society in Minoan Crete', in *Minoan Society* (1983), 33–45.

J. Cherry, 'The emergence of the state in the prehistoric Aegean', *PCPS* 30 (1984), 18–48.

J. Cherry, 'Polities and palaces: some problems in Minoan state formation', in C. Renfrew and J. Cherry (eds.), *Peer-Polity Interaction and Sociopolitical Change* (Cambridge, 1986), 19–45.

D. Evely, *Minoan Crafts, Tools and Techniques. An Introduction* I. (SIMA 92: 1; Göteborg, 1993).

Y. Hamilakis, 'Wine, oil and the dialectics of power in Bronze Age Crete: a review of the evidence', *OJA* 15 (1996), 1–32.

M. S. F. Hood, 'The Early and Middle Minoan periods at Knossos', *BICS* 13 (1966), 110–1.

S. W. Manning, *The Absolute Chronology of the Aegean Early Bronze Age. Archaeology, Radiocarbon and History* (Sheffield, 1995).

J. W. Myers, E. E. Myers and G. Cadogan (eds.), *The Aerial Atlas of Ancient Crete* (London, 1992).

A. A. D. Peatfield, 'Minoan peak sanctuaries: history and society', *Op.Ath.* 18 (1990), 117–31.

A. A. D. Peatfield, 'Rural Ritual in Bronze Age Crete: The Peak Sanctuary at Atsipadhes', *CAJ* 2 (1992), 59–87.

O. Rackham and J. Moody, *The Making of the Cretan Landscape* (Manchester and New York, 1996).

C. Renfrew, *The Emergence of Civilization. The Cyclades and the Aegean in the Third Millennium B.C.* (London, 1972).

M. Tsipopoulou, 'Recenti scoperte di epoca minoica nel golfo di Sitia', *Seminari anno 1990. Istituto per gli Studi Micenei ed Egeo-Anatolici* (Rome, 1991), 105–21.

P. M. Warren, *Myrtos. An Early Bronze Age Settlement in Crete*. (BSA supp. vol. 7; London, 1972).

P. M. Warren, 'The settlement at Fournou Korifi, Myrtos (Crete) and its place within the evolution of the rural community in Bronze Age Crete', *Recueils de la Société Jean Bodin pour l'histoire comparative des institutions* 41 (1983), 239–71.

P. M. Warren and V. Hankey, *Aegean Bronze Age Chronology* (Bristol, 1989).

T. M. Whitelaw, 'The settlement at Fournou Korifi Myrtos and aspects of Early Minoan social organization', in *Minoan Society* (1983), 323–45.

D. E. Wilson, 'The pottery and architecture of the EM IIA West Court house at Knossos', *BSA* 80 (1985) 281–364.

D. E. Wilson and P. M. Day, 'Ceramic regionalism in prepalatial central Crete: the Mesara imports from EM I to EM IIA Knossos', *BSA* 89 (1994), 1–87.

S. Xanthoudides, *The Vaulted Tombs of the Mesara* (London, 1924).

THE OLD PALACE PERIOD

One of the main features in the development of Minoan civilization is the appearance of a new form of social organization, more hierarchical and centralized, soon after 2000 BC, that is the appearance for the first time in the Aegean of what has been defined as a 'state' or 'complex society'.

This social change found its most conspicuous archaeological correlate in the appearance of monumental buildings at sites such as Knossos, Phaistos and Mallia, which were called 'palaces' by their first excavators at the beginning of the twentieth century – a term which has remained embedded in the archaeological literature, in spite of some attempts to show its limitations.

Minoan palaces have a long history, traditionally divided into two main phases, the Protopalatial and Neopalatial – other current terms being the First Palace or Old Palace period, and the Second Palace or New Palace period. The Protopalatial covers the MM IB–MM IIB phases of the ceramic and chronological scheme devised by Evans and Mackenzie, and still in use today.

Although the appearance of the First Palaces is perhaps the most conspicuous material aspect of what is generally regarded as the emergence of the state in Crete, there are many other important and characteristic features of this development. For example, the Protopalatial period also saw the appearance of literacy for economic and bureaucratic purposes in the form of unintentionally baked clay bars and tablets inscribed in the so-called Cretan Hieroglyphic and Linear A scripts. Another characteristic feature is the increase in production of prestige goods, such as the famous polychrome Kamares ware (FIGS. 56 and 57), whose circulation and consumption on Crete and abroad appears to have been limited to élite groups. This period also saw important changes in religion, exemplified by the growth of the Minoan 'Peak Sanctuaries', probably the most important communal cult centres on the island, and by developments in the rituals associated with them. As a final example, one may point to the intensification of contacts with surrounding

FIG. 56 An early postcard of Kamares Ware from the Royal Pottery Stores at Knossos.

FIG. 57 Composite group of pottery from Knossos and figurines from Petsopha; the pottery includes some polychrome vases and fragments of the Old Palace Period. (Ashmolean Museum Oxford)

regions of the Eastern Mediterranean, illustrated by finds of foreign imports in Crete and, vice versa, of Cretan exports to other regions. Concerning the latter, one may note that, at the time of writing, the distribution of Protopalatial artifacts found outside Crete covers most of the Eastern Mediterranean, stretching from the Peloponnese and Kythera in the west to the western coast of Anatolia, Cyprus, Syria and the Lebanon in the east; and from the island of Samothrace in the north to Egypt in the south.

Despite its crucial importance both for its own sake and for helping the understanding of the whole development of Minoan civilisation, the First Palace period has been, on the whole, a relatively neglected phase in Cretan history, as Gerald Cadogan (1988) pointed out in a paper on 'Some Middle Minoan Problems'. It has been overshadowed both by the Prepalatial and Neopalatial periods because the former has been regarded as the crucial phase leading to 'state formation' in the Aegean, while the latter represents the period of the island's maximum influence abroad, Evans's 'golden age' of Crete. Even the 'Postpalatial' or 'Third Palatial' period has received more attention, especially in recent times, partly because of the continuing controversy over the date of the Knossos Linear B tablets. Moreover, the Protopalatial period has been somewhat neglected because, in the evolutionary perspective which, until recently, has dominated Aegean scholarship, it could be understood partly as the outcome of what went before and partly as a less developed stage of what happened afterwards. Finally, another reason why Minoan scholarship, and especially British scholarship, has not focused on the Protopalatial may be due to the central, dominating role played by Evans and, consequently, by Knossos, and to the fact that, of all the Minoan palaces, 'The Palace of Minos' so far has yielded the least spectacular architectural remains for this period.

Nevertheless, British scholarship has offered a very substantial contribution to the present understanding of the Protopalatial period in the last hundred years, starting from the pioneering work of scholars such as Evans and J. L. Myres, and continuing through the work of the generations who followed in their footsteps.

Cadogan, in the above mentioned paper (also written on the occasion of another British centenary), discussing the British contribution to Aegean Bronze Age studies generally, observed that 'pragmatism has been a strength of the archaeology practised by the British School over the last hundred years . . . a pragmatism based on inference and empiricism and imagination, not on the deductive application of generalisations – though a fashion for these has been growing of late'. While this view appears to be fundamentally correct, one might suggest that more theoretical approaches also constitute an important aspect of British archaeology in the Aegean and from the very beginning, starting with Evans. In fact one might argue that it is precisely the variety of more 'pragmatic' and more 'deductive' approaches influencing and stimulating each other that constitutes the major strength of British scholarship, and not just for the Old Palace period. British archaeologists cannot boast the richness of the Protopalatial remains of 'Italian' Phaistos or 'French' Mallia, but their intellectual contribution to the understanding of the period is still substantial, for it is not only the discoveries in themselves that are important in the history of scholarship, but also their interpretations (which are sometimes marked by 'deductive application of generalisations').

British contribution to Protopalatial studies

The British contribution to the field of Protopalatial studies started in the nineteenth century, that is even before Evans and others began excavations in Crete, with W. M. F. Petrie's work in Egypt. Petrie (1890), while digging at Kahun, discovered fragments of a new and strange polychrome ware, which he suspected to be of Aegean provenance. Petrie's suspicions were indeed confirmed by the discovery of fragments and vases of that same ware in the Kamares cave on Mount Ida (FIG. 58), which the Italian archaeologist L. Mariani was the first to illustrate in a lecture given in Rome in 1894 (*Röm. Mitt.* 9 (1894), 100). Although Mariani did appreciate the great antiquity of the Kamares pottery, it was another British archaeologist, J. L. Myres, who in 1895 first established the connexion between the Cretan ware and Petrie's finds, thus providing a secure chronology for one of the most characteristic artifacts of what later became known as the Protopalatial period. Incidentally, Italian archaeologists also led the way in the exploration of the Kamares cave itself, with A. Taramelli's visit in June 1894, but it was the British archaeologists R. M. Dawkins and M. L. W. Laistner who were the first to excavate this important Minoan cult place in 1913.

Thus, there is perhaps a certain justice in the fact that the architectural remains of the First

FIG. 58 Early photograph showing a group of shepherds and their dog outside the entrance to the Kamares Cave. (Ashmolean Museum Oxford)

Palace period found by the Italian archaeologists at Phaistos are the most spectacular, while those of Knossos – arguably the pre-eminent site throughout Cretan prehistory, the first and largest Minoan Palace to be excavated – are rather elusive. Federico Halbherr and Luigi Pernier's excavations at Phaistos started only a few weeks after Evans's at Knossos: the richness of their finds and the amicable relations with their British colleagues meant that Evans and Mackenzie often looked to the 'Italian' palace (FIG. 59) as a source of inspiration for their reconstruction of the architecture of the first 'Palace of Minos', sometimes perhaps forcing the analogy too far (cf. Momigliano 1992). Evans's idea that the Old Palace at Knossos was constituted by various *insulae*, however, owes nothing to Phaistos, and although nowadays this is viewed with some scepticism, it remained unchallenged for a very long time and may even still find some supporters.

Although Knossos cannot boast the impressive architectural remains of Protopalatial Phaistos, or Protopalatial Mallia, these provide only some of the evidence upon which archaeologists can reconstruct this phase of Cretan history. Evans's excavations at Knossos revealed other exquisite and significant finds, illuminating all aspects of this period, from technology to religion, and from literacy to diet. For instance,

FIG. 59 Evans (*right*, in white) and Mackenzie (*left*) visiting Phaistos. (Ashmolean Museum Oxford)

the delicate and appealing 'Kamares' wares found in what Evans dubbed the 'Royal Pottery Stores' of Knossos (FIG. 60) prompted so much admiration among archaeologists and even the general public that they were deemed worthy of reproduction in contemporary black and white postcards (FIG. 56) (even if this medium could never do them justice).

Perhaps the two greatest contributions made by Evans and Mackenzie to our understanding of the Protopalatial period concern the stratigraphic sequence and the interpretation of the significance of the Palaces or, in other words, chronology and social development. The former is based on the 'pragmatic' work carried out in the field and in the pot-shed largely by Mackenzie, the latter is the result of the more

FIG. 60 Knossos 1902. Excavations in the Room of the Jars, Royal Pottery Stores. (Ashmolean Museum Oxford)

'deductive' but also more imaginative work by Evans. It is these two strands of research in which, I believe, the most significant contributions of following generations of British scholars have also been made.

From the very first days of the excavations at Knossos, Evans and Mackenzie paid particular attention to the stratigraphy and pottery sequence of the site. This was done with the aim of producing a systematic chronological scheme valid for the whole island, and which they also tried to apply to the rest of the Aegean. By the end of the first excavation campaign in 1900, Mackenzie had established the three main phases in the history of the Palace, which he called 'Kamarais Palace', 'Mycenaean Palace', and 'Period of decline' and correspond, in modern terminology, to the Old Palace, New Palace, and Re-occupation periods. By 1903, in an article published in *The Journal of Hellenic Studies*, Mackenzie had refined this sequence and produced a classification of Knossian pottery based on a tripartite subdivision into Early, Middle, and Late Minoan phases. Then, in 1904, Mackenzie supervised the excavations of various test-pits in the West Court to investigate

FIG. 61 The West Court at Knossos, looking east, showing the *Kouloures* and, to the left, the area of the 1904–5 test pits. (Ashmolean Museum Oxford)

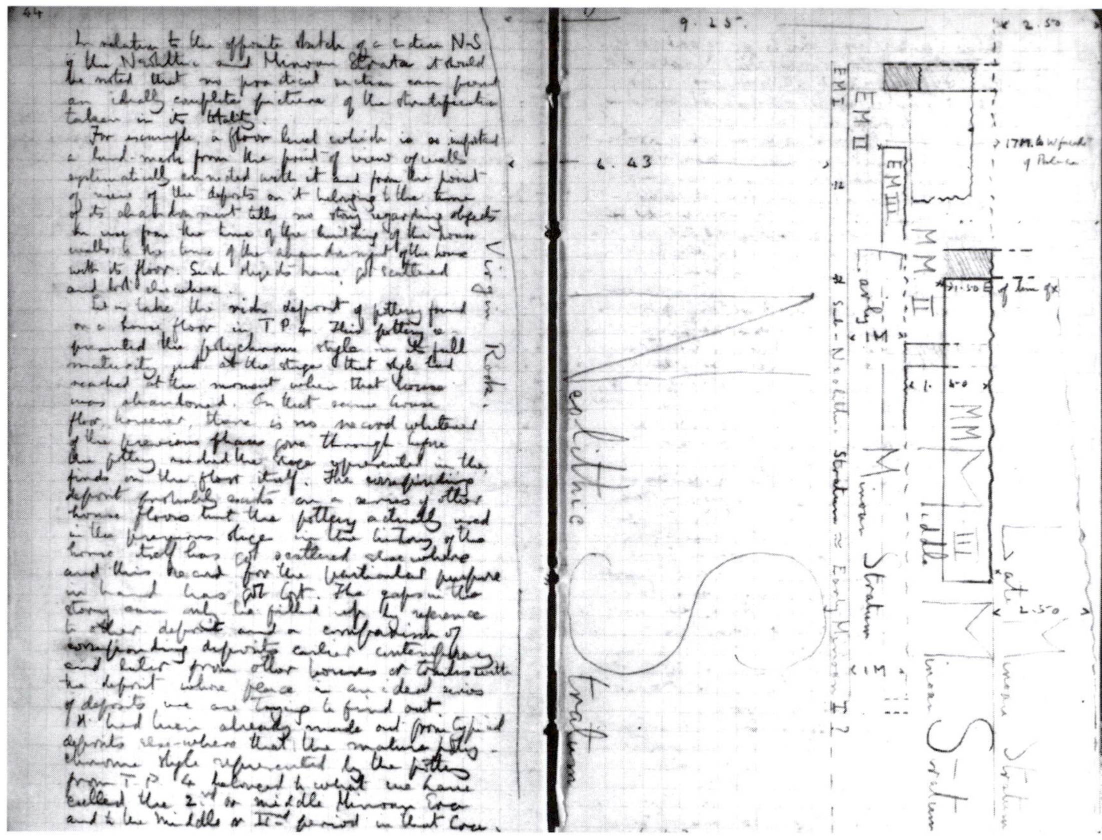

FIG. 62 Mackenzie's Daybook for 1904, showing the West Court section. (Ashmolean Museum Oxford)

the early (Pre- and Protopalatial) history of the site (FIG. 61). The results were summarized by Mackenzie in an interpretative schematic section (FIG. 62), reproduced with only slight alterations in Evans's preliminary report in the *Annual* of the British School at Athens as well as in *The Palace of Minos*. (FIG. 63). This sketch shows that Mackenzie had already envisaged a further tripartite subdivision of each phase, bringing it to a total of nine phases, by the spring of 1904. Then, in 1906, Mackenzie published another article in *JHS* in which he was able to present the first detailed study of the pottery sequence for the Middle Minoan period at Knossos. All this forms the basis of the more elaborate scheme presented by Evans in *The Palace of Minos* and which, with some alterations, is still in use today.

As mentioned above, perhaps Evans's most important contribution to Protopalatial scholarship lies in his more general and historical interpretation of the First Palaces. According to Evans, these represented one of the stages in the gradual and incremental development of Minoan society which culminated in the MM III–LM I phase, the acme of Minoan Crete, and was followed by a period of decline. More specifically, and to use Evans's own words, the Middle Minoan period was 'pre-eminently the Age of the Palaces' in which the 'hierarchical

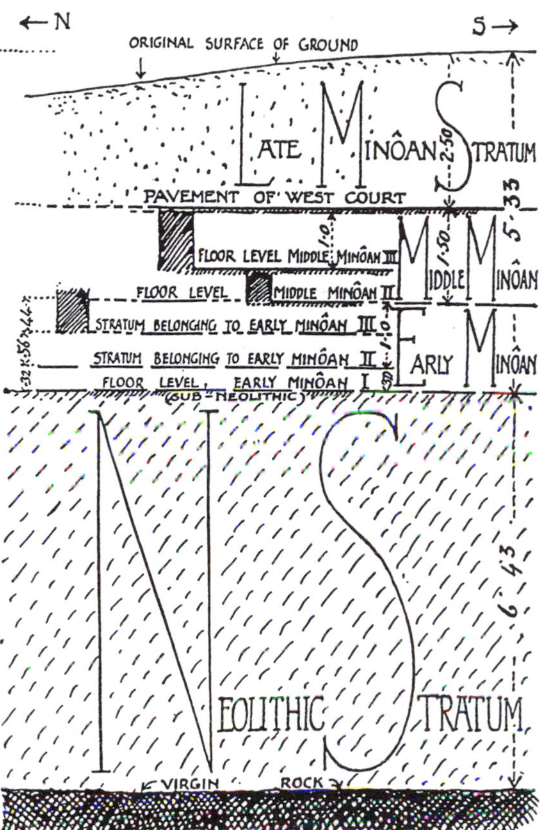

FIG. 63 West Court section as published by Evans in his *BSA* report for 1904 and in *The Palace of Minos* i. 33 fig. 4.

position of the priest-kings was . . . consolidated'; it was also the phase in which the 'final evolution of the Art of Writing' took place (*PM* i. 26–7). The palaces were the 'peaceful abode of Priest-Kings' as well as the main sanctuaries of the Minoan polity: they were the 'royal and sacerdotal abode' of dynasties of rulers who closely resembled the Anatolian theocracies described by Evans's friend and colleague W. M. Ramsay. This similarity, according to Evans, was partly explained by racial affinities between Anatolia and Minoan Crete, for 'the earlier [Middle Minoan] priest-kings themselves belonged to a ruling caste of the old Anatolian type, to which the name "Armenoid" may be given. On the other hand the Late Minoan profiles . . . suggest the intrusion of a new dynastic element of "Mediterranean" stock' (*PM* i. 9).

It is well known that Evans's gradualist views on the development of Minoan civilization owe much to Darwinian evolutionary theories (partly mediated through the social and anthropological 'Darwinism' of E. Tylor and L. Morgan), while his conception of Minoan priestly kings finds its origin in the works of James Frazer (which were also imbued with evolutionary theories). Similarly, the work of contemporary British physical anthropologists such as W. Boyd Dawkins, W. L. H. Duckworth and C. H. Hawes, and especially by the Italian polymath G. Sergi form the background of Evans's opinions on the various ethnic elements in Minoan society.

Naturally, some of Evans's views are now outdated, but he was the first (if not the only one) among the first generation of archaeologists engaged in the discovery of Minoan Crete who attempted a comprehensive historical synthesis, who tried to place the newly discovered civilization within the broader context of human evolution, adopting and adapting theories developed in other disciplines. Few (if any) of his contemporaries had such breadth of vision and shared his capacity to combine a remarkable variety of ideas to create something new.

Evans, inevitably, will always dominate any account of Aegean Bronze Age studies, but his work should not completely overshadow the important contributions made by some of his British contemporaries. At the same time as Evans was recovering the earliest history of the 'Palace of Minos', D. G. Hogarth was conducting excavations in areas around the palace with the aim of discovering its burial grounds. In fact, he revealed that the palace was part of a substantial and complex urban system already in the Protopalatial period. To use his own words: 'I had for objective the cemeteries prior to the Geometric period . . . In the event I found what I had not expected, namely a well-preserved early town' (Hogarth 1900).

Hogarth's collaboration with Evans at Knossos did not last very long. He soon turned towards the east of the island, with excavations at Psychro and Kato Zakros. These two enterprises were not particularly significant for Protopalatial studies, but were soon followed by further British explorations in this part of Crete, namely the work by R. C. Bosanquet and R. M. Dawkins at Palaikastro and by Myres at Petsophas, which offered far more substantial contributions to the study of settlement, burial, and religious practices in the Old Palace period in the far east of the island. Palaikastro, a site extremely rich in finds of all Minoan periods, and which has continued to be investigated by the British School at Athens, yielded notable remains of Protopalatial houses and ossuaries or 'bone-enclosures', while the work of Myres at Petsophas (1903) represents the very first excavation of a Minoan Peak Sanctuary. Amongst the various finds from this remarkable site one should mention a large group of Middle Minoan male and female votive figurines, some wearing fascinating garments and head gear (FIG. 57).

British scholars of the generation immediately after Evans did not offer very substantial contributions to the study of the Old Palace period, although one should mention that remains belonging to this phase were found by John and Hilda Pendlebury and Mercy Money-Coutts during their excavations in the 1930s of the *Kouloures* in the West Court at Knossos (Fig. 61), in the Trapeza Cave and Kastellos Tzermiadhon, and by J. Forsdyke in the Mavrospelio cemetery.

More significant were the excavations conducted by Sinclair Hood in the late 1950s and early 1960s along the Royal Road at Knossos, and those conducted by Mervyn Popham in 1969 ('Trial KV') (Popham 1974). The latter produced an interesting MM IIB ceramic deposit from the Knossian town, while the former, besides other important discoveries, revealed probably the best stratigraphic sequence for Protopalatial Knossos excavated so far, which has helped to refine considerably Evans and Mackenzie's scheme. Hood has been particularly generous in allowing other scholars to study his material, and the results of his work have provided a useful guide to recent publications of Knossian ceramics, especially the important volume by Alexander MacGillivray, discussed below.

The last quarter of the twentieth century has seen a revival of British interest in the Protopalatial period. The main contributions fall into the two broad fields mentioned above: the further refinement of the pottery sequence and chronology, and the interpretation of the significance of the First Palaces in terms of social developments.

Starting with the first, it is well known that Evans and Mackenzie published only a very small proportion of their finds at Knossos. The 1903 and 1906 articles by Mackenzie on Knossian Palace pottery constitute what one may call 'work in progress', while Evans's *The Palace of Minos* is not, and was never meant to be, a site publication, providing a detailed and systematic account of the discoveries at Knossos. Subsequent work on other Aegean sites, and especially Doro Levi's excavations of a new wing of the First Palace at Phaistos, raised a number of questions concerning the stratigraphy and pottery sequence presented by Evans and Mackenzie, and stressed the need for a much more extensive and up to date illustration of the relevant ceramic material. A few years ago the writer was able to make a small contribution to this problem with an article which, although devoted to Evans's 'Prepalatial' (Middle Minoan IA) pottery from Knossos, also illustrated important material of the Old Palace period (Momigliano 1991), but the daunting and difficult task of illustrating Evans's main Protopalatial deposits has now been carried out by Alexander MacGillivray, a scholar of Canadian birth, but with a strong and long association with British scholarship: his doctoral dissertation on pottery groups of the Old Palace Period at Knossos was awarded by the University of Edinburgh in 1984 and he carried out most of the research for it while serving as Curator at Knossos, 1980–84. His dissertation – incorporating the main results of Hood's discoveries and of more recent excavations at Knossos – has been transformed into a BSA Studies volume (MacGillivray 1999), and promises to be one of the major and most useful contributions to the study not only of Knossos in the Old Palace period, but also of Protopalatial Crete in its wider relations with the Eastern Mediterranean, especially with Egypt.

As to the renewed interest in the significance of the First Palaces in terms of social developments, this is well illustrated by a series of articles published in the 1980s and 1990s especially by John Cherry, Keith Branigan and Gerald Cadogan.

Cherry, in a stimulating paper published in 1983, offered an incisive and perceptive critique of the Darwinian perspective which has dominated Aegean Bronze Age studies since Evans, and which considers the emergence of the First Palaces almost as the 'inevitable outcome' of a long and gradual development leading to increasing social complexity. The main argument used by Cherry against this evolutionary paradigm was the fact that recent studies in the field of biology, namely N. Eldredge's and S. J. Gould's theory of 'punctuated equilibria', suggested that evolution does not occur gradually but through a series of relatively rapid changes which follow long periods of 'stasis' or 'equilibrium'. Thus, Cherry suggested that the appearance of the First Palaces in Crete may have also been the result of rapid 'revolution' rather than slow 'evolution', and that this interpretation is in fact more in accordance with the actual archaeological evidence of Pre- and Protopalatial Crete.

While Cherry's criticism of the 'Darwinian' approach is sound, the claim that the archaeological evidence supports the 'revolutionary' model is disputable (see, e.g., Warren 1987 and Branigan 1995). Also, one might legitimately question (on theoretical and methodological grounds) the validity of substituting for a Darwinian biological model a more recent one to explain certain developments in Minoan civilization. Human beings are, indeed, like other animals, subject to certain biological laws, but here a key factor surely is that the First Palaces are not the product of biological but of cultural evolution, which operates in rather different ways (and can actually provide better foundations to argue for rapid or 'revolutionary' changes). Moreover, Cherry's 'revolutionary' model is only of limited use in understanding the emergence of the First Palaces, as it does not really explain its causes, but simply describes the speed of change.

In spite of these limitations, Cherry's 1983 paper, together with other articles published in 1984 and 1986, has been very important and useful for the development of research on Pre- and Protopalatial Crete. The greatest merit of Cherry's work is that it has sparked a most lively and interesting debate on state formation in the Aegean, and has rightly challenged a number of assumptions concerning not only the emergence but also other aspects of the First Cretan palaces, such as the notion that they were systems of basically the same kind as the New Palaces.

The idea that there may have been significant differences between the rôles and functions of the First and Second Palaces has been further developed and combined with the concept of 'social storage' by Keith Branigan in a number of stimulating articles (1987, 1988, 1990). According to this scholar, the more 'active' rôles of the New Palaces – as producers, regulators of internal and external exchange, and as presenters of ritual activities – were barely attested in the First Palaces, whose main use was as depositories of largely agricultural produce. In other words, while storage areas are very visible and very 'public' in the early palaces (e.g. *kouloures* at Phaistos and Knossos), the evidence for craft production, ceremonial activities, and administration is also present, but in a 'scarcely embryonic form' or, at any rate, it shows that these functions operated at a 'relatively low level of intensity'.

Branigan's interpretation of the First Palaces, although influential, has not found wide acceptance. Many scholars still believe in the importance of the ceremonial and religious functions of the First Palaces. For example, MacGillivray (1994), in an article on Protopalatial Knossos, suggested that this 'may have been conceived both as a place of worship and as storehouse for wealth – rather like an early temple, but also as the dwelling of the ruling family – like the contemporary palaces in the Near East'. P. M. Day and D. E. Wilson (1998) also emphasized the religious and ceremonial functions of the First Palaces, functions that seem to go back well before the Protopalatial period, at least at Knossos.

In spite of a healthy disagreement about the main functions of the Old Palaces, most scholars now recognise the need to examine more critically and more closely the potential differences between them and the New Palaces. One important aspect in this line of research is the way in which the palaces (or rather the élites who are represented by these buildings) articulated their power within their territories. One way of tackling this problem is, of course, by means of intensive surveys, of which many have now been carried out by scholars of various nationalities in different parts of Crete: one of the first was, indeed, conducted by two British archaeologists, Keith Branigan and David Blackman, in the Ayiopharango valley in the early 1970s. The British School at Athens has now planned one for the Knossos area, which, it is hoped, will be carried out early in the twenty-first century. This will increase even further the remarkable amount of information already compiled by Hood and David Smyth in their *Archaeological Survey of the Knossos Area* (1981), perhaps the most detailed collection of data on any Aegean Bronze Age site and its immediate territory produced so far. Besides intensive surveys, much useful information on this matter can also be provided by studies such as those carried out by Alan Peatfield (1987 and 1990) on the relationship between Palaces and Peak Sanctuaries, by Peter Warren (1994) on the road network of Minoan Knossos, and especially by Gerald Cadogan (1990 and 1994) on the territories of the Old Palace 'states' of Mallia and Knossos – his work being largely prompted by the abundant Middle Minoan remains discovered during his excavations at Myrtos (Pyrgos).

If there is little agreement among British (and other) scholars as to the origins and functions of the First Palaces, and if the study of their territories is still in its infancy, what about the British contribution to the understanding of how they ended? Evans was a great believer in the power of earthquakes, something which is not unconnected with his personal experience of the one which shook Crete in 1926. That the First Palaces were destroyed by severe tectonic movements is the explanation still followed by many scholars, at least as far as Knossos is concerned. However, as the notion that Crete in the Old Palace period was divided into a number of different competing polities or 'states' gains ground, so does the idea that the end of the First Palaces may have been caused by warfare among these polities, in which Knossos emerged victorious (see, e.g., Cadogan 1994).

To sum up, and to conclude, British scholars in the last hundred years have made important contributions to Protopalatial studies, both in pragmatic and theoretical ways. These contributions cover many aspects of this field, but perhaps have been particularly noticeable in the establishment of a pottery and chronological sequence, and in the interpretation of the social developments represented by the First Palaces, as illustrated, for example, by Mackenzie's and MacGillivray's analyses of the Knossian ceramics, and by Evans's and Cherry's approaches to Minoan social evolution.

The importance and interest of these and of other British contributions, however, should not conceal the fact that the Old Palace period has been, on the whole, rather neglected. Although some advances have been made towards solving or, at least, addressing, some of the many 'Middle Minoan problems' discussed by Cadogan in 1988, there is still much to be investigated in the next hundred years before our understanding of the First Palaces can begin to equal that of the following period. New intensive surveys and new excavations are a priority, but one should not overlook the evidence already accumulated. For British scholars this means, above all, Evans's hefty legacy of unpublished material from his excavations at Knossos. This kept many scholars busy in the last century, and will continue to do so well into the new one.

NICOLETTA MOMIGLIANO

D. J. Blackman and K. Branigan, *Ayiopharango* (1975), 17–36.

D. J. Blackman and K. Branigan, *Ayiopharango* (1977), 13–84.

K. Branigan, 'The Economic Role of the First Palaces', in *Minoan Palaces* (1983), 245–9.

K. Branigan, 'Some Observations on State Formation in Crete', *Greek Prehistory* (1988), 63–72.

K. Branigan, 'A Dynamic View of the Early Palaces', *Proceedings of the 6th Cretological Congress, 1986, Chania* (Chania, 1990), 147–59.

K. Branigan, 'Social Transformations and the Rise of the State in Crete', in R. Laffineur and W.-D. Niemeier (eds.), *Politeia: Society and State in the Aegean Bronze Age* (AEGAEUM 12; Liège, 1995), 33–9.

G. Cadogan, 'Some Middle Minoan Problems', *Greek Prehistory* (1988), 95–9.

G. Cadogan, 'Lasithi in the Old Palace Period', *BICS* 37 (1990), 172–4.

G. Cadogan, 'An Old Palace Period Knossos State', in *Labyrinth* (1994), 57–68.

J. F. Cherry, 'Evolution, revolution, and the origins of complex society in Minoan Crete', in *Minoan Society* (1983), 33–45.

J. F. Cherry, 'The Emergence of the State in the Prehistoric Aegean', *PCPS* 210 (1984), 18–48.

J. F. Cherry, 'Polities and Palaces: Some Problems in Minoan State Formation', in C. Renfrew and J. Cherry (eds.) (1986), 19–45.

R. M. Dawkins and M. L. W. Laistner, 'The Excavation of the Kamares Cave in Crete', *BSA* 19 (1912–13), 1–34.

D. Evely, H. Hughes-Brock, N. Momigliano (eds.), *Labyrinth* (1994).

E. B. French and K. A. Wardle (eds.), *Greek Prehistory* (1988).

R. Hägg and N. Marinatos (eds.), *Minoan Palaces* (1987).

D. G. Hogarth, 'Knossos II. Early Town and Cemeteries', *BSA* 6 (1899–1900), 70–85.

S. Hood and D. Smyth, *Archaeological Survey of the Knossos Area* (BSA suppl. vol. 14; Oxford, 1981).

J. A. MacGillivray, 'The Early History of the Palace at Knossos (MMI–II)', in *Labyrinth*, 45–55.

J. A. MacGillivray, *Knossos: Pottery Groups of the Old Palace Period* (BSA Studies 5; 1999).

D. Mackenzie, 'The Pottery of Knossos', *JHS* 23 (1903), 157–205.

D. Mackenzie, 'The Middle Minoan Pottery of Knossos', *JHS* 26 (1906), 243–67.

L. Mariani, 'Antichità cretesi. Note sulla ceramica cretese. 1. Vasi di Kamares.' *Mon. Linc.* 6 (1895), 333–46.

N. Momigliano, 'MM IA Pottery from Evans' excavations at Knossos', *BSA* 86 (1991), 149–271.

N. Momigliano, 'The "Proto-palatial Facade" at Knossos', *BSA* 87 (1992), 165–75.

J. L. Myres, 'Prehistoric Polychrome Pottery from Kamárais, Crete', *PPS* 15 (1895), 351–6.

J. L. Myres, 'Excavations at Palaikastro II. The Sanctuary-Site at Petsofa', *BSA* 9 (1902–3), 356–87.

A. Peatfield, 'Palace and Peak: the political and religious relationship between Palaces and Peak Sanctuaries', in *Minoan Palaces* (1987), 89–93.

A. Peatfield, 'Minoan Peak Sanctuaries: history and society', *Op.Ath.* 18 (1990), 117–31.

H. W. Pendlebury, *et al.*, Excavations in the Plain of Lasithi. I. The Cave of Trapeza', *BSA* 36 (1935–6), 5–131.

H. W. Pendlebury, *et al.*, Excavations in the Plain of Lasithi. II.', *BSA* 38 (1937–8), 1–145.

J. D. S. Pendlebury, 'Lasithi in Ancient Times', *BSA* 37 (1936–7), 194–200.

W. M. F. Petrie, 'The Egyptian Bases of Greek History', *JHS* 11 (1890), 271–7.

M. R. Popham, 'Trial KV (1969): a Middle Minoan Building at Knossos', *BSA* 69 (1974), 181–94.

C. Renfrew and J. F. Cherry (eds.), *Peer Polity Interaction and Socio-political Change* (Cambridge, 1986)

A. Taramelli, 'A Visit to the Grotto of Camares on Mount Ida', *AJA* 5 (1901), 437–51.

P. M. Warren, 'The Genesis of the Minoan Palaces', in *Minoan Palaces* (1987), 47–56.

P. M. Warren, 'The Minoan Roads of Knossos', in *Labyrinth* (1984), 189–210.

THE NEW PALACE PERIOD

There are several reasons why the British contribution to Minoan archaeology, and especially to the New Palace Period, has been influential and even dominating. The main reason, of course, is Sir Arthur Evans. Minoan archaeology, it is fair to say, was actually created in the first decade of this century and the intellectual achievement was mainly that of Evans. His contribution concerned every aspect of Minoan civilisation. The generations of archaeologists, British and others, which followed, have mainly modified, corrected, corroborated, or added to his views to give us the present picture. Because of Evans, the British have had the good fortune to excavate at Knossos and at several other major Neopalatial sites on the island, planting scientific seeds whose harvest still provides the British School with scholarly challenges. Knossos, famous from many a legend, may have been, if not the political, then surely the cultural capital during the Neopalatial period. Although evidence is preserved of every stage throughout the almost ten thousand year history of the longest inhabited site in Europe, these are the years which provide the richest information. The period with which we are concerned started with a violent earthquake and ended with a devastating wave of fires. In between, however, the Cretan genius produced masterpieces of art and a quality of life that equalled that of the courts of the Egyptian pharaohs.

The British School, and the British educational system for that matter, has been traditionally open-minded and foreigner-friendly. Several of the scholars mentioned in this chapter are indeed not 'ethnically' British: all, however, took part in British School work either because they came from Commonwealth countries or studied at British universities. Some, like the present author, did neither: for them the School provided a scholarly and collegial haven, offering the opportunity for research in Minoan Crete which their respective home countries could not give. This paper, besides honouring the School's work on Crete, is at the same time a token of my gratitude for providing such a haven. Since this volume celebrates British archaeology in Crete, many references to the important work of Greek archaeologists and of those of other nationalities are mostly omitted.

Archaeology and chronology are naturally two sides of the same coin. At the close of the nineteenth century Sir Flinders Petrie's discovery of Kamares ware and Mycenean pottery in dateable Egyptian contexts provided the earliest such glimpse of objects from the Aegean. In his first campaign at Knossos, Evans immediately recognised their importance. At that point a distinction was made only between a 'Kamares' phase and a 'Mycenaean' one. The former was dated around 2000 BC because of its association with the discovery of an Egyptian diorite statue. The destruction at the end of the Mycenaean phase was seen to be dateable to the Age of

Amarna, around the beginning of the fourteenth century BC. At the same time an architectural development was recognised, allowing a distinction to be made between a First and Second Palace, an impression which was strengthened by the work of the Italian team at Phaistos. However at Knossos, unlike Phaistos, the distinction is not so easily discerned, for the palace seems to have developed gradually, expanding organically from its earliest Middle Minoan core to its Late Bronze Age form. As it grew, walls might be razed, or modified, or newly constructed. Evans, writing in 1906 his *Essai de classification des époques de la civilisation minoenne*, provided in a succinct masterpiece a straightforward chronological framework based on sound archaeological and art-historical observations.

To balance the influence of Knossos on the Neopalatial picture, the British School from the start devoted attention to settlements in the central and eastern regions of the island at Petras (1901), Zakros (1901), Palaikastro (1902–6), and Plati (1913), work which was carried out under three of its directors: D. G. Hogarth, R. C. Bosanquet, and R. M. Dawkins. The results at Petras were quite meagre, but they helped to put the place on the archaeological map. On the Lasithi plain Plati, too, was more interesting for its later 'Mycenaean' buildings than for its slight Neopalatial remains. Zakros and Palaikastro, however, provided early evidence for the New Palace Period, added to by the Greek discoveries at Nirou Hani and Tylissos, the American work at Gournia, Mochlos and Pseira, and that by the Italians at Phaistos and Haghia Triadha. The so-called Zakros Pits, for instance, comprising a large quantity of decorated vases, remain one of the most characteristic early Neopalatial pottery deposits (FIG. 64). Because of its unique iconography and its multiple sealing system, the extensive Neopalatial Sealing Archive from House A at Zakros forms a consistent feature of the study of Late Bronze Age administration. Most sites explored by the School outside Knossos were soon abandoned, with the exception of Palaikastro. Its archaeological value was realised immediately and several campaigns were allotted to uncovering what is still the largest excavated Minoan Neopalatial town. Palaikastro has yielded a marvellous assemblage of finds, including many Late Minoan IB Marine Style vases. These discoveries at Zakros and Palaikastro, together with sites discovered by others, allowed Knossian influence on pottery production and architectural style to be seen in proper perspective and often underlined the vitality of the regional centres.

From the beginning of his work and again in his final publication in *The Palace of Minos* (i. 315), Evans maintained that a new era started with Middle Minoan IIIA, immediately after the destruction of the Old Palaces. For him, as in J. D. S. Pendlebury's *A Handbook to the Palace of Minos* (1933), which may well reflect the view of the master quite closely, it was essentially the Middle Minoan IIIA palace which survived, despite an earthquake and some serious rebuilding which had followed the outline of the old structures, at the end of Middle Minoan IIIB. The Late Minoan period, on the other hand, would have left few traces in the architecture. Similarly in Evans' *Scripta Minoa* (i. 22), it is stated that 'The close of the Third Middle Minoan Period was marked at Knossos by a widespread catastrophe in the Palace and its dependencies, followed, perhaps by a certain interval, by a great restoration and partial remodelling of the building . . . during the early part of the Late Minoan Age.' He dated this catastrophe to *c.*1600 BC. He then realised that deposits which epitomised the destruction levels at the other Cretan centres, now called

FIG. 64 Vases from Zakros Pits. (*JHS* 23 (1903), 253 fig. 17)

Late Minoan IB, were more or less absent at Knossos. Knossos itself was, according to Evans, finally destroyed in Late Minoan II 'about the close of the fifteenth or the early part of the fourteenth century BC.' (*Scripta Minoa* i. 38) In the preface to the second volume of *The Palace of Minos* (1928), he corrected himself, dating the great destruction somewhat before the end of Middle Minoan IIIB, at the same time providing it with a slightly later absolute date at *c.*1570 BC, with the new Late Minoan IA ceramic style evolving from about 1550 onwards. Late Minoan IB would, in his view, coincide with the reign of Tutmosis III, then dated *c.*1500–1450 BC.

For Evans then, the palace at Knossos met its end by fire in Late Minoan II. He realized, however, that the walls and the decoration upon them could well be much older than the pottery deposits which dated the final destruction.

> Owing to the archaeological law that the small relics found on floors belong to the last moment of occupation, remains of three distinct LM I epochs are largely or entirely absent. There is practically nothing to show for the very interesting phase which marks the rapid evolution of the LM IA style from the latest Middle Minoan. Mature LM IA itself is only sporadically forthcoming, and the very beautiful LM IB style that succeeds it with its naturalistic marine and rock-work designs, reflecting the fresco style already in vogue, is almost entirely absent within the palace. (*PM* ii. 359).

Nonetheless he attributed a large part of the palace and a considerable number of fine town mansions at Knossos to the Great Restoration late in MM IIIB which he also dubbed the New Era. Foremost were the House of the Frescoes, the South and South-East Houses, the Royal Villa and the Little Palace. Despite his claim that LM IA pottery was only 'sporadically forthcoming', he asserted that most of these buildings were destroyed or abandoned in LM IA; 'in all seven good houses belonging to private individuals had sprung up close around or actually within the borders of the South-West Palace Angle in the period immediately succeeding the great Earthquake, none of which seems to have remained inhabited after the middle of the First Late Minoan Period' (ii. 390), the exceptions being the Palace, the Royal Villa and the Little Palace. A well, excavated on Gypsades in 1913, also yielded a collection of fine mature LM IA pottery (ii. 549). The cause of this widespread destruction was again thought to be an earthquake, and, in view of the large number of bronze hoards found in these town houses, Evans suggested that this indicated 'a wholesale quitting of the site' in favour of a move to Mainland Greece (ii. 626). The fear of earthquakes, he surmised, would have given a sudden impetus to emigration to the Peloponnese. Although Knossos 'remained for many generations an important urban centre' and 'the Palace, at most after a brief set-back, continued to flourish' (ii.627), it was clear to him that the end of the LM IA period represented a real turning point in the history of the site. LM IB was for Evans 'the age of the great expansion overseas' when 'Minoan commanders made use of black regiments for their final conquest of a large part of the Peloponnese and Mainland Greece' (ii. 757).

Some of Evans's theories such as 'Mycenae as a great and civilised city was only just in the making at the hands of Minoan conquerors and colonists' (ii. 564) were to cause a great rift between him and A. J. B. Wace and C. W. Blegen, who rightly, we know now, defended the Helladic component of mainland culture. LM IB Knossos, Evans believed, witnessed the introduction of a new script (Linear B) together with the advent of a more warlike dynasty. The destructions by fire marking the end of the provincial centres in LM IB, as clearly seen at Palaikastro, Zakros and elsewhere, he blamed on 'the tyrannous lust of domination on the part of the lords of Knossos' (ii. 348; iii. 308). During LM II, Knossos remained in sole control over a territory in which a degenerate form of LM I pottery was in use (i. 27, 29). In *The Archaeology of Crete* John Pendlebury further developed this view arguing that the LM II at Knossos was contemporary with LM IB elsewhere on the island. He also considered the destructions by fire of LM IB to be 'a deliberate sacking on the part of the enemies of the most powerful cities of Crete.' As to the identity of the attackers, Pendlebury assessed two hypotheses: first, Wace's theory that the Mainland had established control over the island during LM II, and that the destruction was caused by a revolt against this foreign takeover, or alternatively that rebellious Cretan dominions on the Mainland sailed to the island and sacked it. Pendlebury supported the latter view, influenced perhaps by Evans's own strong feelings.

Although J. Forsdyke's exploration in 1926–7 of the Mavrospelio cemetery showed that it had been in use during the Neopalatial period, after Evans's work no large scale excavations concentrating on this period were made at Knossos until the late 1950s. The first post-war excavations under the direction of Sinclair Hood revealed, close to the Royal Road at Knossos, the first full-scale destruction deposit dating to LM IB, including a large collection of ivories (FIG. 65). It was stratified over classic LM IA, which itself lay above what was already being called transitional MM IIIB/LM IA. Hood also found a good LM IA destruction deposit in the area of the so-called Hogarth's Houses on Gypsades.

The historical importance of these discoveries was not immediately recognised because of an outburst of controversy over the date of the final destruction of the palace at Knossos. The 'Palmer dispute' began a debate which still

FIG. 65 Knossos, Royal Road North, 1961. Hugh Sackett with foreman Manolis Markoyiannakis (wearing cap) and others at work on the ivory workshop site. (L. H. Sackett)

continues, and may be thought, by the violence of the opinions voiced, to tarnish the reputation of Aegean archaeology. Launched initially as a consequence of Michael Ventris's decipherment of the Knossian Linear B tablets as Greek, together with Wace's theory that LM II Knossos was in the hands of Mycenaean mainlanders, it rapidly intensified into an open battle.

Mervyn Popham's work on the entire sequence of Late Minoan pottery, not only on that associated with the final destruction, was instrumental in providing a sound basis on which to try to reconstruct Minoan history. Between 1967 and 1972 his and Hugh Sackett's excavation of the building already named by Evans 'The Unexplored Mansion', offered an ideal opportunity to gain a fresh look at the Late Bronze Age sequence at Knossos. Although its main importance lies with its later deposits, the architecture of the Unexplored Mansion was almost entirely Neopalatial, and so were many of the finds, including fragments of once fine frescoes, as demonstrated by Mark Cameron. The occupational history of the building appears to mirror that of the Palace and the Little Palace: constructed in LM IA, becoming a building site or abandoned during LM IB, restored in LM II, during which a destruction occurred, with minor reoccupation afterwards, and final abandonment in LM IIIB.

Popham's *The Destruction of the Palace at Knossos* (1970) introduced a break in Minoan history by lowering the date of the elimination of Knossos from LM II to early LM IIIA2, around 1370 BC, several generations after the disappearance of the other Minoan centres. The research of both Popham and Hood corrected Pendlebury's old view on the contemporaneity of LM IB and II, but it took another decade before this was universally accepted. The question of the final destruction of the Palace at Knossos and the date of the Linear B tablets found there is still not satisfactorily solved.

Here we have been concerned only with what happened before the LM IB destructions, but excavations since 1970 have helped to complete the picture of the whole Late Minoan I period. Thus, Peter Warren's excavation of 1971–2, south of the Royal Road, revealed a Neopalatial monumental staircase and grandstand, showing how the centre of Knossos and its approaches were formalised in a way that recalls Egyptian architecture. In 1973 Hood found a MM IIIB destruction deposit which confirmed that the New Palace was a later construction. Between 1974 and 1976, Hector and Elizabeth Catling, assisted by David Smyth, excavated some houses on the acropolis at Knossos, which, although they were much ruined, contained some excellent Neopalatial pottery deposits to which we will turn below. Warren directed excavations west of the Stratigraphical Museum from 1978 to 1982 (FIGS. 66 and 67). These, at a distance of about 350 metres west of the Palace, clarified the extent and nature of the LM IB Minoan town, when the area seems also to have been used for industrial activities. Here, moreover, the discovery of children's bones bearing cut marks provided tantalising evidence for probable Minoan sacrifice and possible cannibalism (FIG. 68).

FIG. 66 Marine Style alabastron. Knossos Stratigraphical Museum excavation. (P. M. Warren)

Tests directed by Hood in 1987 also yielded valuable information on the New Palace, especially those by Vasso Fotou and Doniert Evely in the Throne Room area and those by Colin Macdonald in the South-West Wing, since both illustrated substantial architectural modifications during this period. Excavation continued in 1992–3 under Macdonald in the area of the South-West Houses. One of the main discoveries was a house entirely built in gypsum with a fine pier-and-door partition, constructed in LM II, after a destruction by fire in LM IA and a gap in occupation in LM IB. In collaboration with the Archaeological Service, Macdonald also conducted tests near the Hellenistic kilns west of the Palace which yielded a good MM III / LM IA destruction deposit of forty vases (including one inscribed with Linear A) and a mature LM IA level with a lily fresco. Again no LM IB was

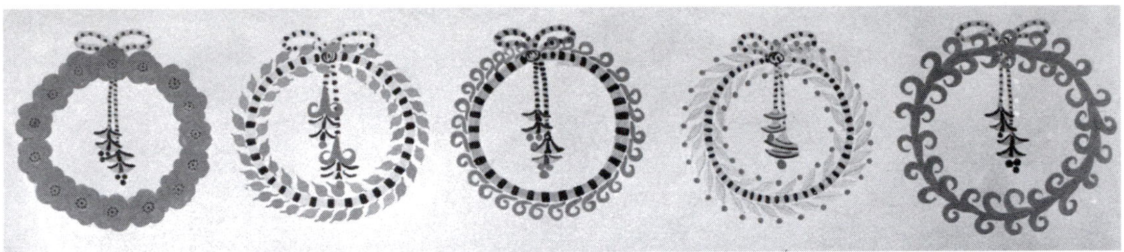

FIG. 67 Fresco of the Garlands. Stratigraphical Museum excavation. (After reconstruction painting by Jeff Clarke)

found. Finally Evely's and Marina Panagiotaki's tests of 1995 in the area of the Temple Repositories also produced evidence of a serious reconstruction in LM IA.

Other Cretan sites excavated by the School in more recent years have also provided valuable insights into the Neopalatial period. The story has it that in the early 1960s, the ephor Nikolaos Platon (the senior Greek archaeological officer on the island) allowed the School to choose at which site to dig from among those in east Crete where there had been earlier British expeditions, namely, Petras, Zakros and Palaikastro. The last was decided upon, undoubtedly because it possessed the largest agricultural hinterland and seemed the most likely to have supported another Minoan palace. Moreover it was seen to be necessary to provide a proper stratigraphical background to the rich material already known from the site. Sackett and Popham, both sometime Assistant Directors of the School, led two campaigns in 1962–3 which yielded the first properly excavated and published LM IB house on Crete, as well as offering interesting stratigraphical information and defining local pottery styles. No palace was found, however, whereas Platon himself discovered the palace at Zakros, and Metaxia Tsipopoulou has recently cleared a small building with all the ingredients of a palace at Petras!

In the 1980s the School once again returned to Palaikastro for work directed by Alexander MacGillivray and Sackett. After an initial survey campaign in 1983, excavations began in 1986 and still continue. Still without a distinctive central building, Palaikastro remains the most eloquent illustration of a proper bourgeois Neopalatial town with extensive paved streets provided with a drainage system and obvious signs of central planning (FIG. 69). The new

FIG. 68 Child's humerus with cut marks. Stratigraphical Museum excavation. (P. M. Warren)

excavations have uncovered several important Neopalatial buildings one of which may have served as an urban shrine, since one of the finest Minoan works of art ever found comes from here: a chryselephantine statue of a young man, fifty-four centimetres high, standing in the traditional pose of worship seen in votive male statuettes found in peak sanctuaries. The fact that the statue was maliciously shattered gives rise to tantalising speculation as to the social factors involved in the LM IB destruction (FIG. 70). The excavation succeeded in further refining the local pottery sequences of the period, together with providing sound evidence for two LM IB destructions by fire. Strong Knossian architectural influence in the form of a Minoan Hall, a type of construction hitherto absent from the site, was made clear.

The other major site investigated by the School and especially rich in New Palace Period data is Myrtos (Pyrgos), excavated 1970–3, under the direction of Gerald Cadogan with Vronwy Hankey assisting in the study of the pottery. The main building here is an exquisitely built country house, a manor, which formed the focus of the hill-top settlement. The

FIG. 69 Plan of Palaikastro. (L. H. Sackett)

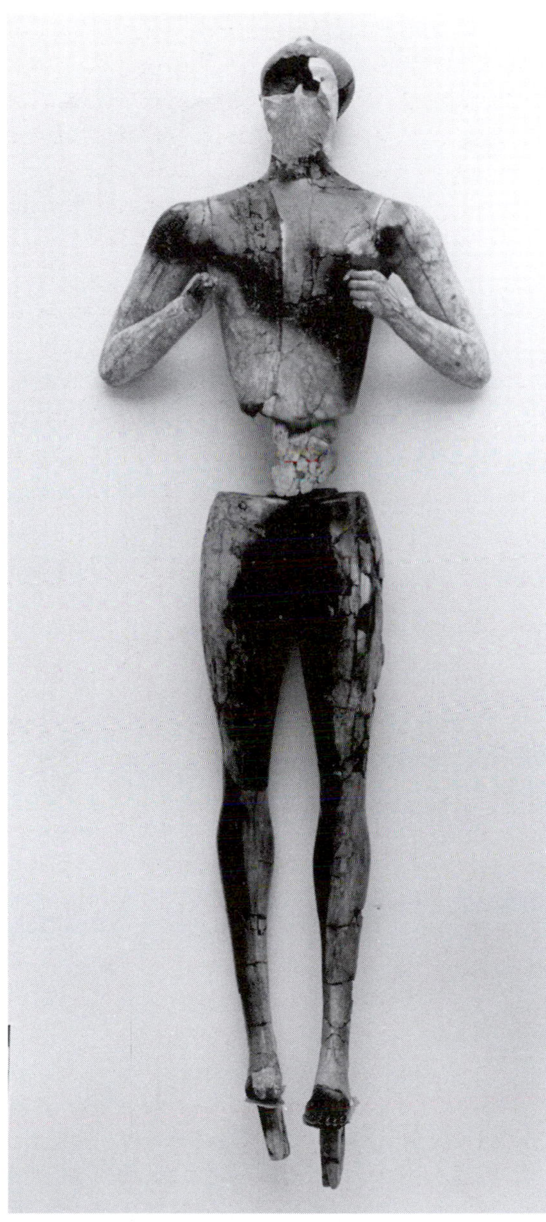

FIG. 70 The Palaikastro *kouros*. (L. H. Sackett)

finest architectural techniques, themselves betraying Knossian influence, make this complex a splendid example of the work of the New Palace Period (FIG. 71). Destroyed by human hand in LM IB, the site contained some pottery of a high standard besides a few Linear A documents. Especially interesting was a house tomb, in use from MM I up to LM IA, containing sixty-five interments and hundreds of LM IA vases. Particularly instructive was the extent of 'Minoanisation' on the south side of the Lasithi mountains, showing how the periphery closely followed central Cretan developments, but at the same time kept some regional diversity, for example, in funerary customs.

Although not strictly speaking in Crete, the joint British School and Pennsylvania University Museum excavations on nearby Kythera, at Kastri, in 1963–5, by Nicolas Coldstream and George Huxley with Richard Hope Simpson, John Lazenby and others deserve a mention. Through its unique strategic position, Kythera provided a staging post on the way to the Peloponnese for the Minoans during the Neopalatial period. The excavations have considerably improved our knowledge of LM IB regional pottery production and the interaction between Kythera and Crete itself. A series of rock-cut chamber tombs, in use up to the end of LM IB, help to some extent to close the gap in our understanding of the contemporary situation in Crete. As it is generally regarded as a Minoan colony, Kythera reawakened consideration of the existence of a Minoan thalassocracy and the recognition of Minoan colonists abroad, for which Keith Branigan has presented a theoretical framework. The quantity of Late Helladic IIA material recognised during the excavation may now warrant some caution and require explanation.

Here should be mentioned the use of new analytical techniques, carried out mainly by the British School's Fitch Laboratory in Athens, and at Oxford, especially by Noel Gale and Sophie Stos-Gale, Richard Jones and Peter Day, on pottery fabrics and metal composition, which

FIG. 71 Myrtos (Pyrgos). The Minoan Villa. (After reconstruction painting by Jeff Clarke)

has allowed statements to be made on connections between the islands of the Aegean. Despite the importance of the Lavrion mines in Attica for Neopalatial Crete, we still need to find the precise source of the large collection of copper ingots found in several LM I sites. As for Minoan pottery outside the Aegean, the fine publication of Barry Kemp and Robert Merrillees has emphasised how only a very few LM IA vases found their way to Egypt in contrast to the situation in LM IB. It may well imply some historical event during the New Palace Period which caused this change, and might also account for the representations of peoples of the Aegean, and the later modifications of those paintings, in the Tombs of the Nobles at Egyptian Thebes.

Eighty years after Evans created his chronological scheme, more recent excavations and studies have allowed Warren and Hankey in their crucially important handbook, *Aegean Bronze Age Chronology* (1989), to outline both the relative and absolute chronology for the cultural development of Prehellenic Archaeology, in which they pay full attention to the problems of the New Palace Period. Although the destructions by fire of the First Palaces in MM IIB are usually considered the beginning of the period under discussion, the initial MM III phase still remains somewhat cloudy, because Knossos and the other palaces, although almost immediately rebuilt in MM IIIA, suffered subsequent further destructions, each followed by massive rebuilding, later in that period and again at the very end of MM IIIB. The rebuildings largely obliterated the architectural evidence for this intermediate period before LM IA. Warren has been able to identify a so-called Transitional MM IIIB/LM IA pottery phase at Knossos by combining evidence from two important Neopalatial contexts: one in a pit in his own Stratigraphical Museum Extension Excavations and the other found by the Catlings in the ruined house on the acropolis. Similar deposits were found by Hood at the Royal Road, by Popham in the

Unexplored Mansion, and by Macdonald in the west part of Knossos town. Almost all were of pottery cleared out after a destruction. Whether we assign them with Evans and Hood to MM IIIB, or with Warren to MM IIIB/LM I Transition, or to very early LM IA is more a matter of terminology than of actual disagreement between different scholars. It may be preferable to look upon MM III as an intermediate phase of attempted rebuilding, while the real Second Palace, as at Phaistos and Mallia, seems almost certainly of LM IA construction. It is to these still visible remains that the term New Palaces is best reserved.

The Second or New Palace Period is then, in ceramic terms, mainly of LM I date. It represents both the acme of Minoan civilisation and the prologue to its ruin. Its spirit seems as though created through havoc: earthquakes regularly brought down monumental constructions so that both the walls and the fine artistic objects kept within them were sealed for the archaeologist's spade. Each time, however, buildings finer than before were raised, and new objects produced, excelling the earlier ones in skill and naturalism. The earthquake at the close of MM III provoked a building boom throughout the island and had a stimulating influence on artistic production, commercial enterprise, and more elaborate ritual. Most of the fine objects sealed into the destruction levels at the very end of LM IB were produced in a palatial context and were charged with symbolism for use in cult, ritual, and the life of the élite.

Apart from the coarse pottery and simple stone tools, most Minoan products are both functionally effective and artistically pleasing. British interest in Minoan artistry, following Evan's footsteps, has seen the publication of E. J. Forsdyke's lecture on *Minoan Art* in 1929, Reynold Higgins's *Minoan and Mycenean Art* in 1967 and culminated in Hood's *The Arts in Prehistoric Greece* (1978), a brilliant analysis, combining the different branches of art in which he not only amassed a vast array of material but was able to place it in a proper context. Recently Warren has continued this line of research, exploring the deeper meanings behind Minoan art. Work of this kind requires a painstaking method, gathering compendia of various art forms, and here British scholars have excelled. Their traditional strength has been in ceramic studies, whether through more traditional typological or stylistic studies, such as those of Popham or Penelope Mountjoy, or through petrography and more analytical procedures such as those of Jones and Day.

Neopalatial pottery could, however, benefit from more attention, compared with, for example, that given to Early or Middle Minoan, especially in view of the existence of regional styles. Recent influential and detailed studies by Hood, Warren, Macdonald and Popham now place in a proper context Philip Betancourt's more general but excellent outline, *History of Minoan Pottery* (1987). Mountjoy's work on Marine Style pottery, (and her work together with that of Jones and John Cherry), clarified the existence of regional production centres, both in Crete and on the Helladic mainland. Hers was one of the first attempts to attribute vases of this period to specific individuals.

In 1968 Warren produced *Minoan Stone Vases*, a synopsis which remains the basic handbook. Stone vases, especially the Neopalatial ones showing relief decoration, are a subject where art and technology are so closely entwined that one cannot master the one without the other. The same applies to Evely's *Minoan Crafts: Tools and Techniques* (1993) which will continue to prove invaluable. The art of fresco painting is also a medium through which the Minoans depicted their natural and spiritual world in a most vivid manner. Apart from a few older fragments, most of the surviving frescoes are Neopalatial. Studies of them by Mark Cameron and Lyvia Morgan, supported by technological analyses by the Fitch Laboratory, deserve special mention. Cameron and Hood worked on the frescoes found by Evans, discovering among them general themes as well as providing a firmer chronological development, for their *Knossos Fresco Atlas* (1967). One of Evans's great strengths had been his knowledge of sealstones, which had indeed been the main reason for his original visit to Crete. Exquisite masterpieces of this craft were produced during the Neopalatial period and were much studied in the 1960s by Victor Kenna. John Boardman, too, used stylistic and art-historical methods in his work on gems, while more recent studies of seals and sealings have been been made by John Betts, John Younger and Paul Yule.

It is generally agreed among archaeologists that a special significance may be seen in the earthquake destruction in the mature phase of LM IA. Previously the Minoans seem to have been stoical where earthquake damage was concerned, but this time something seems to have sapped their skills, heralding their eventual demise and gradual fading away into history. In 1939 Spyridon Marinatos suggested that the eruption of the volcano on Thera (Santorini) be blamed for the destruction of the Minoan sites at the end of LM I; his theory derived tremendous support from his excavations at Akrotiri on that island, which lies just over a hundred kilometres to the north of Crete. The eruption is believed to have been one of the largest in the history of mankind. It sent tons of ash into the air to be blown by the winds to cover several Aegean islands to the south east. Tidal waves may have salinated the coastal plains. John Luce in *The End of Atlantis* (1969), and Sir Denys Page, in his Northcliffe Lectures (1970), having collected together all the relevant evidence, proposed a link between the LM IA destruction at Akrotiri and the widespread ones on Crete in LM IB. The differing dates for the pottery made Page conjecture that there were two eruptions and that most of the damage was done by violent associated earthquakes.

Recent discoveries on Crete, especially at Mochlos by Jeffrey Soles and by Sackett and MacGillivray at Palaikastro, have shown conclusively that the eruption did indeed happen at the end of LM IA, and that the destructions by fire in LM IB require another explanation. Already in the 1970s Hood had dissociated the two events, and collected evidence for human involvement in the second, blaming a Mycenaean invader. This theory provided an explanation for the changing character of Cretan society in LM II–IIIA1. Recently it has been suggested by Macdonald and Jan Driessen that the earthquake which caused damage in LM IA triggered off the eruption. The subsequent changes, reflected in the arts and crafts, that may be observed in society in LM IB, suggest that Crete experienced a crisis which led ultimately to civil war and the wholesale destruction of the settlements and palaces by fire, opening the way for Mycenaeans from the Greek mainland.

It is fair to say that this reconstruction is heavily dependent on fixing a precise absolute date for the eruption, which remains yet another point of dispute among Aegean archaeologists. Many scientists believe the eruption to have had a global impact, so that non-archaeological sources such as ice-cores and long-living trees can provide evidence for its dating. Archaeological evidence, supported by synchronisms with Pharaonic Egypt, favours a low date for the eruption some time in the second half of the sixteenth century BC, which, among British scholars, is especially advocated by Warren. However, Carbon-14 and dendrochronology incline more towards a higher date around 1628 BC, almost a hundred years earlier, in this case favoured by Sturt Manning from Australia and by Betancourt among the Americans (FIG. 72). Consensus still seems far away, with unfortunate consequences, since the uncertainty throws doubt on the historical interpretation of the periods both before and after the eruption. For example: the Middle Minoan II period on Crete appears to be intimately linked to Twelfth Dynasty Egypt and to end around 1700–1650 BC. Following the high chronology, LM IA should have started, at the latest, early in the seventeenth century, leaving far fewer years allotted to MM III than in the traditional scheme. While this would fit well enough with the dearth of MM III material remains, it must follow that LM I Crete was largely contemporary with Hyksos rule in Egypt, which seems unlikely on present evidence. Both the relative and absolute date for the end of LM IB has been established with a fair degree of certainty at around 1450 BC. The reconstruction of events of LM I, such as the social and political crisis recently argued for by Macdonald and Driessen, must depend on the length of time that is allotted for that period. But if it had already started around 1628 BC and lasted more than 150 years, rather than one or two generations as they prefer, the argument for such a crisis would lose some of its impact. One can but present both opinions and let the reader decide.

From the outset, Evans believed that Knossos was ruled by a Priest King. In the first volume of *The Palace of Minos* he drew attention to the relief figure in the south of the palace, and imagined the ruler seated in the Throne Room flanked by the fresco of griffins. Minos, like Pharaoh, was a dynastic and divine title, the 'son of Zeus by Europa, herself, perhaps, an Earth-Goddess' (i. 3). He was convinced of the reality of the Minoan thalassocracy. Crete itself he assumed to have been ruled by the 'beneficent dominion' of a Minoan dynasty. The uniformity in material culture, especially the widespread diffusion of Linear A, suggested to him some central organisation and administration. Pendlebury went

Low dating: P. M. Warren and V. Hankey, *Aegean Bronze Age Chronology* (Bristol, 1989).
High dating: P. Rehak and J. Younger, 'Neopalatial, Final Palatial and Postpalatial Crete', *AJA* 102 (1998), 91–173.

All dates are approximate

	low	*high*
Middle Minoan IIIA	1650–1630	1750–1700
Middle Minoan IIIB	1630–1600	
Late Minoan IA	1600–1480	1700–1580
	(Thera erupts 1520)	(Thera erupts 1628)
Late Minoan IB	1480–1430	1580–1490
Late Minoan II	1430–1390	1490–1430
Late Minoan IIIA1	1390–1360	1430–1370
Late Minoan IIIA2	1360–1330	1370–1320

FIG. 72 Low and high dating in Minoan Chronology

further, assuming that the east Cretan towns kept 'a sturdy individuality' whereas Phaistos and Haghia Triadha 'were mere dependents' during LM IB. Both Evans and Pendlebury were great explorers of the island. Their travels confirmed the gradual expansion of new settlements into the Cretan countryside, among uninhabited valleys and hills, perhaps reflecting increased population pressure in the New Palace Period. It may have been this that forced the Minoans to seek more land overseas on other Aegean islands and on the Anatolian shore.

Extensive survey work (modestly called *Travels*) in the Viannos area, the Amari valley, around Stavromenos, and in the far west of Crete by Hood, Warren and Cadogan in the 1960s added new sites. Since then zealous and often thankless work by energetic Greek archaeologists and local archaeological services has now given us a good idea of the history of Minoan settlement. Intensive surveys of large areas in Crete have not been pursued by the British School to the same extent as by American archaeologists, or as has been the case in mainland Greece. But a pioneering survey was done in the Ayiopharango valley in the southern Mesara area by Keith Branigan and David Blackman, followed recently by Alan Peatfield and Christine Morris with Stavroula Markoulaki and Jennifer Moody in the Ayios Vasilios valley west of Amari, by Branigan in the Ziros area, by James Whitley at Praisos, and now by Cyprian Broodbank in Kythera.

Projects concentrating on the immediate confines of two large settlements – Hood's *Survey of the Knossos Area* (1958, new edition with Smyth, 1981), and Sackett and MacGillivray's survey of the Palaikastro area in 1983 – have provided powerful tools for diachronic settlement analysis. Only recently has equally useful work been done at sites such as Kommos and Mallia. The regional studies and those of individual settlements have together provided the information on which scholars such as R. W. Hutchinson, Keith Branigan, Colin Renfrew, Peter Warren, John Cherry, Gerald Cadogan, Alexander MacGillivray, Lucia Nixon, John Bennet, Colin Macdonald, and Jan Driessen have based their interpretations of urban planning, site distribution, and political organisation in the period of the New Palaces.

The different cultural traditions which existed on the island during the First Palace Period were, it seems, largely superseded during the Neopalatial by a greater uniformity, particularly in pottery and architectural styles, script, and sealing practices. This has invited discussion of the political framework of the period. Many British scholars have believed that Knossos was in sole control of the island in LM I. Cherry's influential analysis of 1986, in which he used Renfrew's Early State Module Scheme, sought to explain the evolution from a Protopalatial mosaic of states to a more unified Neopalatial system. Problems of interpretation remain. John Betts and Judith Weingarten's identification of single, or similar, ring impressions at different sites throughout Crete may suggest a Knossian hegemony or might mean some form of diplomatic exchange.

The arguments for a unitary state have continued to be inconclusive because of the discovery over the last decade of a number of buildings with the traditional lay-out of a palace, as at Petras, Galatas, Kommos, Archanes and elsewhere. Probably for this reason Warren, in an article for *Scientific American,* concentrated on a Knossian state with an eastern port at Zakros, and assuming other largely independent palace polities (FIG. 73), whereas Cadogan in his book on the Palaces of Minoan Crete wisely avoided the question. Macdonald and Driessen have argued for a development during this period from a more centralised and unified organisation

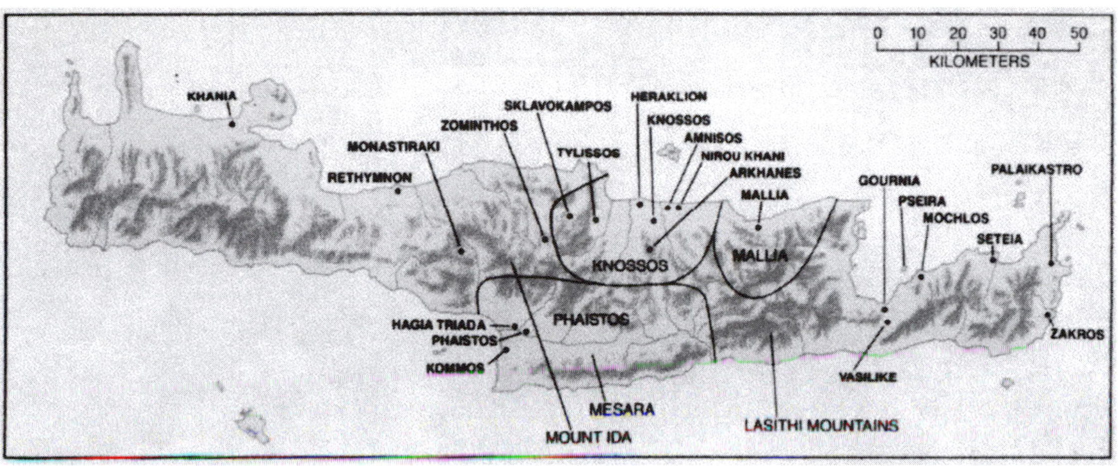

FIG. 73 Map of Crete. (P. M. Warren and Andrew M. Tomko)

under Knossos during LM IA, to a fragmented political landscape during LM IB. Despite a series of conferences devoted to the subject we still lack a secure analysis of Cretan society during the Neopalatial Period. This is partly because we remain ill-informed about funerary practices. What has become clear, however, is the surprising number of regional differences, which, with the proliferation of fine architecture and artifacts, suggests that local élites could have commanded formidable forces and posed a potential threat to any central government. What kind of state did the Minoans cherish before mainland Greek influence established itself? Evans's Priest King, Warren's chief priestess, or some kind of oligarchy, as has been suggested for Palaikastro, all remain possibilities and may even have co-existed in different regions. But neither script nor iconography allows us more than educated guesswork.

The end of the period, as far as Knossos is concerned, remains a contentious issue. While the excavations of Hood and Warren showed the site to have been more or less destroyed at the same time as the other Cretan centres in LM IB, the palace itself seems not to have been harmed. Perhaps damage had been sustained, but was thoroughly cleared away when the palace was repaired in LM II. Or it can be argued that the LM IA earthquake damage was severe enough to require a long term rebuilding programme only accomplished in LM II, in which case the palace was still a site under reconstruction during the LM IB crisis years when the other Cretan centres and the Age of Palaces came to an end.

JAN DRIESSEN

P. P. Betancourt, *The History of Minoan Pottery* (Princeton, 1985).

K. Branigan, *The Foundations of Palatial Crete* (London, 1970).

G. Cadogan, *Palaces of Minoan Crete* (London, 1976).

O. T. P. K. Dickinson, *The Aegean Bronze Age* (Cambridge, 1994).

J. Driessen and C. F. Macdonald, *The Troubled Island: Minoan Crete before and after the Santorini Eruption* (AEGAEUM 17; Liège, 1997).

J. W. Graham, *The Palaces of Crete* (Princeton, 1968).

R. Hägg and N. Marinatos (eds.), *Minoan Palaces* (1987).

R. Higgins, *Minoan and Mycenaean Art* (New York and Toronto, 1981).

M. S. F. Hood, *Home of the Heroes* (London, 1967).

M. S. F. Hood, *The Minoans* (London, 1971).

R. W. Hutchinson, *Prehistoric Crete* (Harmondsworth, 1962).

B. Kemp and R. Merrillees, *Minoan Pottery in second millennium Eqypt* (Mainz, 1980).

R. Laffineur and W.-D. Niemeier (eds.), *Politeia. Society and State in the Aegean Bronze Age* (AEGAEUM 12; Liège and Austin, 1995).

J. V. Luce, *The End of Atlantis* (London, 1969).

O. Krzyszkowska and L. Nixon (eds.), *Minoan Society* (Bristol, 1983).

J. A. MacGillivray, J. M. Driessen and L. H. Sackett (eds.), *The Palaikastro Kouros: a Minoan chryselephantine statuette and its Bronze Age context* (BSA Studies 6; 2000).

W.-D. Niemeier, 'Knossos in the New Palace Period (MM III–LM IB)', in *Labyrinth* (1994), 71–88.

D. L. Page, *The Santorini Volcano and the Desolation of Minoan Crete* (Northcliffe Lectures, 1970).

J. D. S. Pendlebury, *The Archaeology of Crete* (London, 1939).

P. Rehak (ed.), *The Role of the Ruler in the Prehistoric Aegean* (AEGAEUM 11; Liège and Austin, 1995).

P. Rehak and J. Younger, 'Neopalatial, Final Palatial and Postpalatial Crete', *AJA* 102 (1998), 91–173.

J. W. Shaw, *Minoan Architecture: Techniques and Materials* (Rome, 1972).

P. M. Warren, *Aegean Civilisations* (London, 1975 and 1989).

LINEAR B and LINEAR A

On 23 March 1900 Sir Arthur Evans began his excavations at the site of Knossos. A week later, on 30 March, the first tablet inscribed in the script he was to call 'Linear B' came to light. The rest, as they say, is history, a history in which British scholars have played a significant role among an international group.

Was Evans the first to discover Linear B tablets? Almost certainly not. He himself recounts, in *Scripta Minoa* I, the story that the emperor Nero was shown tablets of 'lime-bark' revealed at Knossos by an earthquake (probably that of AD 66). These tablets, Nero was told, were in Phoenician and allegedly contained an account of the Trojan War by one Diktys of Crete. Nero then had them translated into Greek and placed in his library. The story is contained in the prologue to a Latin translation of Diktys's work by L. Septimius. While it is not impossible that Linear B tablets were revealed by earthquake damage at Knossos in Nero's day, we can know nothing of their specific contents at this distance in time, except to say that they certainly did not contain an account of the Trojan War.

The first Linear B tablet Evans actually saw was shown to him in 1895 by a Herakleion chemist, Mr Zachyrakis, probably from the excavations carried out in 1878 by Evans's immediate predecessor at Knossos, Minos Kalokairinos. Even before this date, however, the discovery of a prehistoric, or 'Mycenaean' (the term in general use at the time for prehistoric Greek finds) script had become one of Evans's major goals in seeking to excavate on Crete. As early as 1889 he had noted 'pictographic and linear' signs on a four-sided carnelian seal stone presented to the Ashmolean museum by Greville Chester, an 'antiquarian traveller', and said to be from Sparta (see FIG. 5). Evans and John Myres acquired further examples of these seal stones (known in Greek as 'milk stones', *galópetres*) in subsequent years and discovered that they originated on the island of Crete. When Evans visited the island in 1894 he was able to verify (from its original owner) that the provenance of Chester's donation to the Ashmolean was central Crete. This profound interest in writing is exemplified by two early publications: an article for the *Athenaeum* in 1894 entitled 'A Mycenaean System of Writing', followed, in 1895, by his more substantial (and scholarly) 'Cretan Pictographs and Prae-Phoenician Script'. Perhaps Evans's most notable acquisition, prior to his excavations, is a fragment of a Linear A-inscribed 'libation table' from the Psychro cave in Lasithi purchased in 1896, augmented by two further fragments (one in Oxford, one in the Louvre). (FIG. 74)

The tablet Evans had seen in 1895 – like most of Kalokairinos's other finds – was destroyed in the turmoil of 1899, but Evans himself, once he began finding tablets in his own excavations

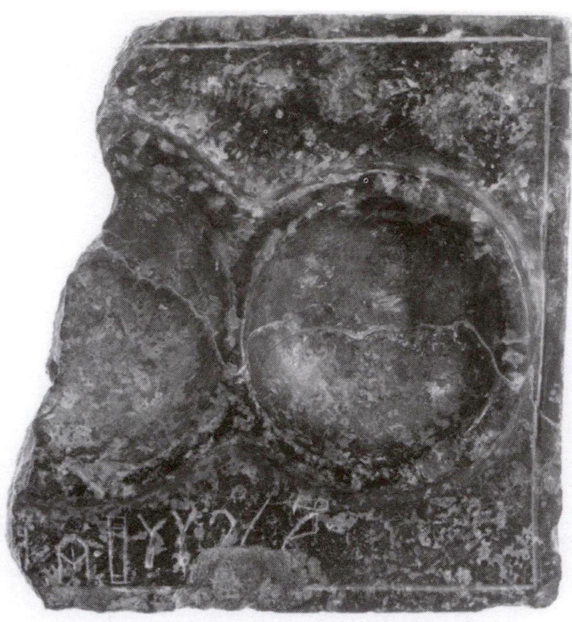

FIG. 74 One of the earliest finds of Linear A, the 'libation table' from the Psychro cave. The bottom right section (AM AE.1) was purchased by Evans in 1896; the fragment to the bottom left was acquired by him in 1923 (AM 1923.661); the joining top right-hand section is a cast of the original, excavated by Demargne in 1897 now in the Louvre (I.P.S. 352) (*GORILA* IV PS Za 2). (Ashmolean Museum Oxford)

(FIG. 75), augmented the numbers by sieving Kalokairinos' spoil heap. Certainly Evans can claim the distinction of finding the first tablets in controlled excavations and the archive he uncovered at Knossos remains the largest yet known, close to 4,000 tablets and fragments (only 1400 of which he considered complete enough for publication). Not only had he discovered documents in Linear B, but he also brought to light a much smaller number of documents in two other scripts he called 'hieroglyphic' or 'conventionalised pictographic' (now more generally termed 'Cretan hieroglyphic') and Linear A.

Small surprise, then, that he was quickly able to apply a system to his finds of written documents at Knossos and publish in 1909 the first volume of *Scripta Minoa*, the work in which his views on the development of, and relationship among, the Cretan scripts were first set out at length. For Evans, the three Cretan scripts represented evolutionary stages: Pictographic or Hieroglyphic (neither term is accurate; the script bears only a superficial resemblance to Egyptian hieroglyphic and it is almost certainly syllabic, not pictographic), giving way to Linear A, which, in its turn, was superseded by Linear B. In 1903, more extensive finds of Linear A documents (tablets, sealings and roundels) were made by the Italian archaeologists F. Halbherr and L. Pernier at the site of Haghia Triadha. This remains the largest single archive of Linear A, although it numbers in the low hundreds, rather than the thousands.

Evans spent the rest of his life publishing his finds from Knossos, but he died in 1941 before

FIG. 75 Linear B tablet Ce 59 from Knossos (AM 1910.212). The text of this tablet featured in a letter from Ventris to Emmett L. Bennett, Jr. dated 18 June 1952, shortly after the decipherment. (Ashmolean Museum Oxford)

he could complete the project of publishing – and deciphering – the Cretan inscriptions. Although he had been granted permission to include the finds from Haghia Triadha in the next volume of *Scripta Minoa*, these eventually appeared in 1945, under the editorship of G. Pugliese Carratelli. The Linear B finds from Knossos, originally destined for the third volume of *Scripta Minoa*, appeared in its second volume, completed by John Myres after Evans's death and published in 1952. Myres's own death in 1954 delayed the third volume, treating Linear A inscriptions from Knossos and elsewhere, which finally saw the light of day under the editorship of W. C. Brice in 1961 as *Inscriptions in the Minoan Linear Script of Class A*.

Evans, given his initial interest in the 'Mycenaean' script, would have dearly loved to decipher Linear B himself. His observations on the nature of the script, beginning in the very first annual reports from Knossos and further developed in the *Scripta Minoa* volumes and in *The Palace of Minos*, particularly its fourth volume, were insightful. He correctly identified the number system and detected some curious patterns, notably the fact that many of the documents which we now know dealt with sheep had figures that added up to round hundreds. These he dubbed the 'percentage tablets'. He also recognised inflectional patterns. Even if he had lived longer, however, two obstacles stood in Evans's way. Firstly, he lacked a training in cryptanalysis acquired during the Second World War by many, including John Chadwick in Britain, and Emmett L. Bennett, Jr. in the U.S.A. More importantly perhaps, Evans's own prejudice – shared by Ventris until the moment of the decipherment – about the primacy of his Minoan civilisation over that of mainland Greece would have stood in the way of his accepting that the language behind the Linear B script was Greek.

However, there is a sense in which Evans can be regarded as 'responsible' for the decipherment. In 1936, at a lecture he gave at Burlington House to celebrate the British School at Athens's Jubilee, the fourteen-year-old Michael Ventris (FIG. 76) was in the audience. His curiosity piqued, Ventris began to work on deciphering the Linear B script. Very much in keeping with scholarly trends of his time, Ventris believed that the language behind the script was anything but Greek, and he even published (at age eighteen) an article suggesting a decipherment of the script as Etruscan in the *American Journal of Archaeology* for 1940, a year before Evans himself died.

After the Second World War, Ventris, now beginning his career as a talented young architect, turned in his spare time to what was now known as the 'Minoan syllabary'. In recent years, a number of scholars had been working on the script, but were very much hampered by the small amount of material available only piecemeal in Evans's publications. Nevertheless, in the U.S.A., Alice Kober of Brooklyn College had brilliantly elucidated patterns of inflection in the script, while Bennett had been given

FIG. 76 Michael Ventris (1922–56), *left,* decipherer of Linear B, with Reynold Higgins. (Tom Blau. Camera Press, London)

access to Blegen's 1939 finds from Pylos and produced, for his 1947 Cincinnati doctoral dissertation, a classification of the tablets by subject as well as an elegant account of the metrical system, published in the *American Journal of Archaeology* for 1950. Feeling the pressure of the fiftieth anniversary of Evans's excavations, at the end of 1949 Ventris sent a questionnaire to a group of twelve scholars working on the script. The replies he incorporated in the now-legendary 'Mid-Century Report', dated 7 March 1950, a summary of the prevailing state of knowledge. It is incredible in these days of instantaneous international communication by electronic mail and fax to think of Ventris producing and circulating multiple copies of his correspondence to these dozen scholars based in Britain, the U.S.A., Finland, Germany, Austria, Czechoslovakia, Italy, Bulgaria, Greece and Turkey.

Over the next two years Ventris circulated a series of 'work-notes' to a larger group of scholars, including Bennett, who published a first transcription of the new tablets from Pylos in 1951. Ventris's efforts culminated in work-note 20, dated 1 June 1952 (not long after *Scripta Minoa* II had finally appeared) entitled 'Are the Knossos and Pylos tablets written in Greek?', and introduced, with characteristic self-effacing modesty as a 'frivolous digression'. Just one month later, on 1 July 1952, he announced on BBC radio that the Linear B script recorded an early form of the Greek language, a result that Evans could never have countenanced.

That broadcast caught the ear of John Chadwick (FIG. 77), at the time on the staff of the *Oxford Latin Dictionary*, about to take up a lectureship at Cambridge University. Chadwick offered Ventris his assistance as a 'mere philologist' in his endeavour to develop the decipherment. The first fruits of their collaboration was 'Evidence for Greek Dialect in the Mycenaean Archives', the first scholarly presentation of the decipherment in *The Journal of Hellenic Studies* for 1953. Only four years after the decipherment, in 1956, there followed the monumental *Documents in Mycenaean Greek*, a sustained commentary by Ventris and Chadwick on a large selection of the newly deciphered documents. Tragically the same year also brought Ventris's death, in a road accident. In 1958, Chadwick published *The Decipherment of Linear B*, a personal account of the decipherment, in which he paid eloquent tribute to Ventris's extraordinary talents.

Just as Champollion's decipherment opened up a new discipline of Egyptology, so the decipherment of Linear B created a new scholarly discipline, 'Mycenaean studies', or, more commonly in the U.S.A., 'Mycenology'. In April 1956 Ventris and Chadwick had been among the twenty participants from seven countries at the discipline's first ever international colloquium, held near Paris at Gif-sur-Yvette. The international spirit, known as the

FIG. 77 John Chadwick (1920–98), Ventris's collaborator in developing the decipherment, with Helen Wace in front of the Treasury of Atreus, Mycenae, in 1953. (John Killen)

'esprit de Gif' among Mycenologists, has continued, fostered by its parent organisation, the Comité internationale permanent des études mycéniennes. To date, colloquia have now been held in Italy, the U.S.A., Britain, Spain, Switzerland, Germany, Yugoslavia, Greece and Austria, and there have been two international congresses (both held in Italy). Sessions on Mycenaean studies formed part of international classical congresses in Czechoslovakia, Ireland, and Hungary.

The decipherment revolutionised the study of the history of the Greek language and Indo-European linguistics in general. British scholars, notably Chadwick and L. R. Palmer and Palmer's successor as Professor of Comparative Philology at Oxford, Anna Morpurgo Davies, rapidly incorporated the results into their own teaching and scholarship, as did their counterparts in Europe, such as A. Bartonek, P. Chantraine, J.-L. García-Ramón, P. Ilievski, M. Lejeune, G. Neumann, E. Risch, C. J. Ruijgh, M. Ruipérez, O. Panagl and others. Chadwick understood that the documents were not mere linguistic data, and his own publications also reflected a more general approach to understanding the workings of the administrations on Crete and the mainland. Among ancient historians, Moses Finley was among the first to realise that the Linear B tablets made the picture of the Bronze Age offered by the Homeric poems anachronistic, a view supported by Chadwick, and now almost universally held by Dark Age archaeologists and historians. Others have used the Linear B data to develop our understanding of Late Bronze Age social history, notably P. Carlier, in France, S. Deger-Jalkotzy and S. Hiller, in Austria, and C. Thomas in the U.S.A.

The move away from narrow philology became increasingly important in the second generation of Mycenaean scholars, among whom John Killen's work on the economic administration of Crete, particularly its textile industry, stands out in Britain, while the work of P. de Fidio, L. Godart, J. L. Melena and J.-P. Olivier holds a similar standing on the continent. Olivier transformed our understanding of the intricacies of Mycenaean administration by identifying the scribal hands working in the Knossos archive, while Bennett, followed by his own pupil T. G. Palaima, carried out similar research on the Pylos archive.

Just how important Chadwick's influence has been is highlighted by his prophetic call, at the 3rd Cretological Congress in 1971, for scholars to integrate the Linear B documentary information with that available from archaeology. It is this approach that has been most fruitful in the past fifteen years through the work of a third generation of scholars. The date of Knossos's destruction still remains controversial, but the sometimes acrimonious controversy of the 1960s has now been dissipated somewhat by Jan Driessen's demonstration that the Linear B documents discovered by Evans in the Room of the Chariot Tablets (including Ce 59: FIG. 75) belong to an earlier horizon than the rest of the archive and there were, therefore, at least two 'Linear B' destruction horizons at Knossos and perhaps as many as six. We understand the workings of the Knossos administration and economy to a considerable degree, if perhaps not quite as well as that of mainland Pylos. John Bennet and others have demonstrated that Knossos controlled and exploited a large part of Crete before its destruction, while P. Halstead, building on Killen's work, has proposed the existence of a substantial non-palatial sector within the overall agricultural economy on Crete. Palaima and R. Palmer in the U.S.A. have also elucidated areas of palatial activity such as seafaring, warfare, and wine production, while C. W. Shelmerdine, well known for her work on the Pylos perfumed oil industry has recently begun a comparative study of administration throughout the 'Linear B world'.

We now have many more Linear B administrative documents than were available to Ventris at the time of the decipherment. Tablets have now been found at Mycenae, Thebes and Tiryns, on the mainland, and Khania, on Crete, raising the possibility of multiple literate administrations on the island. Also the site of Midea has produced inscribed sealings. Similarly, in addition to the finds at Orchomenos known to Evans, more stirrup jars with painted Linear B inscriptions have turned up on the mainland (notably at Thebes, Kreusis, Eleusis, Mycenae, and Tiryns, many of them manufactured in West Crete) and on Crete itself (particularly at Khania, but also at Knossos, Mallia, and Armenoi). Indeed one of the British School's major contributions to the study of exchange within the Aegean has been to use scientific analyses to demonstrate the provenance of these jars, inscribed and plain, a project carried out at the Fitch Laboratory, under the direction of Richard Jones.

What of Linear A and Cretan Hieroglyphic? Our chances of deciphering either of these scripts are very small unless more documents are found. The best way of visualising the problem is to quantify the number of texts in terms of pages of A4 required to carry the preserved signs: over 30 pages for the Linear B corpus, but only 7–8 for Linear A, and 1 for Cretan Hieroglyphic. Unlike the situation in Ventris's day, there are excellent corpora for both scripts. All but the most recently discovered documents in Linear A have been published by the Belgian scholars L. Godart and J.-P. Olivier, in *Recueil des inscriptions en linéaire A* (*GORILA*, for short), while the same team has recently completed a similar corpus of Hieroglyphic seals and documents: the *Corpus Hieroglyphicarum Inscriptionum Cretae* (*CHIC*). Although there have been quite sober attempts to identify the language behind the Linear A as Anatolian (notably by Palmer, G. P. Goold and Maurice Pope) or Semitic (Cyrus Gordon), no decipherment can yet be utterly convincing without either significantly more material, or a Minoan 'Rosetta Stone' – a bilingual inscription. It might well be objects like the 'libation table' acquired by Evans in 1896 (FIG. 74) that offer continuous text, with some repeated formulae, rather than names, commodities and numbers on tablets, that hold the key, as Y. Duhoux has demonstrated.

Our knowledge of the *use* of scripts other than Linear B on Crete has increased enormously since Evans's day through archaeological observations, even though neither script has been deciphered. We owe this knowledge partly to discoveries of more material by continental scholars, notably the Italians at Phaistos and Haghia Triadha, the French and Belgians at Mallia, and Greeks throughout the island. British and American excavations have also revealed Linear A at Phylakopi on Melos and Ayia Irini on Keos respectively, while Greek excavations on Samothrace and Thera have turned up further examples in recent years. Moreover, we now know that Evans's evolutionary scheme for the development of the scripts is not strictly accurate. While there appears to be only a very small overlap between Linear A and Linear B, it is now clear that Linear A originated in south-central Crete and was in use at Phaistos in the Protopalatial period, while Cretan Hieroglyphic was in use at Protopalatial Knossos and Mallia (and some other smaller sites, including the recently excavated site of Petras near Siteia). Only in the Neopalatial period did Linear A become the predominant script on the island. J. Weingarten and E. Hallager have elucidated the way in which administration worked in pre-Linear B Crete by examining sealing systems, while I. Schoep, in a recent doctoral dissertation, has integrated our knowledge of Hieroglyphic and Linear A to reconstruct how administration developed and changed on the island from the Protopalatial to Neopalatial periods.

As the millennium ends and the century following those first discoveries by Evans at Knossos comes to a close, our understanding of the linguistic history and administration of the Late Bronze Age Aegean has increased enormously. The future still holds many discoveries that will modify the picture. Just as Knossos was the only site on Crete to provide Linear B tablets for eighty-nine years prior to the first discoveries at Khania, so future discoveries will modify the picture we have now reconstructed. Given sufficient quantities of new material (or a bilingual), it is likely that the twenty-first century will see the decipherment of Linear A, even Cretan Hieroglyphic . . . maybe even Cypro-Minoan, the related but even more enigmatic script of Late Bronze Age Cyprus, with all the possibilities that that might offer for links with the cultures of the East Mediterranean.

JOHN BENNET

J. Bennet, 'The Structure of the Linear B Administration of Knossos', *AJA* 89 (1985), 231–49.

E. L. Bennett, Jr., 'Fractional Quantities in Minoan Bookkeeping', *AJA* 54 (1950), 204–22.

W. C. Brice, *Inscriptions in the Minoan Linear Script of Class A* (Oxford, 1961).

A. Brown, *Before Knossos . . . Arthur Evans's Travels in the Balkans and Crete* (Oxford, 1993).

H. W. Catling, J. F. Cherry, R. E. Jones, and J. T. Killen, 'The Linear B Inscribed Stirrup Jars and West Crete', *BSA* 75 (1980), 49–113.

J. Chadwick, *The Decipherment of Linear B*, 2nd edition (Cambridge, 1967).

J. Chadwick, *The Mycenaean World* (Cambridge, 1976).

J. Chadwick, *Linear B and Related Scripts* (London, 1987).

J. Chadwick *et al.*, *Corpus of Mycenaean Inscriptions from Knossos*, 4 vols. (Cambridge/Rome, 1986–1999).

J. M. Driessen, *An Early Destruction in the Mycenaean Palace at Knossos: A New Interpretation of the Excavation Field-Notes of the South-East Area of the West Wing* (Leuven, 1990).

Y. Duhoux, 'Le linéaire A: problèmes de déchiffrement', in Y. Duhoux, T. G. Palaima and J. Bennet (eds.), *Problems in Decipherment* (Louvain-la-neuve, 1989), 59–119.

A. J. Evans, *Cretan Pictographs and Prae-Phoenician Script . . .* (London, 1895).

A. J. Evans, *Further Discoveries of Cretan and Aegean Script . . .* (London, 1898).

A. J. Evans, *Scripta Minoa* i. (Oxford, 1909).

A. J. Evans, *Scripta Minoa* ii. edited by J. L. Myres (Oxford, 1952).

M. Finley, 'Mycenaean Palace Archives and Economic History', (reprinted in M. I. Finley, *Economy and Society in Ancient Greece* (Harmondsworth, 1982), 199–212).

L. Godart and J.-P. Olivier, *Recueil des inscriptions en linéaire A*, 5 vols. (Paris, 1976–1985).

E. Hallager, *The Minoan Roundel and Other Sealed Documents in the Neopalatial Linear A Administration*, 2 vols. (Liège-Austin, 1996).

E. Hallager, M. Vlasaki and B. P. Hallager, 'New Linear B Tablets from Khania', *Kadmos* 31 (1992), 61–87.

P. Halstead, 'Lost Sheep? On the Linear B Evidence for Breeding Flocks at Knossos and Pylos', *Minos* 25–26 (1990–1991), 343–65.

J. T. Killen, 'The Wool Industry of Crete in the Late Bronze Age', *BSA* 59 (1964), 1–15.

A. Morpurgo Davies and Y. Duhoux, (eds.), *Linear B: A 1984 Survey* (Louvain-la-neuve, 1985).

J.-P. Olivier, *Les scribes de Cnossos* (Rome, 1967).

J.-P. Olivier, 'Cretan Writing in the Second Millennium B.C.', *World Archaeology* 17 (1986), 377–89.

J.-P. Olivier and L. Godart, *Corpus Hieroglyphicarum Inscriptionum Cretae* (Paris, 1996).

T. G. Palaima, *The Scribes of Pylos* (Rome, 1988).

I. Schoep, *Minoan Administration on Crete.* Ph.D. dissertation, Katholieke Universiteit Leuven (Leuven, 1996).

C. W. Shelmerdine, 'Workshops and Record Keeping in the Mycenaean World', in R. Laffineur and P. P. Betancourt (eds.), *TEXNH: Craftsmen, Craftswomen and Craftsmanship in the Aegean Bronze Age* (Liège-Austin, 1997), 387–96.

M. Ventris, *Work Notes on Minoan Language Research and Other Unedited Papers*, edited by A. Sacconi (Rome, 1988).

M. Ventris and J. Chadwick, 'Evidence for Greek Dialect in the Mycenaean Archives', *JHS* 73 (1953), 84–103.

M. G. F. Ventris and J. Chadwick, *Documents in Mycenaean Greek*, 2nd edition (Cambridge, 1973).

J. Weingarten, 'Three Upheavals in Minoan Sealing Administration: Evidence for Radical Change', in T. G. Palaima (ed.), *Aegean Seals, Sealings and Administration* (Liège-Austin, 1990), 105–20.

MINOAN RELIGION

Arthur Evans's first work on Minoan civilisation was his 'The Mycenaean Tree and Pillar Cult'. This set the scene for future study of Minoan religion. From the beginning, scholarly perception has been that religion so permeated Minoan society, that to separate it would be to unravel our pattern of understanding. Thus almost every scholar who has written about Minoan civilisation includes something pertinent to Minoan religion. This creates a complex task for a limited discussion: how does one avoid a mere bibliographic list or descriptive repetition of familiar objects? How does one tease out the meaningful strands of the pattern, and yet be fair to the myriad of individual ideas? More complex still, how does one establish an individually British contribution to a study whose virtue lies in its integration of international and cosmopolitan insights?

British scholars have made key contributions to every aspect of Minoan religious study: iconography, artifact analysis, socio-religious interaction, linguistic study, cult places. Many of these have been generated from fieldwork: explorations, excavations, and surveys. Interpretation has been driven by new discoveries and a strong practical approach to artifacts. It would be wrong, however, to assume that British studies of Minoan religion, are merely concerned with artifacts. It is commonly observed of Evans that he was influenced by anthropology and the interpretative fashions of his day. Though not uniquely British, this may reflect something of an intellectual tradition. The influence of anthropology and a concern for interpretative structure clearly underpin many of the most significant British contributions to the understanding of Minoan religion. The present study therefore will explore this intellectual theme as a way of approaching key elements of Minoan religion, and the ideas of the British scholars who have written on them.

Intellectual Context of Evans's Minoan Goddess

Evans used the publication of the Palace of Minos at Knossos to establish a comprehensive structure for the understanding of every part of Minoan culture. Of the objects fundamental to his, and later, reconstructions of Minoan religion, perhaps the most famous is the smaller faience 'snake-goddess' from the Temple Repositories at Knossos (FIGS. 78 and 79). She is probably the one single Minoan object recognisable everywhere. She embodies much of Evans's interpretation of Minoan religion, one which wields enormous influence in later studies. As Lucy Goodison and Christine Morris rightly observe, she has been appropriated as an icon of the modern Goddess Movement.

The Knossos 'snake-goddess' represents in microcosm the image of the female, which Evans perceived to be the primary Minoan

FIG. 78 Early photographs from the Evans Archive of the 'snake goddess' found in the Temple Repositories of the Palace of Minos at Knossos. (Ashmolean Museum Oxford)

symbol of the divine, and the main focus for Minoan rituals, such as those evocatively recorded on frescoes, e.g. the Sacred Grove and seal rings like the Isopata Ring (FIG. 80). Evans's explicit statement of his Minoan Goddess model may be found in *The Palace of Minos* ii. 277:

'At the same time we do not encounter any such multiplicity of divinities as in the Classical World, and in fact are constantly brought back to the same Great Mother with her Child or Consort whose worship under various names and titles extended over a large part of Asia Minor and the Syrian regions beyond. The Goddess, indeed, is seen with doves perched on her head in a celestial relation, or with serpents twined round her as Lady of the Underworld and averter, we may believe, of the constantly recurring scourge of earthquakes. As Mother Goddess we see her with her hands on her

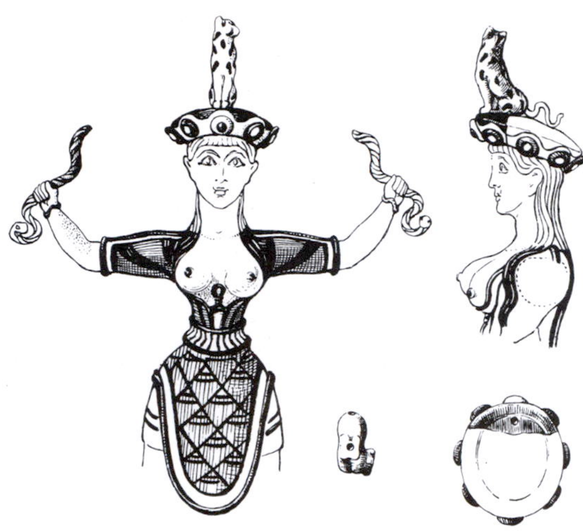

FIG. 79 Later reconstruction of the 'snake goddess' with tiara and seated animal. (A. J. Evans, *The Palace of Minos* i. 504, Fig. 362)

matronly breasts, but with the same tiara, and the same apparel even to the patterns of her dress. As the source of all vegetation she holds corn and poppy-capsules and lilies, and rises from the ground like

FIG. 80 The Isopata Ring. (A. J. Evans, 'The Tomb of the Double Axes', *Archaeologia* 65 (1914), 10, Fig. 16)

Demeter in later myth. With bow and arrow she hunts the roe like Artemis, or, wielding her symbolic double-axe, takes on an Amazonian aspect. At times she holds an anchor as Mistress of the Sea. But throughout these changing impersonations we still feel ourselves in the presence of essentially the same divinity rather than separate mythological deities, like those of later Greece.'

In such passages commentators have discerned the influence of Frazer's *The Golden Bough*. Indeed one might speculate that the title of 'The Mycenaean Tree and Pillar Cult' is a deliberate evocation of *The Golden Bough*. Among recent British critics, Oliver Dickinson states the case for Frazer's influence most strongly, and remarks of the Minoan Goddess model: 'unfortunately a very large proportion of this depends on accepting highly questionable hypotheses.' The first edition of *The Golden Bough* was published in 1890, four years before Evans set foot on Crete in 1894. The subsequent enlarged editions were all published in the early years of the century, up to the 1920s, precisely the same time period when Evans was excavating, writing, and publishing *The Palace of Minos*. Evans and Frazer even shared the same publisher, Macmillan.

Curiously, however, there seems to be only one reference to Frazer in Evans, and that to his lectures on kingship. Therefore, rather than any direct linear influence between Frazer and Evans, the relationship may be more complex. The Greek archaeologist Nanno Marinatos, places Evans within the broader context of the universalist notions of nineteenth-century European social evolutionism and its studies of 'primitive' cultures. Like contemporary anthropological writings, 'The Mycenaean Tree and Pillar Cult' is filled with comparisons with other ancient and contemporary tribal cultures. Marinatos, following Burkert, also cites the concepts of fertility, vegetation, and renewal stressed by the German scholar Mannhardt in 1870. R. Hutton identifies the even earlier work of Gerhard (1849), who postulated the existence of a single great goddess, preceding Greek Classical goddesses. The contributors to Goodison and Morris's *Ancient Goddesses* drew similar conclusions about the origins and evolution of the Goddess idea within the broader realms of European and Near Eastern, as well as Mediterranean, archaeology.

Viewed in this way, the origin of Evans's Minoan 'Mother Goddess' model should not be seen in a direct linear relationship to Frazer. Rather, the theories of both authors, and others, are responses to a spirit of the age, where ideas mutually evolve and recreate in an interactive set of relationships.

Minoan Deity – one or many?

Whether influenced by Frazer or more broadly developed, Evans's interpretative model of the Minoan Goddess is the source of the most contentious theme in the study of Minoan religion: the debate between 'monotheism' and 'polytheism.' Evans' statement, quoted above, about the universality of the Minoan Goddess has been characterised as 'Minoan monotheism'. Dickinson rightly criticises the loose and uncritical acceptance of the Goddess model. Absolute monotheism is misleading here, as Evans refers to the essential companion of the conventional Mother Goddess, a junior male deity, with various roles as 'Child or Consort.' D. G. Hogarth coined the term 'Dual Monotheism' in support of this interpretation.

The Swedish scholar M. P. Nilsson also quoted private correspondence with Evans, where the latter asserted 'it is convenient, in default of more definite knowledge, to treat the Goddess as essentially the same great Nature Goddess under various aspects.' Nilsson quotes this in contrast to his own views on the 'polytheistic' nature of Greek Bronze Age religion. In *The Minoan-Mycenaean Religion* Nilsson was not content simply to demonstrate that many symbolic and iconographic features of later Greek religion have their origin in Aegean Bronze Age religious art. He also argued that there was an essential continuity of belief, focused on the personages of the divinities themselves: that the major classical deities, especially Athena, Hera, Artemis, Zeus etc., were worshipped in the Bronze Age. Nilsson has rightly been criticised for presenting his argument from the later Greek perspective, rather than perceiving that Bronze Age beliefs evolved into the later deities. Nevertheless he did have a wider purpose, which was to demonstrate the fundamental Greekness of Aegean civilisation, a view against which the conventional philological classicists of his time were prejudiced. This does, however, create a flaw in Nilsson's otherwise remarkable account, and one which goes against his own 'leading principle to interpret the Minoan monuments, as far as possible, from themselves'.

The Minoan 'polytheist' cause received a major boost with the decipherment of Linear B. Evans had already surmised that some of the Minoan texts might have a religious content, as did the scripts of contemporary cultures. Michael Ventris's decipherment in 1952 proved Evans correct. John Chadwick, applying Ventris's values to the Knossos tablets, recognised on V52 the name *Potinija Atana* – Potnia (Lady) Athena (FIG. 81). Subsequent studies of the Linear B texts have revealed the names of other Greek deites: Diwios (Zeus), Diwia, Damata (Demeter), Dionysos, Paiawon, Eileithyia, and others. Many of these names also appear on tablets from the Mycenaean Mainland, which raises problems about the identification of these names as specifically

FIG. 81 Linear B tablet from Knossos (V 52).
a-ta-na-po-ti-ni-ja 1 [. . .
e-nu-wa-ri-jo 1 pa-ja-wo-[ne? 1] po-se-da[-o-ne 1?
(Mycenaean Epigraphy Room, Faculty of Classics, Cambridge)

Minoan deities. Among the names unique to the Knossos tablets are several which seem to be female epithets rather than individual names.

For the study of religion, the Linear B decipherment has been frustrating. There are no religious or ritual texts similar to those in Egyptian Hieroglyphic or Hittite. These tantalising names are recorded only as the recipients of offerings.

Other British scholars have sustained the monotheism/polytheism debate. The literature about Minoan religion often referred to two conventional images of Minoan female divinity, the Mistress of Animals (a proto-Artemis) and the Household or Snake Goddess (a proto-Athena). These terms were used by both sides of the debate, as representing either aspects of a single deity or two separate deities. Keith Branigan demonstrated that many of the symbols and iconographic features conventionally attributed to each 'Goddess' do in fact overlap. His altogether reasonable conclusion was that these two aspects should be perceived as a single figure. The article's very real contribution was in demonstrating the essential artificiality of a division between the Mistress of Animals and the Household Goddess. Once established, these labels took on a life which was quite independent of, and at times obscured, the actual evidence for the identification of Minoan deities.

Within the debate Peter Warren has modified his view. His identification of the Myrtos Goddess (FIG. 48) as one of a group of Early Minoan female vessel figurines led him to suggest that they were all individual and different deities. A more 'monotheist' interpretation has been implicit in his later writings, but was made explicit in a perceptive, unpublished lecture at Knossos in 1997. He took the notion of environmental domains: animals, water/sea, vegetation, the urban setting, and pointed out how they are combined in the shrine material of the Temple Repositories, and in one of the most explicit divine images in Aegean art, the goddess in the Thera Xeste 3 fresco. Warren's conclusion, that this multiplicity of domains incorporated into a single image clearly suggests an essential divine unity, not a polytheistic variety, should stand as one of the stronger arguments of Minoan 'monotheism.'

Goodison and Morris have moved the debate

into its latest phase. Their suggestions about Minoan animism (already developing in Goodison's *Death, Women, and the Sun*) and the symbolic significance of gender and nature raise fundamental questions about the whole definition of Minoan divinity.

An archaeology of religion

The most far-reaching analysis of Aegean religion attempted to date is surely Colin Renfrew's publication of his excavations at Phylakopi on Melos. Renewing British interest in the prehistory of Melos, Renfrew uncovered a complex of rooms whose finds included a group of figurines. The largest and finest of this group occupied a position of prominence in one room. Female, she was termed the Lady of Phylakopi (FIG. 82), and was interpreted as a goddess idol. The characterisation of the Phylakopi complex as a shrine allowed Renfrew to address the broad methodological issue of archaeology's treatment of religion, and specifically how to apply the New Archaeology to the identification and interpretation of religious material – a subject previously avoided. The evolution of these ideas was clearly instrumental in the development of Renfrew's notion of Cognitive Archaeology, a significant, if still controversial step for theoretical archaeology.

In setting out his interpretative framework, Renfrew argued it should be applicable to all excavated shrines, not just Phylakopi. He began by trying to establish a definition of religion, derived from anthropological work, notably that of Spiro and Geertz. They set up two opposed definitions of religion, still current in anthropology. Spiro's definition is 'an institution consisting of culturally patterned interaction with culturally postulated superhuman beings'. Geertz defines religion as 'a system of symbols which acts to establish powerful, pervasive and long-lasting moods and motivations in men by formulating conceptions of a general order of existence, and clothing these conceptions with such an aura of factuality that the moods and motivations seem uniquely realistic'.

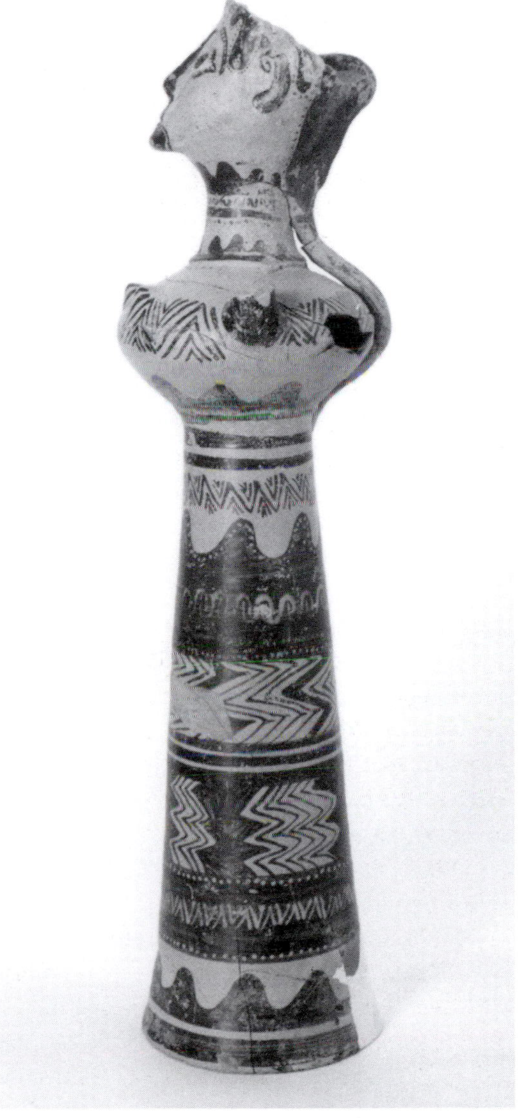

FIG. 82 The 'Lady of Phylakopi', Melos. (L. Morgan in *The Archaeology of Cult: The Sanctuary at Phylakopi*, BSA supp. vol. 18; London, 1985)

Not surprisingly Renfrew rejected Geertz's definition, criticising its vagueness. This was a little unfair, especially as Geertz later refined his ideas. More significantly, in preferring Spiro's definition of religion, Renfrew was aligning himself with an approach which Tambiah has defined as 'neo-Tylorian' (after the nineteenth-century anthropologist, E. B. Tylor). The problem is that religion is here defined only in terms of western religious experience, characterised by belief in panthea of deities, or Judaeo-Christian monotheism. This approach tends to undervalue the performative, experiential aspects of religion, where experience of the transcendent need not be defined in personalised terms.

Part of the reason for the monotheism/polytheism debate in Minoan religion having remained unresolved despite a century of vigorous debate is perhaps because it asks the wrong questions. If we take a non-theist, or 'anti-Tylorian' approach to Minoan religion we can ask more interesting questions, such as, did the Minoans express their experience of the transcendent by personalising it in terms of deity? Or even more fundamental, how did the Minoans experience the transcendent?

The problematic nature of religious definitions apart, Renfrew's analytical framework for interpreting religious material is more successful. He established four basic criteria for identifying religious artifacts within their context, and presented a longer series of interpretative correlates. But it was his most basic point which was the most important: 'In practice the recognition of cult must be on the basis of *context*: single indications are rarely sufficient in themselves. Any single find of supposedly cult significance, could, for instance, be dismissed in the absence of other evidence as either a toy or as a secular object'. In other words, the assemblage is more important than any single object within it.

It may seem a simple point for an archaeologist to make that context is important, but it is sometimes worth stressing the obvious. The lack of a coherent approach to religion has meant that archaeologists have often lost their intellectual rigour, relied too much on intuition, and thus have strayed into the 'speculative stratosphere' when interpreting religion. Curiously Renfrew's methodology has been used relatively little in subsequent studies of Aegean religion. (Alan Peatfield used it as framework for the preliminary report of the Atsipadhes peak sanctuary excavation). This is regrettable because the principles of contextuality can be used as an interpretative methodology. The American archaeologists Kent Flannery and Joyce Marcus term it 'holistic archaeology' in their contribution to Renfrew's *Ancient Mind*. Furthermore Peatfield has argued that the methodology of context has broader applications than for archaeology alone; even anthropology and social sciences have something to learn from archaeology here.

Ritual action

The dichotomy between the 'neo-Tylorian' approach to Minoan religion centred on the divine being, and the more performative perspective also emerged in Warren's analysis of Minoan ritual action.

One of the achievements of international Minoan scholarship is the sophistication of iconographic interpretation. For a prehistoric culture, iconography, with its interaction of symbols, figures, and actions, offers a visual narrative of cult practice and belief that replaces verbal description. Warren drew all this together in his 1986 Felix Neubergh Lecture *Minoan Religion as Ritual Action*. He observed that the study of objects, places, and texts, can produce a static picture of Minoan religion, and set about creating a more dynamic perspective. Borrowing the vocabulary of Eleusinian mystery cult, Warren defined ritual action as things done, things said or sung, and things displayed or envisioned in epiphany. These were then illustrated through an analysis of Minoan iconography, wherein he identified rituals based on the manipulation of objects, baetyls, robes, and flowers, as well as dance and sacrifice.

Warren's particular contribution here is his perception of a structure to Minoan religion, which he terms 'the operation of belief' (FIG. 83). He does fall prey to the divine-being definition of religion by suggesting the immediate purpose of ritual was 'to invoke the presence of the divinity and to gain communion with her.' This refers to Evans's notion of epiphany, enacted or envisioned, in Minoan ritual, a purpose which Mark Cameron argued was fundamental to the understanding of the Knossos frescoes and the pageantry they imply. Nevertheless Warren does seem to be attempting to resolve the afore-mentioned dichotomy, by suggesting that through the performance of their rituals in their natural context, 'the Minoans display a positive, enquiring response, a proto-European attempt to understand and explain their environment and their cosmos'. The similarity to Geertz's definition of religion is obvious.

Peatfield made a similar structural approach to Minoan religion in his discussion of the concepts and actions involved in the Minoan ritual manipulation of liquid. Examining symbols and images of libation, purification, sacrifice, and rites of passage, the key point in

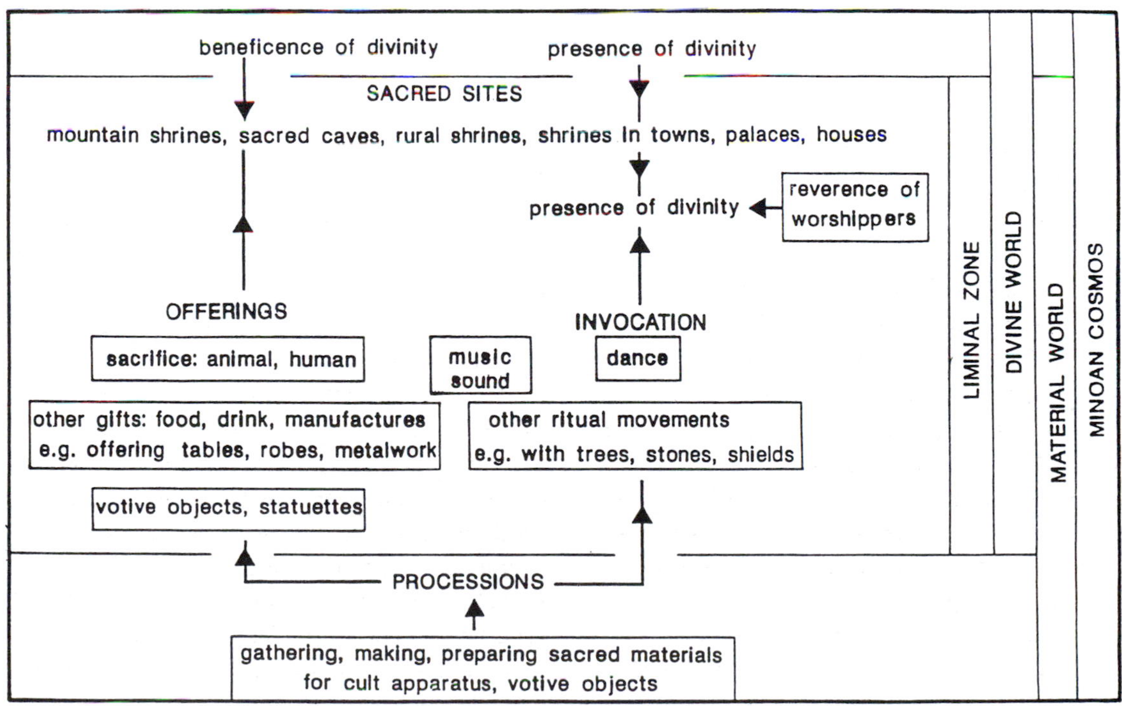

FIG. 83 The operation of belief. (P. M. Warren)

his article is that ritual action can hold together a multi-dimensional series of meanings, wherein religion becomes a dynamic counterpart to the ambiguity of poetry. Thus he argues that the performative element is itself the fundamental structure of religion, upon which beliefs may be articulated and transformed, in the continual process of becoming.

Cult places – peak sanctuaries

Most studies of Minoan religion are primarily artifact-orientated, focused on interpretation of the rich Minoan iconography found on frescoes, rings, seals and sealings, carved stone vases, vase-painting. In the early days of Minoan archaeology, however, this iconographic focus came at a price: the relative dearth of analytical discussion of shrines and sanctuaries. This was further restricted by the power of the language Evans used to define the religious character of rooms: throne-rooms, bench sanctuaries, lustral basins, pillar crypts etc. After Evans, the most consistent analysis came from the Greek archaeologist Nikolaos Platon, who wrote about various settlement and rural shrines. It was not until the 1970s and the work of the Polish archaeologist Bogdan Rutkowski, and the American Geraldine Gesell that the study of cult places was established as a specific field of study within Minoan religion, with its own parameters and methods.

FIG. 84 Atsipadhes Korakias peak sanctuary. A view of the mountain peak. (A. Peatfield)

FIG. 85 Atsipadhes Korakias peak sanctuary. Votive figurines *in situ*. (A. Peatfield)

In the early, exploratory phase of Minoan archaeology, sanctuaries in the Cretan countryside were identified, notably cave and peak sanctuaries. The excavations at the Kamares Cave by R. M. Dawkins and M. L. W. Laistner, and at the Psychro Cave by D. G. Hogarth, were key events in Minoan archaeology. Peak sanctuaries were defined by Myres's excavation in 1903 of Petsophas and Evans's exploration of Juktas in 1909. The material from these sites was poor in relation to the immense wealth of finds from the great palaces excavated in this period. Beyond excavation reports, therefore, these sanctuaries were summarily considered, even in Nilsson's otherwise comprehensive treatment of Minoan religion.

Rescue excavations necessitated by Cretan post-war economic expansion discovered many new rural sanctuaries. Platon wrote the first synthetic study of peak sanctuaries in 1951, and his colleague C. Davaras excavated many peak sanctuaries in the 1960s and 1970s. In 1974 another Greek, Alexandra Karetsou began a major campaign of excavation on Juktas; her extensive preliminary reports were the fullest account of a peak sanctuary since Myres's report of Petsophas.

British interest in peak sanctuaries was renewed by Peatfield in the 1980s. Until then peak sanctuaries had been inconsistently defined. Through study of the sites and their finds, Peatfield established criteria based on

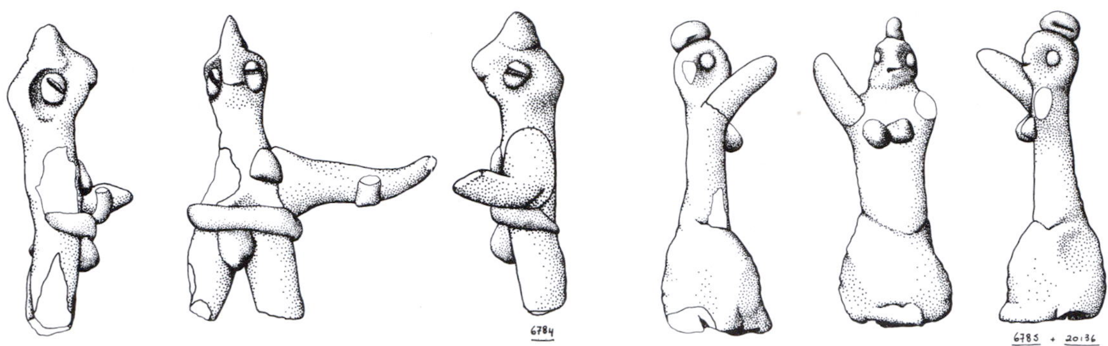

FIG. 86 Atsipadhes Korakias peak sanctuary; male and female figurines with outstretched arms in ritual postures. (A. Roberts and J. Doole)

common features of topography and offerings. Peak sanctuaries were also perceived to have a historical evolution which interacted with the social development of the Minoan palace state. This research contributed to the increased appreciation within Minoan studies of ideology and socio-religious interaction.

Peatfield's excavation of the Atsipadhes peak sanctuary in 1989, followed by the Ayios Vasilios survey, was designed to test his general ideas about peak sanctuaries, functional, historical, and topographic (FIG. 84). But part of the excavator's purpose was to take the traditional archaeological techniques in which the British School excels, and to stretch their interpretative possibilities. Thus, the precise three-dimensional recording of all the material on Atsipadhes enabled the recovery of the spatial dynamics of the sanctuary in remarkable detail (FIG. 85). Study of the pottery has implications for the general identification of ritual assemblages, Minoan and Neolithic. The application, for the first time, of the methodologies of ceramic attribution to peak sanctuary figurines reveals the character of non-élite Minoan religion and its expression within the ritual landscape. Moreover, their previously unappreciated postures, their ritual action frozen in time, are emerging as fundamental witnesses to the nature of Minoan religious experience (FIG. 86).

It would seem to be an inherent contradiction to conclude that archaeology, the interpretative science of the physical and material, should devote so much study to religion, the supremely metaphysical creation of mind and spirit. Yet surely one of the lessons of a century of Minoan scholarship is that the analysis of the performed allows at least a glimpse of the creative soul. It remains for the scholars of the next millennium to draw on the intellectual legacy of Evans and his heirs, and to demonstrate how the study of Minoan religion can transcend narrow regional and chronological specialities, contributing insights of universal significance to the very nature of human spiritual experience.

ALAN PEATFIELD

K. Branigan, 'The Genesis of the Household Goddess', *SMEA* 8 (1969), 28–38.

K. Branigan, *The Foundations of Palatial Crete* (London, 1970), 92–113.

J.H Chadwick, *The Mycenaean World* (Cambridge, 1976), 84–101.

G. Cadogan, 'Clay tubes in Minoan religion', *3rd Cretological Congress, Rethymnon 1971* (Athens, 1973), 34–8.

M.A.S. Cameron, 'Theoretical interrelations among Theran, Cretan and Mainland frescoes', in *Thera and the Aegean World I* (London, 1978), 579–92.

M.A.S. Cameron, 'The "palatial" thematic system in the Knossos murals', in *Minoan Palaces* (1987), 320–8.

C. Crowther, 'A note on Minoan Dikta', *BSA* 83 (1988), 42.

O.T.P.K. Dickinson, *The Aegean Bronze Age* (Cambridge, 1994), 257–94.

O.T.P.K. Dickinson, 'Comments on a popular model of Minoan religion', *OJA* 13(2) (1994), 173–84.

A.J. Evans, 'The Mycenaean tree and pillar cult', *JHS* 21 (1901), 99–202.

A.J. Evans, 'New light on the cult and sanctuaries of Minoan Crete', *3rd Int. Congress for the History of Religions*, vol. 2 (Oxford, 1908), 195–7.

J.G. Frazer, *The Golden Bough* 1st edition (London, 1890).

L. Goodison, *Death, Women and the Sun* (BICS supp. vol. 53; London, 1989).

L. Goodison and C. Morris (eds.), *Ancient Goddesses* (London, 1998).

D.G. Hogarth, 'The Dictaean Cave', *BSA* 6 (1899–1900), 94–116.

M.S.F. Hood, 'Minoan town-shrines?' *Greece and Eastern Mediterranean. Studies presented to Fritz Schachermeyr* (Berlin, 1977), 156–72.

J.T. Hooker, 'Minoan religion in the Late Palace period', in *Minoan Society* (1983), 137–42.

R. Hutton, 'The Neolithic Great Goddess: a study in modern tradition', *Antiquity* 71 (1997), 91–9.

J.T. Killen, 'Piety begins at home; place-names on Knossos records of religious offerings', in P.H. Ilievski and L. Crepajac (eds.), *Tractata Mycenaea. 8th International Colloquium on Mycenaean Studies*, 1985 (Skopje, 1987), 163–78.

L. Morgan, 'Idea, idiom, and iconography', in P. Darcque and J-C. Poursat (eds.), *L'iconographie minoenne.* (BCH supp. vol. 11; Paris, 1985), 5–19.

C.E. Morris and V. Batten, 'Final Neolithic pottery from the Atsipadhes Korakias peak sanctuary', in *8th Cretological Congress, Rethymnon 1996* (in press).

C.E. Morris and A.A.D. Peatfield, 'Feeling through the body: gesture in Cretan Bronze Age religion', in Y. Hamilakis and S. Tarlow (eds.), *Thinking Through the Body* (Lampeter, 1998) (in press).

J.L. Myres, 'Excavations at Palaikastro II. The sanctuary-site of Petsofa', *BSA* 9 (1902–3), 356–87.

A.A.D. Peatfield, 'The topography of Minoan peak sanctuaries', *BSA* 78 (1983), 273–9.

A.A.D. Peatfield, 'Palace and peak: the political and religious relationship between palaces and peak sanctuaries', in *Minoan Palaces* (1987), 89–93.

A.A.D. Peatfield, 'Minoan peak sanctuaries: history and society', *Op.Ath.* 18 (1990), 117–31.

A.A.D. Peatfield, 'Rural ritual in Bronze Age Crete: the peak sanctuary at Atsipadhes', *CAJ* 2 (1992), 59–87.

A.A.D. Peatfield, 'After the Big Bang: Minoan shrines and symbols beyond Palatial collapse', in S. Alcock and R. Osborne (eds.), *Placing the Gods: Greek Sanctuaries in Space* (Oxford, 1994), 19–36.

A.A.D. Peatfield, 'Cognitive Aspects of Religious Symbolism: an archaeologist's perspective', *CAJ* 4 (1994), 149–55.

A.A.D. Peatfield, 'Water, fertility, and purification in Minoan Religion', in C.E. Morris (ed.), *KLADOS: essays in honour of J.N. Coldstream*. (BICS, supp. vol. 63; London, 1995), 217–27.

A.A.D. Peatfield, 'Minoan religion for ordinary people', in *8th Cretological Congress, Iraklion Crete, 1996*. (in press)

A.C. Renfrew, 'Questions of Minoan and Mycenaean cult', in *Sanctuaries and Cults* (1981), 27–33.

A.C. Renfrew, 'The sanctuary at Phylakopi', in *Sanctuaries and Cults* (1981), 67–79.

A.C. Renfrew, *Towards an Archaeology of Mind* (Cambridge, 1982).

A.C. Renfrew, *The Archaeology of Cult. The Sanctuary at Phylakopi*. (BSA supp. vol. 18; London, 1985).

A.C. Renfrew, 'The archaeology of religion', in C.

Renfrew and E.B.W. Zubrow (eds.) *The Ancient Mind: Elements of Cognitive Archaeology* (Cambridge, 1994), 47–54.

S. Wall, J. Musgrave, and P. M. Warren, 'Human bones from a Late Minoan Ib house at Knossos', *BSA* 81 (1986), 333–88.

P.M. Warren, 'The beginnings of Minoan Religion', in *Antichità Cretesi. Studi in onore di Doro Levi* (Catania, 1980), 137–47.

P.M. Warren, 'Minoan Crete and ecstatic religion. Preliminary observations on the 1979 excavations at Knossos', in *Sanctuaries and Cults* (1981), 155–66.

P.M. Warren, 'The Minoans and their gods', in B. Cunliffe (ed.), *Origins: the Roots of European Civilisation* (London, 1987), 30–41.

P.M. Warren, 'The Ring of Minos', in *EILAPINI* (1987), 485–500.

P.M. Warren, *Minoan Religion as Ritual Action,* SIMA 72 (Gothenburg, 1988).

P.M. Warren, 'Of baetyls', *Op. Ath.* 18 (1990), 193–206.

THE POSTPALATIAL PERIOD

If Knossos was the most powerful of Minoan palaces in Late Minoan I, it was undoubtedly the capital of the island after the Late Minoan IB destructions. Since any discussion of post-palatial or, let us say, post-LM IB Crete, involves Knossos, the destruction date of the Palace and its Linear B archive is a key issue for the reconstruction of not only Knossian but also Late Bronze Age Aegean history. Duncan Mackenzie, A. J. Evans's field director, in a letter of 1901 addressed to his employer, expressed explicitly his views on the last days of the Palace at Knossos and convinced Evans that the latest occupation phase was of a non-palatial character, a 'reoccupation' representing a period of decadence after the Palace and its Linear B archive were destroyed by fire. Evans associated this destruction, which preserved the Linear B tablets, with pottery of the so-called Palace Style dated to LM II, at about 1425 BC (FIG. 87). It is not an exaggeration to say that the field of post-LM IB studies is still dominated by Mackenzie's interpretation of the stratigraphy at Knossos.

Some fifty years after their discovery, the decipherment of the Linear B script by Michael Ventris was the next most exciting moment in the study of LM III Crete. However nobody could anticipate the sweeping changes it would bring to the field in the following decade. The seeds of doubt were planted by C. W. Blegen in 1958, when, following the decipherment of Linear B, he suggested that the archives of Knossos and Pylos were roughly contemporary, the Pylos destruction being dated around 1190 BC. In 1963 the publication of *On the Knossos Tablets*, by the linguist L. R. Palmer and the archaeologist John Boardman, launched the most lively and highly controversial debate in Minoan archaeology regarding the date of the destruction by fire which baked and preserved the Linear B archive of the Knossos Palace. Although originally intended as a combined publication on the date and findplace of the Linear B archives, the radically different opinions of the two authors resulted in the publication of two highly opposing accounts within the same volume. Palmer followed up Blegen's idea in concluding that the last Palace at Knossos was constructed and destroyed at the end of LM IIIB, *c.*1200 BC. Boardman, in defence of Evans's views, proposed that the Knossos Palace was destroyed by fire at the end of the LM II period, in about 1400 BC, and that all subsequent occupation, which ended in LM IIIB, was not associated with an archive. A different opinion regarding the destruction of the Palace was expressed in 1965 by Sinclair Hood who suggested a middle position in terms of dates and stratigraphy by associating certain deposits with the Palace destruction which Evans had assigned to the squatter re-occupation. In 1989, Peter Warren returned to Hood's idea by suggesting that a large number of deposits from

FIG. 87 Knossos, an early excavation photograph of the Throne Room, with the pottery found *in situ.* (Evans Archive, Ashmolean Museum Oxford)

the Palace were contemporary but belonged to an LM IIIA2 late destruction. According to Warren, all subsequent re-occupation was probably for cult purposes, centred around the Shrine of the Double Axes (FIG. 88).

The Knossos controversy initiated the re-examination of all aspects of Evans's work at Knossos embracing stratigraphy, architecture, frescoes, tablets, sealstones, sealings, stone vases and, last but not least, pottery. Since the debate was about the date of the Linear B archives at Knossos, much reference was made to the relevant pottery deposits excavated by Evans and Mackenzie. The need for a detailed pottery analysis brought on to the scene of Minoan archaeology Mervyn Popham, a scholar whose exemplary studies since the 1960s have defined the field of LM II and LM III Knossos. His publications on the LM IIIA and LM IIIB pottery from the Palace and surrounding houses at Knossos remain classic works of reference, not only for the study of LM III Knossos but for the stylistic analysis of contemporary ceramic material throughout the island. Popham's studies have brought a slight modification to Evans's dating of the destruction of the Palace to early LM IIIA2, a date which still remains a strong candidate for the end of palatial Knossos.

FIG. 88 Knossos, excavation of the Shrine of the Double Axes. (Evans Archive, Ashmolean Museum Oxford)

The pioneer work of British scholars in the 1960s and 1970s on the Knossos Palace initiated a re-examination of Evans's excavations through the detailed study of his excavation archive in combination with the preserved archaeological material. The work of Jean-Pierre Olivier on the scribes of Knossos, and of Erik Hallager and Wolf-Dietrich Niemeier in favour of an LM IIIB destruction of the Palace, were followed by the more recent work of Jacques Raison, Jan Driessen, Sieglinde Mirié, Sinclair Hood, Doniert Evely, Vasso Fotou, Nicoletta Momigliano, Marina Panagiotaki, and Eleni Hatzaki on different areas of the site.

Although the controversy around an early LM IIIA2 as against a late LM IIIB date for the Palace destruction had died down, recent discoveries have revived the dispute with new complications. The 'unity of the archives' has been doubted as a result of Driessen's re-examination of the Room of the Chariot Tablets in addition to the discovery at Khania of two Linear B tablets, from an LM IIIB1 deposit, written by a scribe well known for his administrative work at Knossos. The Linear B archive or archives of Knossos, regardless of their potential date, remain the largest corpus of written records for prehistoric Crete, providing an insight into Minoan-Mycenaean society in a way which will never be surpassed by material culture.

From the early days of his excavations, Evans's attention turned to the town and cemeteries of Minoan Knossos. The Royal Villa, the Little Palace, the High Priest's House and the Temple Tomb remain classic examples for the re-use of LM I buildings in LM II and LM III. The publication of the Zapher Papoura and Isopata cemeteries remains the basic work of reference for the burial customs of LM III Knossos. To these we can add a series of LM II–IIIA chamber tombs excavated by British archaeologists since the 1930s. Certain chamber tombs, such as those at Ayios Ioannis and Sellopoulo (FIG. 31), are classified as 'warrior graves', so-called because of the amount of weaponry found in them, providing a strong case in favour of the existence of an élite society at Knossos which adopted a mixture of Minoan and Mycenaean customs. Further evidence for such a mixture was produced by Popham's excavation of the Unexplored Mansion, which took place under the spell of the Knossos controversy (FIG. 89). The publication in 1984 of this Minoan building has confirmed that the stratigraphy of Knossos can be extremely complex and unpredictable. Although the Unexplored Mansion excavation did not solve the problem of dating the Knossos tablets, its results were highly rewarding, for prior to its publication, LM II was known only from Evans's excavation of the Temple Tomb and various chamber tombs in the Knossos valley. LM II has become one of the best defined and illustrated ceramic phases at Knossos with pottery derived from a purely domestic context. Furthermore it was the first time that stratified LM IIIA and LM IIIB deposits from settlement contexts were published. The definition of Knossian LM II laid the groundwork for the identification of contemporary deposits throughout the island either in the form of local productions as at Kommos and Khania, or direct imports such as those from Palaikastro. Warren's excavations at the Stratigraphical Museum Extension Site proved that for LM II, the sequence of events at the Unexplored Mansion was not isolated but wide-spread along the west part of the town. Driessen's re-assessment of the South East Area of the West Wing showed that the LM II destructions also affected the Palace. Finally Colin Macdonald's 1992–3 excavation at the House West of the South West House also produced evidence for construction in LM II.

FIG. 89 Knossos, the site of the Unexplored Mansion in a photograph of 1910, showing the Roman House of the Diamond Frescoes. (Heaton 17A; Ashmolean Museum Oxford)

Although not the means to an end, pottery is basic to the study of prehistoric societies of the Aegean. Knossian potters were blessed with good sources of raw materials and a strong tradition for high quality potting, thus providing ceramic specialists with a first class array of material. Although Knossos has set the standard for different aspects of Minoan Crete it is the study of its ceramic tradition that cannot be overlooked when excavating or surveying on the island. The considerable advances in the 1980s and 1990s in pottery studies have illustrated the need for defining a ceramic typology for regional workshops, which usually follow their own traditions with a varied degree of influence from Knossos. It is however the Knossos LM III typology as defined by Evans and Mackenzie, Popham and Warren that provides useful synchronisms for different parts of the island. But an aspect of post-palatial Knossos which remains a minefield for pottery specialists, and still requires the excavation at Knossos of a good stratigraphical sequence, is the ceramic period from LM IIIA2 down to LM IIIB. The Unexplored Mansion and Stratigraphical Museum Extension Site produced only minor deposits which remain our basic references for these periods, together with Hood's 'Kitchen at Makritikhos', published in 1959. The proceedings of the 1994 Danish Institute at Athens Conference on LM III pottery illustrates the importance of Knossian ceramic studies for all post-palatial Crete. Pottery studies in the 1980s turned to technology by employing petrographical and chemical analysis of the clay as a means of defining its provenance. For LM III, the pioneer work of Hector Catling, Richard Jones, John Cherry and John Killen on imported stirrup jars has been more recently followed by analysis of stirrup jars from Crete itself by Peter Day, Halford Haskel and Richard Jones.

The decipherment of Linear B implied that Greek-speaking Mycenaeans were involved in the bureaucratic organisation of the Palace at Knossos. Archaeologists started searching for signs in the material culture which would confirm the presence of a Mycenaean population on the island. The excavation of a series of chamber tombs in the Knossos valley together with the results of the Unexplored Mansion and the Stratigraphical Museum Extension Site excavations provide much evidence for a mixture of customs. The introduction of the kylix, the squat alabastron, of 'tinned' vases, burials in pit-graves and chamber tombs with a long *dromos* sometimes containing 'warrior graves' or 'burials with bronzes', have been interpreted as Mycenaean features. The placement of the dead on blue-painted wooden biers and their adornment with jewellery including sealstones and gold rings, and gold or faience necklaces have been considered Minoan. The LM IIIA1 Dancing Circles at the Stratigraphical Museum Extension Site illustrate a strong Minoan religious tradition, where the worship of a female divinity is often associated with ritualistic dancing (FIG. 90).

Outside Knossos, the presence of Mycenaean influence varies considerably, possibly a sign of its highly uneven distribution. A good case study for the character of Minoan society and culture after the LM IB destructions is Palaikastro, a site closely related to the work of British scholars since the early 1900s. The land of the Eteocretans in the east of the island, with its dramatic landscape and dense remains of ancient habitation, had attracted a number of British archaeologists. The five year excavation campaign of R. C. Bosanquet at the site of Roussolakkos at Palaikastro coincided with D. G. Hogarth's work at Zakros and Evans's at Knossos (FIG. 91). Its outcome was the discovery and extensive excavation of a thriving and

FIG. 90 The larger of the two Dancing Circles found in the Knossos Stratigraphical Museum extension site. (P. M. Warren)

long-lived Minoan town, which produced significant information on post-palatial Crete. Although largely understressed by the excavators, the site revealed strong evidence for a thorough re-occupation after the wholesale LM IB destructions. Amongst the best known post-LM IB deposits from Palaikastro is the so-called 'bathroom deposit' in Block Gamma, which remains a hallmark of local and imported LM IIIA2 pottery. Block Delta produced a highly intriguing group of votive material which has been interpreted as furnishings for a domestic shrine dated by the decorated pottery to LM IIIA2. The group of four votive figurines, three dancing while the fourth plays the lyra, highlights the importance of ritual dancing in post-palatial Crete, recently confirmed by the Dancing Circles at Knossos.

It is only with the more recent excavations at Palaikastro that the significance of the pioneer work of Bosanquet and R. M. Dawkins can be appreciated. Hugh Sackett and Mervyn Popham's 1962–3 excavations at Block N gave an opportunity to explore the relationship between the LM IB destructions and later re-occupation phases. The discovery of early LM IIIA occupation levels stratified above the wholesale destruction by fire in LM IB anticipated what has now become a normal stratigraphical situation in several of the newly excavated Palaikastro houses. In 1985 an ambitious excavation programme commenced at

FIG. 91 Palaikastro at the time of the first excavations. (*BSA* 8 (1901–2), pl.16)

Roussolakkos under the joint directorship of Sackett and Alexander MacGillivray (FIG. 92). Several of the buildings so far excavated have produced ample evidence for a thorough re-occupation after the LM IB fire destructions. The final publication will improve our knowledge of LM III settlement patterns in East Crete. The presence of LM II pottery in occupation levels confirms that the Minoan town of Palaikastro was re-occupied very soon after the LM IB destructions. Evidence for damage by fire in early LM IIIA could signify an event contemporary to the destruction at Knossos. The town was once again repaired and remained active until late LM IIIA2 or sometime in early LM IIIB, when it was abandoned possibly after earthquake damage. Popham's study of the local pottery prepared the groundwork for a more thorough study of LM III local ceramic styles. The current work on stratified pottery groups deriving from two LM IB wells, subsequently used as dumping grounds, confirm that the local 'Minoan' ceramic traditions continued unchanged at Palaikastro, with little Knossian influence in LM II and LM III. Shapes and decoration remain purely Minoan, hence the total absence of locally made kylikes, 'champagne cups' and stirrup jars, whereas technological advances follow the developments seen in other LM III pottery workshops, such as better fired, slipped and polished clays.

On the eve of the Second World War,

FIG. 92 Excavation at Roussolakos, Palaikastro, 1993. View north over Buildings 7 and 1 to Kastri. (L. H. Sackett)

members of the British School, under the directorship of J. D. S. Pendlebury, excavated a highland LM IIIC settlement in the Lasithi mountains (FIG. 93). Karphi is famous for several of its bench sanctuaries located either in houses or independent structures, recognised as temples by the excavator. The large clay female figurines, identified as goddesses, were found *in situ* sometimes together with other 'cult objects' such as triton shells, rhyta and snake tubes. The type of objects found here testify to the continuity in cult practices from the heyday of Minoan civilisation to its closing era. The site as depicted in Pendlebury's photographs is remarkable for its resemblance to contemporary Cretan mountain villages (FIG. 94). The Karphi pottery, published by Mercy Seiradaki in 1960, remained the single detailed source of reference on LM IIIC pottery until Popham's publication of contemporary pottery from Kastri at Palaikastro. Stratigraphical tests on the hilltop of Kastri confirmed the results produced in the early 1900s in discovering evidence for extensive LM IIIC occupation levels. Both British sites are typical examples of the so-called 'refuge settlements' established after widespread population movements both in Crete and on mainland Greece. Although only a small section of the LM IIIC settlement of Kastri was explored, its prompt publication has provided detailed evidence for a period in Minoan history little known before the extensive excavations and surveys conducted in the 1980s

FIG. 93 Karphi. The site in the Lasithi mountains. (*BSA* 38 (1937–8), pl. 15.1)

and 1990s by the Archaeological Service and a number of foreign Schools in Greece. LM IIIC Knossos was virtually unknown until the Stratigraphical Museum Extension Site excavations produced evidence, not only for the establishment of a new settlement early in the period, but for continuous habitation down through the Sub-Minoan period.

FIG. 94 Karphi. A closer view of the excavated site. (*BSA* 38 (1937–8), pl. 15.3)

The discovery and publication of new sites throughout the island together with the re-examination of 'old sites' such as Knossos and Palaikastro are constantly changing our views on post-palatial Crete. The British contribution to these studies colourfully illustrates how fascinating is the study of the period which led to the collapse of the Bronze Age Aegean palatial systems and the movement of peoples around the Eastern Mediterranean, before the transition into the Iron Age, which at Knossos inaugurated a new and prosperous period for Crete.

ELENI HATZAKI

The Palace and the Linear B archive

Articles by M. Popham, J. Weingarten and J.-P. Olivier in *Labyrinth* (1994).

J. Bennet, 'The structure of the Linear B administration at Knossos', *AJA* 89 (1985), 231–49.

J. Bennet, 'Knossos and LM III Crete: A post-palatial Palace?', in *Minoan Palaces* (1987), 307–12.

J. Driessen, *An Early Destruction in the Mycenaean Palace at Knossos.* (Acta Archaeologica Lovaniensia Monographiae 2; Leuven, 1990)

M. Gill, 'The Knossos sealings: Provenance and Identification', *BSA* 60 (1965), 58–98.

E. Hallager, *The Mycenaean Palace at Knossos: Evidence for a Final Destruction in the Late Minoan IIIB Period* (Stockholm, 1977).

E. Hallager, 'The history of the Palace at Knossos in the Late Minoan period', *SMEA* 19 (1978), 17–33.

W.-D. Niemeier, 'Mycenaean Knossos and the Age of Linear B', *SMEA* 23 (1982), 219–87.

W.-D. Niemeier, 'The Character of the Knossian Palace Society in the Second Half of the Fifteenth Century BC: Mycenaean or Minoan?' in *Minoan Society* (1983), 217–36.

W.-D. Niemeier, *Die Palaststilkeramik von Knossos*. (AF 13; Berlin, 1985).

J.-P. Olivier, *Les Scribes de Cnossos.* (Incunabula Graeca, 17; Rome, 1967).

J.-P. Olivier, 'KN 115=KH 115. Un Même Scribe à Knossos et à la Canée au MR IIIB: Du Soupçon à la Certitude', *BCH* 117 (1993), 19–33.

L. R. Palmer and J. Boardman, *On the Knossos Tablets* (Oxford, 1963).

L. R. Palmer, *The Penultimate Palace at Knossos.* (Incunabula Graeca, 33; Rome, 1969).

M. Popham and M. Gill, *The Latest Sealings from the Palace and Houses at Knossos.* (BSA Studies, 1; Oxford, 1995)

P. Warren, 'A stone vase-maker's workshop in the Palace at Knossos', *BSA* 62 (1967), 195–206.

P. Warren, 'The destruction of the Palace of Knossos', in V. Karageorghis (ed.), *The Civilizations of the Aegean and their diffusion in Cyprus and the Eastern Mediterranean, 2000–600 BC* (Larnaca, 1989) 32–7.

Recent settlement excavations and pottery studies at Knossos

M. Popham, *The Last Days of the Palace of Knossos. Complete Vases of the Late Minoan III B Period.* (SIMA 5; Lund, 1964)

M. Popham, *The Destruction of the Palace at Knossos. Pottery of the Late Minoan IIIA Period.* (SIMA 12; Göteborg, 1970)

M. Popham, 'Late Minoan IIIB pottery from Knossos', *BSA* 65 (1970), 195–202.

M. Popham, *The Minoan Unexplored Mansion at Knossos.* (BSA supp. vol. 17; London, 1984).

P. Warren, 'Knossos: Stratigraphical Museum excavations, 1978–80. I', *AR* (1980–1), 73–92.

P. Warren, 'Knossos: Stratigraphical Museum excavations, 1978–82. II', *AR* (1982–3), 63–87.

P. Warren, 'Circular platforms at Minoan Knossos', *BSA* 79 (1984), 307–23.

LM II–III tombs in the Knossos Valley

G. Cadogan, 'Late Minoan IIIC pottery from the Kephala tholos near Knossos', *BSA* 62 (1967), 257–65.

H. W. Catling, 'The Society of Antiquaries and the British School at Athens, 1886–1986: The Cemeteries of Knossos and Mycenae', *Ant. J.* 67 (1987), 223–36.

A. J. Evans, 'The Prehistoric Tombs of Knossos', *Archaeologia* 59 (1905), 391–562.

A. J. Evans, 'The Tomb of the Double Axes', *Archaeologia* 65 (1914), 1–94.

M. S. F. Hood and P. de Jong, 'Late Minoan Warrior Graves from Ayios Ioannis and the New Hospital site at Knossos', *BSA* 47 (1952), 247–77.

M. S. F. Hood, G. Huxley, and N. Sandars, 'A Minoan Cemetery on Upper Gypsadhes', *BSA* 53–54 (1958–9), 194–262.

M. S. F. Hood and D. Smyth, *Archaeological Survey of the Knossos Area* (London, 1981).

R. W. Hutchinson, 'A Late Minoan Tomb at Knossos', *BSA* 51 (1956), 68–73.

R. W. Hutchinson, 'A Tholos Tomb on the Kephala', *BSA* 51 (1956), 74–80.

M. Popham, E. A. and H. W. Catling, 'Sellopoulo Tombs 3 and 4. Two Late Minoan graves near Knossos', *BSA* 69 (1974), 195–257.

Palaikastro

BSA reports 1901–5; 1965; 1970; 1984; 1987– .

R. C. Bosanquet and R. Dawkins, *The Unpublished Objects from the Palaikastro Excavations* (BSA supp. vol. 1; London, 1923).

L. H. Sackett, M. Popham and P. Warren, 'Excavations at Palaikastro VI', *BSA* 60 (1965), 248–315.

L. H. Sackett and M. Popham, 'Excavations at Palaikastro VII', *BSA* 65 (1970), 203–42.

Karphi

H. W. and J. D. S. Pendlebury and M. B. Money-Coutts, 'Excavations in the Plain of Lasithi. III. Karphi: A City of Refuge in the Early Iron Age on Crete.' *BSA* 38 (1937–8), 57–145.

M. B. Seiradaki, 'Pottery from Karphi', *BSA* (1960), 1–37.

K. Nowicki, 'The History of Refuge Settlement in Crete' *JRGZM* (1987), 235–56.

B. Rutkowski, 'The Temple at Karphi' *SMEA* 26 (1987), 257–79.

Further studies on LM III Crete

J. Driessen and A. Farnoux (eds.), *La Crète Mycénienne. Actes de la Table Ronde Internationale organisée par l'Ecole francaise d'Athenes, 26–28 Mars 1991* (Paris, 1997).

E. and B. P. Hallager, (eds.), *Late Minoan III Pottery Chronology and Terminology. Acts of a Meeting held at the Danish Institute at Athens, August 12–14, 1994* (Athens, 1997).

A. Kanta, *The Late Minoan III Period in Crete. A Survey of Sites, Pottery and their Distribution* (SIMA 58; 1980).

I. Sakellarakis and E. Sakellaraki, *Archanes, Mia Nea Matia stin Minoiki Kriti* (Athens, 1997).

L. V. Watrous, *Kommos III: The Late Bronze Age Pottery* (Princeton, 1992).

EARLY GREEK and CLASSICAL CRETE

Amid the troubles accompanying the final collapse of Minoan civilisation, many Cretans took refuge in the mountains. One of their largest refugee strongholds was excavated by John Pendlebury in 1937–9 at the aptly named site of Karphi, the 'needle' that looms over 1100 metres high above the north-west wall of the Lasithi range. On a saddle below this inhospitable peak, Pendlebury excavated a town of 150 stone-built houses, a network of narrow streets, a cobbled public square, 21 built tombs on the slopes below and, overlooking an impregnable cliff, a sanctuary containing several large terracotta goddesses made on the wheel, raising their arms in the Minoan gesture of epiphany (FIG. 95). With the return of more peaceful conditions, the whole site was abandoned, including the shrine with the goddesses. Pendlebury placed the abandonment in Protogeometric times (tenth century BC), but most scholars today think that it occurred during the Subminoan phase of the eleventh century.

FIG. 95 Karphi, terracotta goddesses. (J.N. Coldstream. *BSA* 55 (1960) pl. 14a.)

Karphi still poses a number of puzzles. In winter the site is snowbound and bitterly cold. To raise their crops, their olives and their lambs, the Karphiots would have needed winter quarters well below the snow line; several sites have been proposed, but none has been tested by excavation. And we still have much to learn about the subsequent experiences of the Karphiots after their final descent from the heights. A likely site for their new home was found by Pendlebury on the nearby lower hill of Ayiou Georgiou Papoura (the Mound of St George) overlooking the Lasithi plain; there he dug several Geometric *tholos* tombs related to those of Karphi, but the settlement remains unexplored. At all events Karphi, with its houses, its sanctuary and its tombs, remains to this day the largest and best preserved site of the early Dark Age, not only in Crete but in the entire Aegean world. Indeed, Karphi exemplifies the survival of urban life in Crete at a time when it seems to have lapsed in the Greek mainland.

At Knossos, too, urban continuity is evident; but there the evidence has had to be laboriously recovered from scattered deposits and flimsy traces of domestic architecture, buried under the deep foundations of the Roman city. In the surroundings of the Palace, Evans dug rapidly through later occupation in his enthusiasm to reach Minoan levels as soon as possible; nevertheless, he kept a large quantity of his later finds from which the eastern limits of the early Greek town can be plotted. Subsequent excavations by Sinclair Hood near the Minoan Royal Road (1957–61), by Mervyn Popham and Hugh Sackett above the 'Unexplored Mansion' (1967–72), by Peter Warren behind the Stratigraphical Museum (1978–82) and, most recently, by Colin Macdonald at the south-western border of the Palace (1992–3) have all produced many well-stratified deposits of early Greek pottery, published by Nicolas Coldstream. These, together with well-fills in peripheral areas, help to outline the extent of the town from the eleventh until the seventh century BC.

It is the cemeteries, however, that offer the most enlightenment concerning the civilisation of Early Greek Knossos. The practice of collective interment in solidly constructed chamber tombs cut in the rock – another symptom of continuity from Minoan times – has allowed many thousands of pots to survive whole and in good condition; and, as cremation became the prevailing rite from the Protogeometric period onwards, the large urns invited elaborate and often ambitious decoration. The first excavations of these tombs were by D. G. Hogarth (1899), A. J. Evans (1907) and Humfry Payne (1927). To begin with, their contents hardly excited enthusiasm. 'The Geometric ware of Crete' wrote F. B. Welch in 1900, 'so far appears to be certainly the poorest found in any Greek land, and to be of a peculiarly local character – as we might expect from a people who were always outside the current of ordinary Greek life and politics'. For Welch it appears that the Dipylon vases of Athens provided the exemplars of what Geometric pottery ought to look like, and his crudely adverse value-judgment foreshadows a difficulty felt by all subsequent students of Early Iron Age pottery in Crete. The orthodox labels for phases – Protogeometric, Geometric and Orientalizing – were first invented to suit the pottery of Athens, Corinth and other regions of the Greek mainland; but, for reasons that will soon become evident, they are often not easy to reconcile with the pottery sequence in Crete.

In 1928 Payne offered a more sympathetic account of Cretan Geometric pottery in one of his earliest articles, publishing the tombs dug by Evans and himself. His main interest, however, lay in the Orientalizing vases, especially in the uniquely Knossian pithos-urns with polychrome decoration, and their possible debt to Near Eastern sources. As yet, there was still too little material to work out in full the development of the earlier phases. But, very soon, it was Payne himself who made this possible, through a major excavation of twenty more tombs, directed in 1933 and 1935 by himself and Alan Blakeway; three of them lay near the main road to Herakleion at the southern limit of what we now call the North Cemetery, but the main group formed a row behind the hill on which the village of Fortetsa stands. Sadly, both excavators died in the year following the second campaign. The huge task of publication was left to a student member of the second excavation, James Brock, who was also able to include the finds from the richest of all the Fortetsa tombs, excavated by Nikolaos Platon, and the source of all the now famous Fortetsa bronzes displaying oriental influences long before the conventional 'Orientalizing' period of Greek art.

Brock completed his work *in situ*, assisted by his wife, in the course of two post-war winters. His magisterial volume, *Fortetsa*, appeared in

1957 – a volume to which all those who have subsequently dealt with the Early Iron Age of Crete will have been profoundly indebted. It was Brock's great achievement to have elucidated for the first time the entire Early Iron Age sequence of Knossos, from the Subminoan of the eleventh century BC to the Orientalizing of the seventh. But even with the large corpus at his disposal, the task was not easy. In contrast to the regional styles of the Greek mainland, the Cretan phases could not be documented in single grave groups, each one encapsulating a collection of contemporary offerings. In the family chamber tombs of Knossos, the goods from individual cremations could only rarely be separated out with complete certainty. Nevertheless, the large quantity of whole pots enabled Brock to work out a convincing sequence through the four centuries, datable at many points through association with Attic and other imports, thereby providing a life-line through the Greek Dark Age and its immediate sequel. 'Quite the most remarkable phase in Cretan vase-painting', as he put it, was his newly discovered Protogeometric B phase of the late ninth century, well illustrated by the straight-sided urn Fortetsa 1440 (FIGS. 96–97) with a reminiscence of the Minoan snake goddess under the handles, supported by wild curvilinear ornament chiefly of Near Eastern origin.

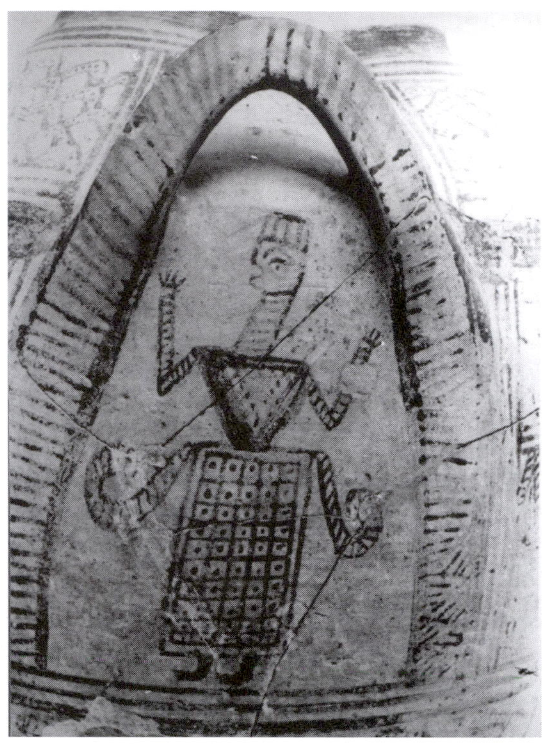

FIG. 97 Detail of Fortetsa no. 1440.

FIG. 96 Fortetsa no. 1440, pithos-urn, Protogeometric B. (J.N. Coldstream. *Geometric Greece* (London, 1977) 69, fig. 21a and b)

Brock's sequence was at first viewed with some scepticism, not least by some continental scholars. To those accustomed to the orderly development of pottery style on the Greek mainland, how illogical it might seem that the Knossians should have been toying with Orientalizing ornament even before they had evolved their own Geometric style! Nevertheless, Brock's sequence and chronology has been amply vindicated, both by contexts in later excavations in the settlement, and also by the even larger corpus of tombs dug in the North Cemetery between 1975 and 1980. What is more, as we shall see, the unusually early appearance of Near Eastern influence in Protogeometric B pottery proves to be quite in tune with the peculiar character of early Cretan work in metal relief.

The excavation of over 300 tombs between 1975 and 1980, the largest ever mounted by the British School at Knossos, was invited by the Cretan Ephoreia as a huge rescue operation, principally to prepare for the construction of the Medical Faculty building of the new University of Crete. Thence came much new enlightenment concerning early Greek Knossos. The early Iron Age here was represented by no less than one hundred collective tombs; their close packing, their sheer numbers, and the plot's unbroken continuity of use through four hundred years all served to confirm Payne's earlier suspicion that the main cemetery of Knossos must have lain to the north, founded well outside the settlement in the eleventh century BC – even so, the North Cemetery's outer limits have yet to be defined. Hector Catling, studying the earliest interments, published some surprisingly well-furnished warrior burials, encouraging a more positive view of the Subminoan period among those who had seen it as the doldrums of the Dark Age. Although few tombs had escaped plundering, Catling and Anthony Snodgrass were able to work out a social hierarchy, based on the presence of warlike gear and other metal offerings. From the cremated bones the anatomist Jonathan Musgrave could detect not only the age and sex of many incumbents, but also details of pathology (anaemia, arthritis and dental hygiene) and even some signs of consanguinity within the same tomb. Study of the abundant pottery by Hector Catling (Subminoan), Nicolas Coldstream (Protogeometric and Geometric) and Elizabeth Moignard (Orientalizing), consolidated and at some points modified Brock's sequence. There were some surprisingly ambitious experiments in figured scenes during the ninth century BC,

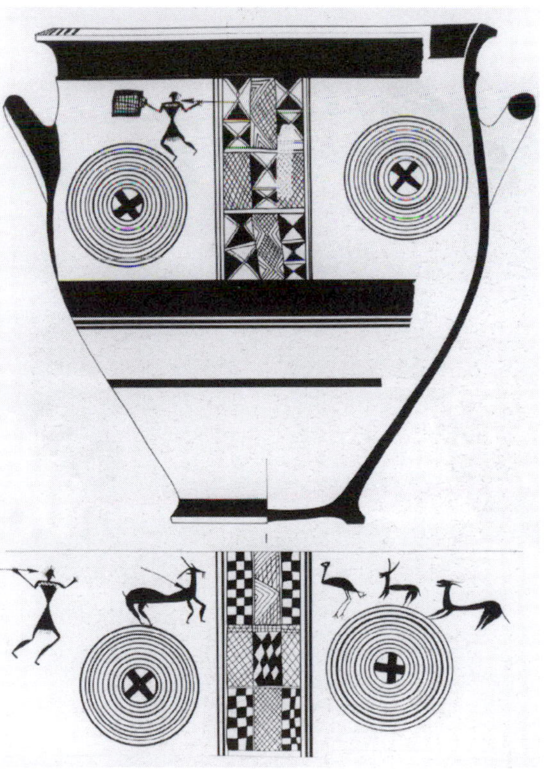

Fig. 98 Knossos, Teke F 1, bell-krater, Middle Geometric. (Elizabeth Catling drawing. *KNC* Fig. 59)

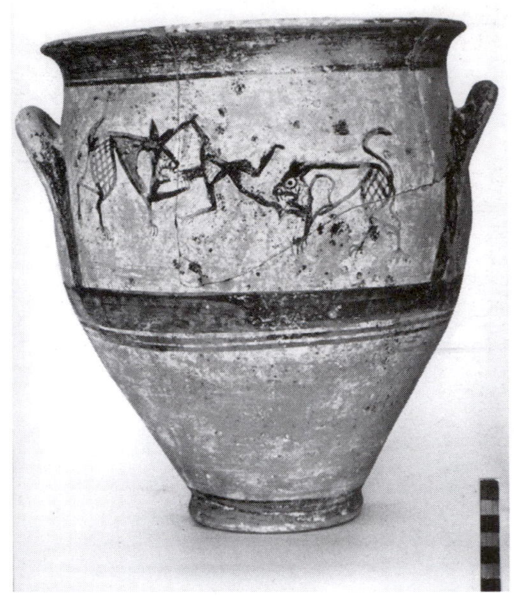

FIG. 99 Knossos, Teke E 3, bell-krater, Late Geometric. (J.N. Coldstream)

among the earliest in Greek vase-painting: for example, a bell-krater (FIG. 98) bearing an extended hunt scene, another (FIG. 99) showing a warrior in danger of being eaten by two lions, and a straight-sided urn of Protogeometric B with, on one side (FIG. 100), a nature goddess arriving on a simplified chariot in spring and, on the reverse, departing in late autumn.

No less striking among the finds from the North Cemetery is the wide variety of imports, both from other Aegean centres (especially Athens) and from the East Mediterranean; these establish early Greek Knossos as an unusually outward-looking place during the Dark Age, receptive of foreign visitors and always prepared to profit from them. The eastern imports, much more numerous than in other Greek regions, include a steady flow of eighth-century unguent flasks from Cyprus, preceded

FIG. 100 Knossos, KMF 107.114, pithos-urn, Protogeometric B. (Nicola Coldstream drawing. *KNC* Fig. 109)

FIG. 101 Knossos, Teke J f1, bronze bowl with Phoenician inscription. (J.N. Coldstream. *AR* 23 (1977) 13, figs. 27–8)

by a bronze bowl of *c.*900 BC bearing a Phoenician owner's inscription (FIG. 101) – the earliest known appearance of the alphabet in Greece, long before the Cretans themselves were to acquire alphabetic literacy. The various precociously early manifestations of Near Eastern contacts and influence in Crete called for a special explanation, other than casual trade and piecemeal copying of Eastern artifacts.

Here we need to follow another line of research, which goes right back to the first excavation of the Idaean Cave by Frederico Halbherr in the 1880s. The votive bronze shields, with their figured repertoire of eastern monsters, lion fights and hunt scenes, were fully published by Emil Kunze in 1931. Their imagery was orientalizing in a peculiarly Cretan way, with very little trace of hellenization; and for many years after their discovery, their chronology and the

FIG. 102 Fortetsa no. 1569, detail of bronze quiver. (J.M. Carter. *BSA* 67 (1972) 43, fig. 1. After *Fortetsa* pl. 169)

circumstances of their manufacture remained mysterious. Some enlightenment eventually came from the closely related bronzes in Platon's Fortetsa tomb – for example, the scene on the bronze quiver (FIG. 102), an only slightly hellenized version of an oriental hero dominating two lions. The tomb context of this and similar metal work suggested to Brock a date not later than the early eighth century – a date unacceptable to most specialists at the time of writing. Figured scenes in Greek art were then supposed to have begun on the monumental funerary vases from the Athenian Dipylon cemetery; how could it possibly be that Cretan metalworkers should be experimenting, at least a generation earlier, with a fully orientalizing repertoire of lion combats, sphinxes and griffins? One possible explanation was put forward by Tom Dunbabin in a monograph appearing in the same year as Brock's *Fortetsa*. Considering the parallel phenomenon of the votives from the Idaean Cave, Dunbabin argued that the earliest bronze shields (which Kunze had already put back in the ninth century) were the work of immigrant Near Eastern smiths who had settled in Crete, and then 'took Cretan apprentices, who over a long period retained many of the externals of the Phoenician style, while their own Greek sense of form asserted itself in the arrangement of the material'.

Four years later John Boardman, publishing the Cretan collection in Oxford (mainly from the Dictean Cave), applied this notion to all early Cretan metalwork including the Fortetsa bronzes. He grouped the quiver with a wholly oriental gold band (FIG. 103), showing Mesopotamian heroes fighting rampant lionesses; here in his view, was a good sample of the prototypes introduced to Crete by these resident oriental craftsmen. Now this band

FIG. 103 Teke tholos, gold band. (Th. Phanourakis drawing. *BSA* 62 (1967) pl. 12)

forms part of the exotic gold treasure buried in the reused Minoan *tholos* tomb of Teke or Ambelokipi, near the outer limits of the North Cemetery, excavated in 1940 by R. W. Hutchinson. In a later article (1967) Boardman revised the stratigraphy in the Teke *tholos*, concluding that most of the goldwork must have accompanied the earliest incumbent in the reused tomb, dated by Protogeometric B pottery to the late ninth century. Furthermore, the many unworked pieces of gold seemed to have been the stock-in-trade of an immigrant eastern goldsmith buried in the tomb, creator of the various masterpieces of jewellery in the

FIG. 105 Teke tholos, penannular gold pendant. (J. Boardman. *BSA* 62 (1967) pl. 11)

FIG. 104 Teke tholos, gold pendant with rock-crystal and amber inlays. (J. Boardman. *BSA* 62 (1967) pl. 10)

treasure – the band, the large lunate pendant inlaid with rock crystal (FIG. 104) and an even more elaborate pendant, a penannular crescent enclosing a cross and four birds, ending in two female heads wearing *polos* crowns, and covered with oriental cable pattern (FIG. 105).

And so the sudden and startling appearance of the Protogeometric B style could be plausibly explained: Knossian potters began to cover their vessels with cables and other freehand curvilinear motifs of a proto-orientalizing kind, simply because eastern master-craftsmen in metal had already begun to settle among them, and their work could be seen, admired and imitated. In this way, long before the conventionally named Orientalizing movement in the rest of the Aegean, the Cretans were already obtaining their own private view of Near Eastern art and imagery, which they gradually adapted to their own taste. However, since other Greeks took very little notice of Cretan artifacts at this time, these precociously early experiments with oriental themes were to have virtually no effect on the art of the Greek mainland.

Thanks largely to the abundance of well-furnished early Greek tombs excavated by the School at Knossos, British scholars have been able to make a substantial contribution to our understanding of Cretan archaeology in the

FIG. 106 Knossos, Royal Road, Attic black-figure krater. (J.N. Coldstream. *BSA* 68 (1973) pl. 22)

Early Iron Age. In the early years of the twentieth century, when the available evidence was meagre and unimpressive, the island was considered something of a backwater by the standards of the Greek mainland. More recently, as the material accumulated in quality as well as in quantity, Knossos has come to be regarded as one of the major centres of the early Greek world, comparable with Athens, Corinth, Argos and the Euboean cities in size, in importance, and especially in its overseas connections.

This early prosperity of Knossos came to a sudden end with the universal abandonment of the cemeteries with chamber tombs some time in the late seventh century BC. The next hundred years are almost a blank in the archaeological record of Knossos, not only in the cemeteries, but also in the settlement and even in the sanctuaries where, in a continuously flourishing city-state, complete continuity in votive offerings should be expected. For this apparent recession, followed by a long desolation, the causes remain mysterious. Various possible explanations have been briefly put forward by Dunbabin, Brock, Boardman and Hood, and a recent article by Coldstream and George Huxley brings in some clues from the literary record to argue for a disastrous defeat in war by the rival city of Lyttos and its Spartan allies. Be that as it may, not all of Crete was desolate during the sixth century. Two sites in the extreme east, Praisos and Palaikastro, were extensively excavated by Bosanquet in the first years of the twentieth century; both produced numerous terracotta and other offerings of the sixth century, and in both places Bosanquet argued for a cult of Dictaean Zeus. From both sites these finds require, and are receiving, further study.

Quite recently, evidence has been emerging from excavations at Knossos for a revival of its fortunes around 500 BC. Within the settlement, every major sounding has produced large deposits of Late Archaic pottery, always including copious imports of Attic black-figure (FIG. 106) and black-glaze. With their help, an extensive repertoire of plain Knossian shapes can be dated to the early fifth century BC, and their progress can be followed throughout the Classical period. A later deposit of whole pots from a kiln site, published by Mrs B. Homann-Wedeking (1950), offers much enlightenment on the local pottery around 400 BC. As in the Early Iron Age, however, remains of domestic architecture are still very scarce, and the public centre of the Classical city still eludes discovery.

Concerning the Classical sanctuaries of Knossos we are better informed. Still enigmatic is the date of an oblong stone building imposed upon the ruins of the Minoan palace and constructed out of reused Minoan blocks; Evans, following a clue from Diodoros, identified it as a temple of the mother-goddess Rhea, set in a sacred grove. Whatever its date and deity, it is clear that a cult flourished here from the early fifth century onwards, to judge from a sequence of votive pottery reviewed by Peter Callaghan (1978). A new paved road of the fifth century, found in Macdonald's excavation of 1993, seems to lead directly towards this building from the centre of the town.

Callaghan also excavated a small shrine ascribed to the local hero Glaukos, son of Minos and Pasiphaë, drowned in a *pithos* of honey and then miraculously restored to life. He associates this shrine with the Cretan harvest festival of the Thiodaisia, at which adolescent boys were initiated into manhood. Ritual drinking clearly formed an important aspect of this cult; a mass of cups and kraters, carefully stacked in cabinets and happily found complete, provides a useful source for reconstructing the sequence of Knossian drinking vessels throughout the Classical period.

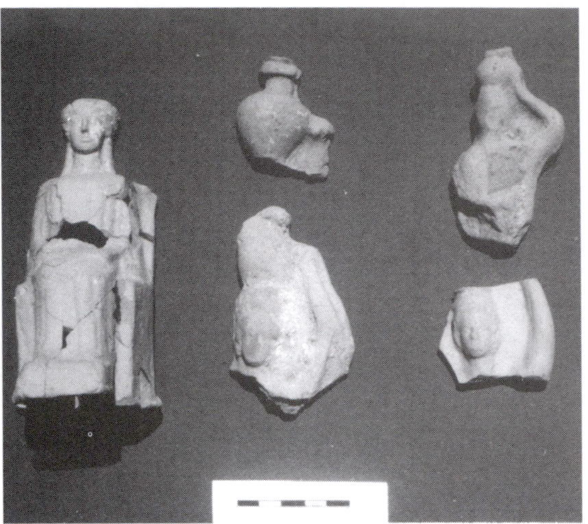

FIG. 107 Knossos, Sanctuary of Demeter, terracottas. (J.N. Coldstream. Selected from BSA supp. vol. 8, (1973) pls. 40, 53.)

FIG. 109 Knossos, Sanctuary of Demeter, silver rings. (J.N. Coldstream. BSA supp. vol. 8, pls. 83, 85.)

The most extensively excavated sanctuary is that of Demeter, situated on the Gypsades hill to the south of the Minoan palace. Most numerous among the votives are some six thousand *disiecta membra* of clay figurines ranging in date from the eighth to the second century BC, from which Reynold Higgins published a compact and masterly *catalogue raisonné* of 273 pieces; this was the first comprehensive presentation of Greek terracottas from Knossos, and has proved invaluable for the study of other sanctuaries of Demeter more recently discovered in Crete. Worship here began in the open air, and the earliest terracottas (eighth-seventh centuries BC) include wheelmade boars and bulls: as Higgins put it, 'boars, because the sanctuary was dedicated to Demeter; bulls, doubtless, because we are in Crete'. After the usual Archaic *lacuna*, there was a vigorous revival of the cult in the fifth century, when the votives began to be locally mass-produced. These consist of miniature pots and mouldmade figurines, persisting into the third century and in ever-increasing numbers. A small deposit, also containing multiple lamps and Attic imports, dates the

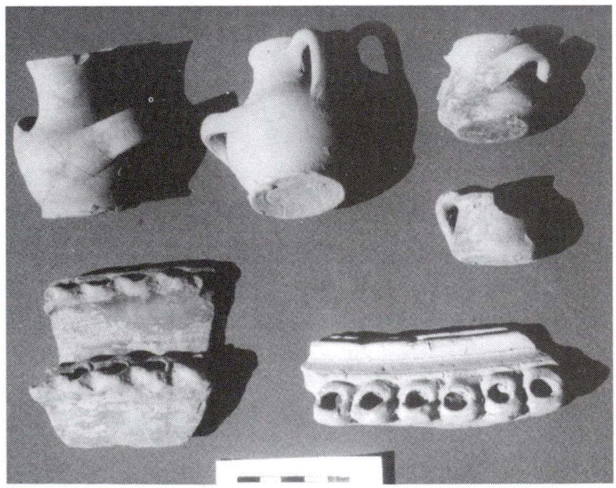

FIG. 108 Knossos, Sanctuary of Demeter, miniature pots and lamps. (J.N. Coldstream. Selected from BSA supp. vol. 8, pls. 15, 18.)

building of an oblong stone temple like that ascribed to Rhea (of which nothing remains except seven reused Minoan blocks). The miniatures are of hydriai and kraters (FIG. 108), while among the figurines the most usual types are of seated goddesses and girls carrying hydriai (FIG. 107). The hydriskai and hydrophoroi allude to Demeter's concern with watering the crops; and among the animal sacrifices there is now a marked preponderance for her favourite animal, the pig. The multiple lamps (FIG. 108) suggest use at the nocturnal mystery celebrations in the open air, remembered by Diodoros. Among the more precious offerings are silver rings bearing the goddess's name in the Doric dialect: DAMATRI (FIG. 109).

NICOLAS COLDSTREAM

J. Boardman, *The Cretan Collection in Oxford: the Dictean Cave and Iron Age Crete* (Oxford, 1961).

J. Boardman, 'The Khaniale Tekke Tombs, II', *BSA* 62 (1967), 57–75.

R. C. Bosanquet, 'Dicte and the Dictaean Temples of Zeus', *BSA* 40 (1939–40), 60–77.

J. K. Brock, *Fortetsa. Early Greek Tombs near Knossos* (Cambridge, 1957).

P. J. Callaghan, 'KRS 1976: Excavations at a Shrine of Glaukos, Knossos', *BSA* 73 (1978), 1–30; also ibid. 186–7 on pottery from Evans's 'Greek Temple'.

J. N. Coldstream, 'Knossos 1951–61: Protogeometric and Geometric Pottery from the Town', *BSA* 67 (1972), 63–98.

J. N. Coldstream, 'Knossos 1951–61: Orientalizing and Archaic Pottery from the Town', *BSA* 68 (1973), 33–64.

J. N. Coldstream (ed.), *Knossos. The Sanctuary of Demeter* (BSA supp. vol. 8, 1973).

J. N. Coldstream and H. W. Catling (eds.), *Knossos North Cemetery. Early Greek Tombs* (BSA supp. vol. 28, 4 vols., 1996).

J. N. Coldstream and G. L. Huxley, 'Knossos: the Archaic Gap', *BSA* 94 (1999), 279–97.

J. N. Coldstream and C. F. Macdonald, 'Knossos: area of South-West Houses, early Hellenic occupation', *BSA* 92 (1997), 191–245.

T. J. Dunbabin, *The Greeks and their Eastern Neighbours* (JHS supp. vol. 8, 1957).

D. G. Hogarth, 'Knossos: Early Town and Cemeteries', *BSA* 6 (1899–1900), 70–85.

B. Homann-Wedeking, 'A Kiln Site at Knossos', *BSA* 45 (1950), 165–92.

R. W. Hutchinson and J. Boardman, 'The Khaniale Tekke Tombs', *BSA* 49 (1954), 215–28.

H. G. G. Payne, 'Early Greek Vases from Knossos', *BSA* 29 (1927–8), 224–98.

H. W. and J. D. S. Pendlebury and M. B. Money-Coutts, 'Excavations in the Plain of Lasithi. III Karphi: a City of Refuge of the Early Iron Age in Crete', *BSA* 38 (1937–8), 57–145.

L. H. Sackett, 'A new Figured Krater from Knossos', *BSA* 71 (1976), 117–29.

L. H. Sackett (ed.), *Knossos: from Greek City to Roman Colony* (BSA supp. vol. 21, 1992).

P. M. Warren, 'Knossos: Stratigraphical Museum Excavations, 1978–82, Part III', *AR* 31 (1985), 124–9.

F. B. Welch, 'Knossos: Notes on the Pottery', *BSA* 6 (1899–1900), 85–92.

HELLENISTIC and ROMAN CRETE

For the Hellenistic and Roman periods British research in Crete is a story more of survey than of excavation. The names of the Cretan cities, and the ups and downs of their tempestuous relationships, are recorded in the histories of Diodorus and Polybius. Pashley and Spratt identified many of these sites. Dramatic settings, towering ruins of buildings and of fortification walls, the evidence of inscriptions and coins, even the garbled survival of ancient names, all contributed to these identifications. Within this skeleton framework of cities, some large and many quite small, the pattern of habitation throughout the island in the Greco-Roman period has been gradually filled in by survey. Villages, houses, farms, shrines, cemeteries, waterworks, industrial installations such as potteries and wine and olive presses all play their part; these are not the sorts of things that are mentioned in literature or history and they can only be found by looking for them.

During the 1890s, before starting to dig at Knossos, Sir Arthur Evans travelled through Crete in search of ancient sites of all periods. While John Pendlebury was Curator of Knossos journeys of this kind became an important part of the tradition of British research in Crete. Pendlebury set out to revisit the sites discovered by Sir Arthur and to find new ones, noting every sort of find from Minoan *tholos* tombs to caves full of stalactites, from cities to scatters of sherds. The purpose was to make a complete register of all ancient remains on the island. The first list of post-Minoan sites appeared in 1939, as part of the gazetteer in Pendlebury's *The Archaeology of Crete*. Of the 150 or so Roman sites listed there more than a third had been found by Pendlebury himself in his tremendous walking tours throughout the island. Some of the discoveries were quite haphazard, such as the small Roman site found on one of these expeditions when Captain Wyndham sat down heavily on the sharp point of a sherd.

During the war T. J. Dunbabin noted about twenty-five unrecorded Hellenistic and Roman sites in the Amari, although he said he found it ill gleaning after Pendlebury. The tradition of survey, started by Evans and carried on by Pendlebury, was continued by Sinclair Hood during the 1950s and 1960s. In 1962, with Peter Warren and Gerald Cadogan, he investigated three regions of Crete, to the west of Hierapetra, to the east of Rethymnon, and the Amari valley, in order to revise Pendlebury's lists in *The Archaeology of Crete*. The finds were of all periods from Neolithic to Byzantine, and many sites of the Classical, Hellenistic and Roman periods were described and added to the map. These included a sizeable Greco-Roman city just east of Rethymnon which may have been ancient Allaria, and other small towns of the Classical to Roman periods, as well as several Roman villas or small settlements and some groups of Roman farms. Many of these were noted here for the first time, and more than one of them had disappeared without trace less than fifteen years later.

On Sinclair Hood's next expedition in 1965, again with Peter Warren, he recorded thirty-six sites in the province of Ayios Vasilios, half of this number being Classical or later; these included seven which produced pottery of Late Roman or Early Byzantine date. One Greco-Roman settlement found high up above Sellia was probably the ancient city of Phoinix; another, below on the shore, may have been the site of Apollonia. The Greek and Hellenistic city site near Kerame was found to possess hitherto unnoticed fortification walls, strengthening the probability of its identity as ancient Bionnos. A small city at Pantanassa appeared to be Classical to Hellenistic, although Pendlebury had reported Roman material from the site. Throughout the area traces of Roman buildings, villas, farmhouses and bath houses were noted and added to the distribution map. Journeys in the western part of Crete produced sparser evidence of Greco-Roman occupation; indeed, some sites (for example, Nokhia, and Ayia Irini near Grimbiliana) formerly thought to be Greco-Roman turned out to be Minoan. But a substantial settlement was found at Palaiokhora at the extreme south-west corner of the island, and possibly a villa at Ayios Giorgios east of the Pelekaniotikos river, and the remains of a group of Roman villages and farms further east at Patsianos near Frangokastelli.

These surveys added enormously to what was known of settlement patterns in Crete throughout antiquity; no one could possibly have said of them that sites of later periods were in any way neglected in favour of the prehistoric. But the importance of Bronze Age Crete is so great that there came to be a feeling (largely no doubt unfounded) that many archaeologists dismissed the Roman remains of the island as negligible; that because the antiquities of the Roman period were not unique, in the way that the Minoan remains were unique, they were to be regarded as somehow inferior by Roman standards too. It was a feeling of this kind that first inspired Ian Sanders to take up the study of Roman Crete. In 1968 he was a member of the team excavating the Early Bronze Age site of Phournou Koryphi, near Myrtos on the south coast. The team was lodged in the village, and it seemed strange to Ian that the massive remains of Roman Myrtos, its bath building with hypocaust, mosaic floors and great concrete vaulted roof tumbled onto the beach, its cistern and the other Roman buildings appearing here and there throughout the village, should count for so little. Not far to the east the considerable remains of the once rich city of Hierapytna lay apparently neglected in the fields, and indeed in those days the same indifference to Roman antiquities seemed to pertain throughout the island, except at Gortyn where the Italians had been excavating for many years.

When Ian Sanders had completed his first degree he embarked upon a doctoral thesis at Oxford; a thesis that was in the end, after his tragically early death, to constitute the most valuable British contribution to this aspect of Cretan studies: the survey and gazetteer of late Hellenistic, Roman and early Byzantine Crete entitled *Roman Crete*. In the autumn of 1973, after a year's preparatory work in libraries, he and his wife Janet (also an archaeologist) set out on ten months systematic exploration of the island, to check known sites and add new ones to the list. They had one student grant to share between them, and an elderly Landrover in which they travelled and also lived; they were young and enthusiastic, and luckily that winter was a mild one. From time to time they returned to the Taverna at Knossos for a breather and to prepare the next stage of the campaign, but even there they could not afford the meals and continued to cook for themselves on a camping stove in their room in the Annexe. In 1975 they returned to Crete for three weeks to check a few last details, but by then Ian was already ill. He finished his dissertation only weeks before his death, and his doctorate was awarded posthumously. Janet saw to the publication of the thesis as a book; it is the foundation on which all subsequent studies of Crete in the historical period of antiquity are, and will continue to be, built, and is a lasting memorial to the courage of a great scholar.

Roman Crete brought together a great deal of research by scholars of different nationalities in many different fields. Besides the gazetteer of 429 sites it has chapters on the history, administration, economy, art, architecture and religion of Crete during the Roman and Early Christian period, and appendices listing the administrators of the Roman province of Crete-and-Cyrene and the known Roman magistrates of Cretan origin. One useful section summarizes the evidence for the changes in sea-level round the coasts of Crete, first recorded by Spratt at Phalasarna and afterwards noted at many sites around the island. In 1955 a campaign of underwater survey, directed by Sinclair Hood and John Leatham, investigating harbour remains and other waterside installations such as fish-tanks at Chersonisos and Mochlos, paid particular attention to this problem, finding at both these places that the sea-level had risen by about one metre since Roman times. At the little city of Lasaia on the south coast, however, a survey by David Blackman and Keith Branigan in 1971 found only a slight rise in sea-level. The phenomenon was clearly not a question of a simple see-saw effect, with the western end of the island rising while the eastern end sank, nor was it something that could be pinned down in time to a single cataclysm. Sanders concluded that there had probably been both a land rise in western Crete in the late Hellenistic times and a general rise in sea-level since the end of the Roman period, but that the story was a complicated one, with many regional variations.

These surveys in the fifties, sixties and the early seventies were carried out in a Crete which had not changed very much since the days of Pendlebury's expeditions before the war; no national roads or village web-sites then, no tourists swarming everywhere in brightly-coloured little cars to muffle the effect of foreigners asking strange questions. Even the main roads were often tyre-shredding tracks, usable only by the toughest vehicles; once one had got to the base camp for a survey one walked, with baggage carried when necessary by mule. The distances recorded by Pendlebury, accurate maps not being available, were in walking hours, and allowance has generally had to be made since then for his great turn of speed (indeed in trying to trace the footsteps of any of these legendary survey teams it is as well to estimate their handicap before starting). Everywhere the archaeologists met with local knowledge and assistance. Occasionally there were slight problems; Dunbabin reported a story of some villagers who, on hearing that archaeologists were approaching, dumped a lot of bones into a chasm in a cave, for fear that excavation would delay the construction of their new cheese houses, and Pendlebury records that he once had a five-hour-long quarrel with a boatman off Cape Sidero. But on the whole, although conditions were austere, enquiries, however baffling, seem always to have been met with great helpfulness and most generous hospitality by the Cretans.

The biggest problem with surveys, however scientific and modern the system on which they are run, is dating; much of the material is pottery, for the most part dismal scraps of cruelly abraded coarseware, and the dating of such pottery depends on reliable comparison with stratified material from excavations. For the Hellenistic and Roman periods the British contribution to excavation has mostly taken place at Knossos, with a very few exceptions such as Humfry Payne's brief campaign in 1929 at Eleutherna, and it is from excavations at Knossos that most of the stratified pottery sequences for these centuries have come. Knossos has of course always been the chief focus of research by British scholars in Crete. Remains of the Hellenistic and Roman periods have been recorded and excavated there on many occasions during the past hundred years, sometimes as a corollary to the investigation of the Bronze Age and sometimes for their own sake. All these finds were collected together by Sinclair Hood and David Smyth, in the *Archaeological Survey of the Knossos Area* (1981). The *Survey* is as rich a gold mine of information on the Greco-Roman period as it is on the prehistoric finds of the Knossos valley. It provides in close-up a highly detailed view of the territory of this one city, as Ian Sanders's book had portrayed on a broader scale the island as a whole. This overall multi-period picture of Knossos shows how very lucky it is that the *agrimensores* who laid out the Colonia Julia Nobilis Cnossus in the late first century BC were wary of building on made ground: if the centre of the new city had been planned to coincide with that of Bronze Age Knossos the buildings and contents of the Palace, as well as the delicate layers of Minoan occupation, would certainly have been annihilated by vast concrete foundations for Roman public buildings. Instead, the monumental centre of the colony was placed further to the north, and there are some indications that the classical, or at any rate the Hellenistic city, also had its focus in that area. A rather rambling 'old town' continued, however, to exist more or less on earlier lines around the lower slopes of the acropolis west of the Palace, and this area has provided much of the material on which the pottery sequences are based.

In 1935 a statue of the emperor Hadrian was found by chance at Knossos, just across the road from the vast Roman basilica; it had been buried in a pit, apparently not long before, and had probably come from some public building nearby (FIG. 110). The head was missing, and when the Curator of Knossos, R. W. Hutchinson, set out to search for it he discovered a fine mosaic. Within the next two months he had uncovered a large part of the Roman house now known as the Villa Dionysos, with its colonnaded peristyle court and magnificent mosaic floors. The excavation was continued after the war by Michael Gough (FIG. 111) who cleared the remaining rooms on the western and southern sides of the courtyard. Gough, a Byzantinist, was director of the British Institute at Ankara and is best known for his work on early churches in Cilicia; at Knossos he made himself unpopular by shouting orders in Turkish at the Cretan workmen, and is not remembered with affection (FIG. 112). After his death in 1973 the task of publishing the Villa Dionysos and conserving the building and its mosaic floors proceeded rather slowly and suffered many setbacks. Full publication of the Villa and the excavations is now being prepared by Sara Paton. The columns of the peristyle courtyard were restored in 1975 under the supervision of David Smyth; and the conservation programme has gathered momentum and is entering its final phase. The rooms will be protected by new architect-designed shelters, the mosaic floors will be cleaned and conserved, and the Villa Dionysos should soon be ready to be opened to the public. It will be the only example of this type of grand *villa urbana* on permanent display in the Roman province of Crete-and-Cyrene.

FIG. 110 Statue of the Emperor Hadrian found at Knossos in 1935. (Graham Norrie)

The pottery from the great fill which had been dumped in the ruins of the Villa Dionysos after its destruction in *c.*AD 200 was published by John Hayes. Although best known for his wider studies of the pottery of the later Roman Empire and the early Byzantine period, Hayes's publications of the second and third century AD pottery from the Villa Dionysos and of several earlier groups from Knossos have contributed a large part of the framework for the Roman pottery sequences in Crete. For the Hellenistic period the work of Peter Callaghan has been invaluable. His excavation, in 1976, of the Shrine of Glaukos at Knossos produced a great quantity of votive pottery deposited over a period of at least four hundred years, and in his publication he was able to relate this material to finds from many other sites, as well as revealing the practices of this fascinating Cretan cult. Full classification of the Hellenistic pottery of Crete is a task that has now been taken up by Jonas Eiring; this too will provide us with a chronological tool of great value.

More of the Hellenistic and Roman city of Knossos came to light in the upper levels of the Unexplored Mansion excavations where a street with houses on either side produced much new evidence for domestic life and minor industry. The meticulous publication of all the finds from this site, edited by the excavation director Hugh Sackett, has provided an unequalled record of the range of material in everyday use at Knossos during the various phases of the Roman period. The sequence of stratified material has now been extended into the Early Christian period by the Roman Knossos excavations carried out in 1993 and 1995 by a Birmingham University team directed by Kenneth and Diana Wardle; the Roman pottery from the site is being analysed by Gary Forster. This is the first time a major project at Knossos has been planned from the outset with the specific purpose of investigating the Roman city, and the results are already very interesting. In several areas domestic material of the fourth and fifth centuries AD has been found overlying grand private houses of the second and third centuries, while a massive wall, 20 metres long and preserved to a height of nearly 6 metres, with a wave-crest mosaic at its foot, is most probably part of a vast public bath building.

FIG. 111 Excavation of the Villa Dionysos at Knossos in 1958. (Michael Gough)

FIG. 112 Michael Gough sitting on the Throne of Minos. (Mary Gough)

Knossos constantly turns up surprises. One very striking find from the Roman Knossos excavations of 1995 was part of a damaged mosaic floor portraying two athletes – boxers, or perhaps pancratiasts – with their names written above their heads. One of men is named (in Greek) SATORNILOS, and is almost certainly to be identified with the Satorninos, a Cretan from Gortyn, who was an Olympic victor in AD 209. The mosaic is thus both a fresh illustration of the well-known sports-mania of the Severan period and also a very useful piece of dating evidence, since the fan who commissioned the pavement must have done so while the victory was still hot news. Another remarkable find came from the North Cemetery, where an Early Christian tomb was found to be constructed from components of a second century AD Corinthian portico (FIG. 113) which had been supplied by the Pentelic quarries in building-kit form, with instructions for assembly inscribed on the blocks – a unique feature (FIG. 119). This tomb was excavated by Jill Carington Smith, who is an unsung heroine of Hellenistic and Roman Knossos. During her years as Knossos Fellow she carried out innumerable rescue digs of all periods, often under very difficult conditions and with minimal backup. While excavating at the North Cemetery she had, for example, no transport, and was once obliged to hire a taxi to ferry six Early Christians back to the Stratigraphical Museum, first prudently disguising them as groceries since four is the maximum number of passengers allowed in a taxi. Although she is a prehistorian her publication of a Roman chamber tomb, the 'Glass Tomb', found intact by chance in 1978 and excavated by her, is a model of its kind (FIG. 114).

The Knossos of Hellenistic and Roman times is taking shape, and since the publication of *Roman Crete* the island of Crete is itself gradually resuming its proper place in the Greco-Roman world, no longer to be seen as a dowdy and impoverished backwater. Its settlements, which often appear at first sight insignificant and isolated, can show astonishingly sophisticated cosmopolitan connections and taste. Of all the British contributions to the history of Crete in this period perhaps one story best exemplifies the odd encounters, the surprises and the contrasts to be encountered in this small half-province of the Roman world. In the Fitzwilliam Museum in Cambridge there is a magnificent relief sarcophagus of the second century AD representing the Triumph of Dionysos. It is made of Italian marble from Carrara (*marmor lunense*); it was almost certainly the product of an *atelier* in Rome, and probably a special commission since it was shipped out to the small town of Arvi (ancient Arbion) on the south coast of Crete, presumably for the burial

FIG. 113 Epistyle block from the Corinthian building being lifted out of Knossos North Cemetery Tomb 244. (David Parfitt)

FIG. 114 *Lagynos* from the Glass Tomb, a Roman chamber tomb on Monasteriaki Kephala, Knossos. (*BSA* 77 (1982), Pl. 36f)

FIG. 115 The Pashley Sarcophagus. (Fitzwilliam Museum, Cambridge)

of a local personage. There it was found by Pashley in the 1840s, while Crete was deep in the struggle for independence from Ottoman rule. He collected the pieces (not without difficulty) and sent them off on another long journey across the Roman world, to England (FIG. 115). In 1962 the survey team led by Sinclair Hood visited Arvi and there met someone who claimed to have known, as a boy, the man who owned the land where the sarcophagus was found. When Pashley asked the owner what he wanted in exchange for the sarcophagus the simple answer was 'gunpowder'.

SARA PATON

D. J. Blackman and K. Branigan, *Ayiopharango* (1975), 17–36.

P. J. Callaghan, 'Excavations at a shrine of Glaukos, Knossos', *BSA* 73 (1978), 1–30.

J. Carington Smith, 'A Roman chamber tomb on the south-east slopes of Monasteriaki Kephala, Knossos', *BSA* 77 (1982), 255–93.

T. J. Dunbabin, 'Antiquities of Amari', *BSA* 42 (1947), 184–93.

J. W. Hayes, 'The Villa Dionysos excavations at Knossos: the pottery', *BSA* 78 (1983), 97–169.

S. Hood, P. Warren and G. Cadogan, 'Travels in Crete, 1962', *BSA* 59 (1964), 50–99.

S. Hood, 'Minoan sites in the far west of Crete', *BSA* 60 (1965), 97–113.

S. Hood and P. Warren, 'Ancient sites in the province of Ayios Vasilios, Crete', *BSA* 61 (1966), 164–89.

S. Hood, 'Some ancient sites in south-west Crete', *BSA* 62 (1967), 48–56.

S. Hood and D. Smyth, *Archaeological Survey of the Knossos Area* (BSA supp. vol. 14, 1981).

J. Leatham and S. Hood, 'Sub-marine exploration in Crete, 1955', *BSA* 53–54 (1958–1959), 261–80.

S. Paton, 'A Roman Corinthian building at Knossos', *BSA* 86 (1991), 297–318.

S. Paton, 'The Villa Dionysos at Knossos and its predecessors', in W.G. Cavanagh and M. Curtis (eds.), *Post-Minoan Crete: Proceedings of the First Colloquium, 1995*, (BSA Studies 2, 1998), 123–8.

J. D. S. Pendlebury, *The Archaeology of Crete* (London, 1939).

L. H. Sackett (ed.), *Knossos: from Greek City to Roman Colony. Excavations at the Unexplored Mansion* (BSA supp. vol. 21, 1992).

I. F. Sanders, *Roman Crete: an archaeological Survey and Gazetteer of Late Hellenistic, Roman and Early Byzantine Crete* (Warminster, 1982).

EPIGRAPHY

Students of the British School at Athens have had a distinguished record in the study of inscribed texts of the Greek period on Crete. This section will concentrate on the material uncovered in excavations by the School, but it would be unbalanced without recognition of the broader field. Two scholars stand out: Ronald Willetts for his dedication to the legal texts of the island, culminating in a definitive edition of the Great Code of Gortyn and the innumerable questions of social structure and epigraphical paragraphing entailed; and L. H. Jeffery whose review of archaic and classical Cretan inscriptions laid the foundations for all later discussions. The Code is also briefly treated by two other eminent epigraphists, Russell Meiggs and David Lewis, in their re-edition of Marcus Tod's *Selection of Greek Historical Inscriptions to the End of the Fifth Century B. C.*; they set it alongside a rare Cretan classical text of a more political nature, the regulations passed by the Argives to monitor a treaty between Knossos and Tylissos, fragments of which have yet to be found at Knossos itself.

With respect to material that has been discovered in the course of work by the School, there follows an overview running from east to west of the island.

Palaikastro

Excavations at the meagre remains of the shrine of Zeus Diktaios at Palaikastro (probably ancient Dikta) yielded just one Greek text (FIG. 116), while a few others reused in the vicinity may originally have stood in the temenos. The famous hymn to Zeus was recovered, incomplete, in

FIG. 116 The Palaikastro Hymn to Zeus, 'rough' copy. Limestone. Third century AD. Width 0.49. Herakleion Museum. (After *BSA* 15 (1908–9) pl. 20)

FIG. 117 Eteocretan stele from Praisos (Duhoux, PRA. 3). Limestone. Fourth or third century BC. Width preserved 0.20. Herakleion Museum 101. (Charles Crowther)

FIG. 118 Latin text regulating affairs of the sanctuary of Asklepios, with damnatio of Nero, from Knossos. Limestone? Width 0.38. Herakleion Museum inv. 189. (Herakleion Museum)

May 1904 and consists of a 'rough' and a 'fair' copy on its two faces. It remains a rare example of the genre and was, ironically, cut well into the Christian era, though dialect and vocabulary demonstrate that it is based on an original of the classical period. It recalls Zeus's upbringing under the Kouretes and asks his blessing on the land and the works of its people, who dance in his honour at the altar.

Praisos

In the excavations conducted by R. C. Bosanquet in 1901 and 1904 a single inscribed vase rim of late Hellenistic date came to light, and a good number of fragmentary stone texts. Many of the latter were just scraps, but two, also of the later classical or early Hellenistic period, added to the small corpus of Eteocretan texts from Praisos and neighbouring sites (FIG. 117). Despite a spirited attempt by Paul Faure to translate them as Greek, the texts are generally accepted to be in a language that may not even be Indo-European. Also in a more complete shape are an honorific decree of the Praisian koinon for two Athenians, fourth to third century BC, and a second to third century AD funerary stele.

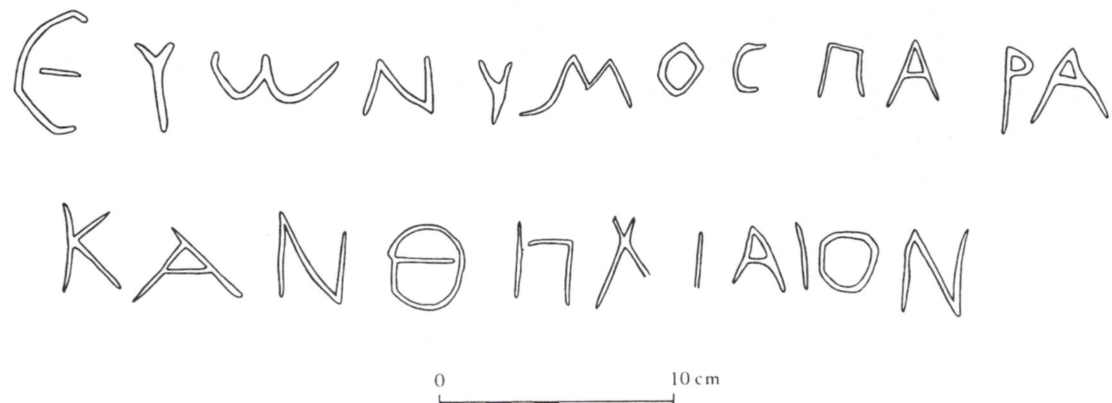

FIG. 119 Architect's note on pediment block of 'temple-tomb' in the North Cemetery, Knossos. Pentelic marble. Second century AD. Knossos Stratigraphical Museum Annexe. (After *BSA* 86 (1991), 302, Fig. 4)

Knossos

The body of written material from Iron Age Knossos is a pale thing compared with the riches of Linear A and B, but it has peculiarities that are well worth attention, especially if we compare the material with that of contemporary poleis, in Crete or elsewhere in the Greek world.

'Inscriptions' are normally taken to be texts on stone, and here the number found in the area of Knossos, and published or mentioned in literature, is some seventy. A good number of these were found before the British School began its involvement in the region, or have been discovered subsequently by our Greek colleagues in modern buildings or foundations. They range from the seventh century BC to the late Roman period, but include no substantial text that is fully preserved. An important earlier, Phoenician text may be added (FIG. 101). There are mere scraps of the early legal texts so striking in other Cretan towns, though one preserves for us an early example of fines to be paid in *darkmas* (drachmai). Similarly there are few Hellenistic honorific decrees, though Knossians find mention for a variety of reasons in such texts from Asia Minor. While the School has excavated at several cemetery sites, the number of inscribed stelai remains small, and it is no surprise that dedicatory bases are few. Knossos of course became a Roman colony, and at least thirteen Latin inscriptions are now known, including *IC* 49, confirmation of a grant of land to the cult of Asklepios by Nero, whose name has been duly expunged from the stone after his death (FIG. 118). The stone 'surfaced' in the late nineteenth century, and was published alongside Evans's first report on the palace excavations. It gives the abbreviated title of the colony CINC – Colonia Julia Nobilis Cnosos, which appears as a stamp on a number of tiles from the excavations.

On stone, but not meant for display is an interesting series of architectural notes on some blocks in the North Cemetery of what was perhaps a mausoleum, in Corinthian order, constructed in the second century AD; it is the most striking of a modest number of texts, yet

FIG. 120 Graffito owner's inscription on a bucchero aryballos, from Tomb 107, North Cemetery, Knossos. Present height 0.06. 650–625 BC. Herakleion Museum. (J. N. Coldstream)

to be published in full, from the cemetery. The most loquacious note ordains 'the left one from the saddle [apex] block', to clarify its position in the raking geison (FIG. 119).

The number of casual writings found in cemetery excavations is normally slight, and Knossos fits this pattern, offering little more than a tidy mid-seventh century owner's text on a bucchero aryballos (FIG. 120). Such owner's texts, together with those displaying the basic *anetheke* formula, are also frequently met on objects dedicated in sanctuaries throughout the Greek world, yet at Knossos we find a strange pattern, since most of the known dedicatory texts are on silver rings from the sanctuary of Demeter (FIG. 109), including that offered by a certain Nothokartes; 'normal' usage is as yet scarcely attested. Here we must take into consideration the dip in central Cretan fortunes in the period *c.*575–475, the time when such usages were particularly prevalent elsewhere (e.g. Naukratis, the Athenian Acropolis and Himera – home of the exiled Knossian athlete Ergoteles, whose Olympic dedication is part-preserved). Even for the later classical and Hellenistic periods the harvest of casual texts is meagre. Many of them are imports (amphora stamps, sigillata stamps), and others cannot assuredly be located as Knossian-produced, though fitting marks for well-drums of probably Hellenistic date presumably were (*The Palace of Minos* iii, 255–8).

The Roman colony sees the continued import of sigillata, while its bilingual nature is nicely characterised by a bone counter inscribed in Greek and Latin with a notation '8'; the makers of lamps also stamp their products in either language. A fine but battered mosaic is of a known type of celebratory agonistic composition, with the victor named, and so a useful chronological peg for the architectural setting. And while one funerary plaque from the North

FIG. 121 Funerary plaque for G. Kanpanios Philephebos and his wife(?) Kanpania Kledon. From the North Cemetery, Knossos. Limestone. Width 0.64. First century AD. Knossos, Stratigraphical Museum Annexe 26. (J.A. MacGillivray)

Cemetery is in Greek, it commemorates members of a family clearly of Italian servile extraction, the Kanpanioi (FIG. 121). We are told by Dio Cassius that Octavian endowed Capua with land in the vicinity of Knossos and here is some epigraphic evidence to support the idea that the new owners may not have been wholly absentee landlords.

ALAN JOHNSTON

L. H. Jeffery, *The Local Scripts of Archaic Greece* (Oxford, 1961; revised with supplement by A.W. Johnston, 1990).

R. Meiggs and D. M. Lewis, *Greek Historical Inscriptions to the End of the Fifth Century B.C.*, revised edition (Oxford, 1988).

R. F. Willetts, *The Law Code of Gortyn* (Kadmos supp. vol. 1; Berlin, 1967).

Palaikastro

R. C. Bosanquet, 'The Palaikastro Hymn of the Kouretes', *BSA* 15 (1908–9), 339–65.

C. Crowther, 'A note on Minoan Dikta', *BSA* 83 (1988), 37–44.

M. Guarducci, *Inscriptiones Creticae III* ii (Rome, 1935–50).

M. L. West, 'The Dictaean Hymn to the Kouros' *JHS* 85 (1965), 149–59.

Praisos

R. C. Bosanquet, 'Inscriptions from Praesos', *BSA* 16 (1909–10), 281–9.

Y. Duhoux, *L'Étéocrétois; les textes, la langue* (Amsterdam, 1982).

P. Faure, 'Les sept inscriptions dites "étéocrétoises" reconsiderées', *Kr. Chron.* 28–9 (1988–9), 94–109.

M. Guarducci, *Inscriptions Creticae III* vi.

Knossos (selected)

J. N. Coldstream, *Knossos. The Sanctuary of Demeter* (BSA Supp. vol. 8, 1973), index, s.v. graffiti, inscriptions.

M. Guarducci, *Inscriptions Creticae III* viii.

S. Paton, 'A Roman Corinthian building at Knossos', *BSA* 86 (1991), 297–318.

L. H. Sackett, *Knossos from Greek City to Roman Colony; Excavations at the Unexplored Mansion* (BSA supp. vol. 21, 1992) ii. 137–46.

J. Whitley, 'Cretan laws and Cretan literacy', *AJA* 101 (1997), 635–61.

THE BYZANTINE and ARAB PERIODS

Little attention has been directed specifically to early Christian, Byzantine or Arab monuments of Crete. The medieval material that overlays most ancient sites seems to have been considered (not only by British excavators) much more as an impediment to the real work of archaeology than as worthy of study, let alone conservation, in its own right. Evans may bear some responsibility for the disastrous attitude which cheerfully recorded the demolition of Byzantine churches in order to get down to the serious levels. That Knossos continued in occupation in the Roman and early Christian periods is clear from numerous stray finds of coins as well as the basilica church and Christian bone deposit (*osteotheke*) eventually excavated there (*BSA* 1962, 1976). British excavators did regularly note the presence of Byzantine pottery and of course coins, found in and around Knossos, at Gortyn and other sites. The pottery, however, was not always published in the final excavation reports, adding to a sense of frustration for the would-be historian or archaeologist of medieval Crete.

Given the strategic position of the island within the Byzantine empire, its continuous occupation through Christian times is hardly surprising, but the early history of Crete is more fully documented from written sources, conveniently brought together by Dimitris Tsougarakis, in his book *Byzantine Crete*. These indicate a flourishing church, led by the Metropolitan of Gortyna, which formed part of the diocese of East Illyricum. It therefore remained under the authority of the church of Rome, until the early eighth century when Emperor Leo III transferred the diocese to the control of Constantinople. In contrast, the island was placed within the administration of the civilian province of Macedonia from the late third century, and its officials, *archontes*, were appointed from the eastern capital. Recent study of the medieval inscriptions and seals confirms the existence of a network of ecclesiastical and secular officials who governed the island from the early Christian period to the Arab conquest, *c.*828; and again from the recovery of the island by Nikephoros Phokas to its fall to the Venetians in *c.*1210. In both the first and second Byzantine phase of Crete's history, this evidence adds an important dimension to the sparse record of excavated material.

One factor which may help to account for the relatively small interest shown by British archaeologists in early Christian Crete might derive from the fact that few pagan temples were converted into churches, as happened at Athens, Ephesus or Syracuse. For where such conversions took place classical archaeologists were often obliged to investigate the later Christian use of the building, as well as its primary use as a temple. It is also the case that even where new basilica churches were identified, excavation was not by any means an

FIG. 122 Knossos North Cemetery. Excavation of a vaulted cistern under the atrium of the Mortuary Church. (H.W. Catling)

automatic result, or it was undertaken as essential rescue work as, for example, on the large construction revealed at the site of the new Medical Faculty of the University of Crete described in *Archaeological Reports* for 1978/9. Surrounded by a substantial enclosure wall, this three-aisled basilica, 40 metres long by 18 metres wide, probably dating from the fifth century, was associated with twenty ossuaries, perhaps indicating a mortuary church established on the site of a Roman cemetery. Little remained of the building itself from which most of the stone had been robbed. The unusual trefoil-shaped sanctuary, stray finds of marble column bases and glass tesserae, the substructures of the floors, and below the atrium a large vaulted cistern, carefully constructed of baked brick, suggest the high quality of the original structure. The site was studied by A. H. S. Megaw, and is now built over (FIGS. 122–5).

In contrast, another basilica church at Knossos, one of the major monuments of the early Christian period, was fully investigated by W. H. C. Frend and D. E. Johnston and published (*BSA* 1962). It was dated to the late fifth or early sixth century, despite an anomalous coin find on the natural clay below the ruined nave, identified as one of Herakleios overstruck on one of Phokas in the third year of his reign (612/3). In his 1982 survey of the sixty-eight basilicas then known on Crete, Ian Sanders observes that since the coin appeared to be crushed by fallen masonry, it may in fact date the destruction of the church rather than its

FIG. 123 The Mortuary Church. Bases of the internal colonnade of the south enclosure wall. (H. W. Catling)

foundation. In addition to the discovery of many outbuildings and tombs (some associated with an earlier cemetery which contained Jewish as well as Roman burials), some early Byzantine coarse pottery was found. Curiously, this type of pottery was not replicated at the nearby Osteotheke excavations of Hector Catling and David Smyth, (*BSA* 1976). Here 35–50 individual skeletons were identified buried in five levels, with pottery more similar to the early Christian finds at Corinth, Athens and Kornos Cave (Cyprus). This discrepancy suggests that it will be necessary to study a wider range of excavated ceramic material from the island in order to construct a useful typology.

The scale and lavish decoration of a five-aisled basilica at Mitropolis, near Gortyn, recently uncovered by an Italian team and reported by Antonino di Vito (*ASA* 1990–1), reflect both the strategic importance of the island as a port of call between North Africa and Constantinople, and of Gortyna as its ecclesiastical centre. Acclamations of the Emperor Herakleios, his wife and son, dated 612, may indicate that *en route* from Carthage to the imperial capital, he called at the southern port. The grandeur of the second phase of this building, constructed immediately after 618, suggests imperial patronage of the metropolitan see of the island. Crete was represented by several bishops at all major church councils of the period, and in those of 681/2 and 692, Metropolitan Basil took a leading role as the representative of the bishop of Rome. In the light of this prominence it is particularly sad that so little is recorded of work at the basilica of St Titus at Gortyn, where several Byzantine seals were found. Metropolitans of Crete frequently chose to depict their patron saint on the reverse of their seals, for example, Stephanos, Andreas, and two later metropolitans, (see D. Tsougarakis, *Seals*, nos. 1, 3, 11, 13, 62).

Ayios Andreas of Crete, appointed metropolitan in the early eighth century, was one of the notable scholars of the Byzantine period who wrote many sermons, hymns and developed the great kanon, a much longer form of *kontakion*. Among several seals attributed to him, one was found in the ruins of Knossos and preserves a bust of St Titus on the obverse. Interestingly, this is the only seal with a clear association with Crete which has been found on the island to date. Like coins minted on Crete, which are regularly found elsewhere, these small objects which travel easily are often

FIG. 124 The Mortuary Church. Sub-floor foundation of brick and tile, set on edge (H.W. Catling)

acquired by collectors who are not especially interested in their provenance.

The importance of Crete in imperial defence became clearer as the Mediterranean came under threat from the Arabs from the 640s. Its ports sheltered naval forces and supported troops on campaigns against the conquerors of North Africa, (Herrin, 1986). But the military and naval resources under the command of *archontes* failed to prevent the attacks launched by Arab pirates from Spain, who overran the island in *c.* 828. The period of Arab domination is poorly documented from the Byzantine side, marginally better from the Arabic by coin finds. So the excavation by Peter Warren of a monument securely dated by coin finds *in situ* is especially significant, and was then unique, (*BSA* 1972). Near the village of Makryteikhos at Knossos, close to the river Kairatos, a small building constructed of rounded river boulders in an unusual style was dated by the discovery of nine coins minted on Crete during the Arab occupation (*c.* 828–961). Since there was no obvious entrance at ground level, and fragments of several large mill stones were found, the building may possibly have been used for pressing olives (FIG. 126). The building was apparently abandoned *c.* 900 when the river began to wash away its foundations, leaving a deposit of yellow river sand banked up against the outer east wall. The coins, all bronze, do not bear dates but four commemorate Shu'ayb b. abi Hafs 'Umar, son of the Arab conqueror of the island.

Through this unique discovery, which also included twenty-six strong iron nails, it is clear that the Arab occupation involved the serious use of local resources, for example in iron working, coin minting and the use of mill stones. Similar activity is documented at other sites where Arab presence can be detected, as, for example, by E. Borboudakis at Ayios Petros

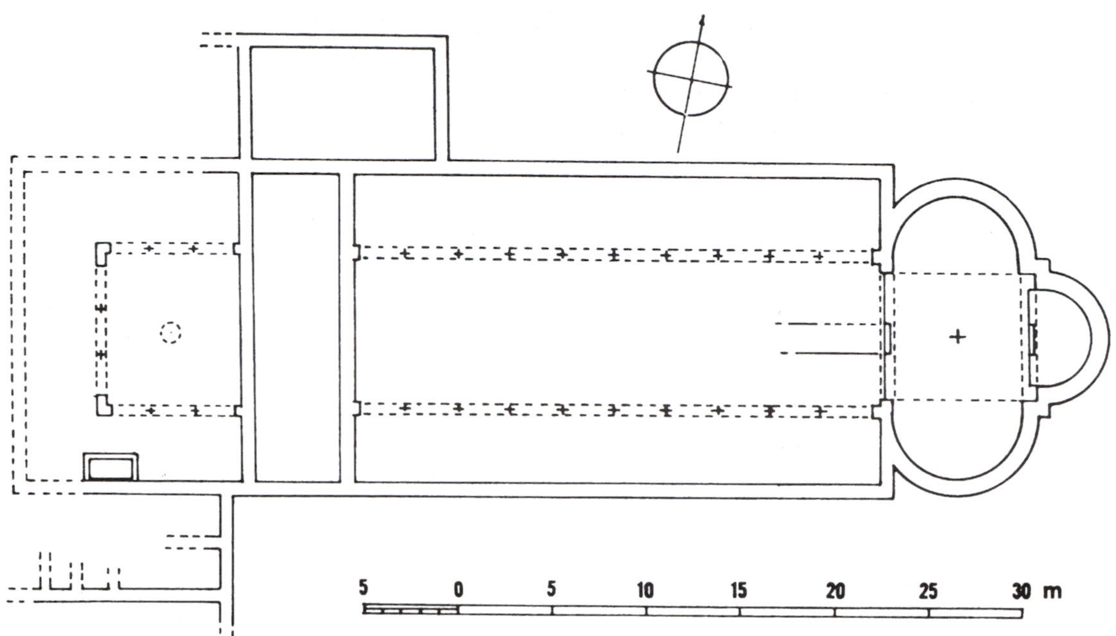

FIG. 125 Restored plan of the basilican Mortuary Church. (A. H. S. Megaw)

FIG. 126 Knossos. Building of the Arab period (9th century) beside the Kairatos stream. (P. Warren)

ton Dominikanon, with an Islamic bowl of local production, and five coins. And at the basilica at Syvritou, with two coins of the ninth century, found by K. D. Kalokyres in the south-west entrance to the narthex, and associated ceramics and nails. From this firm base, the Arabs raided other islands in the Aegean and harassed the coastal regions, as many Byzantine saints' lives record. On Crete itself, the Christian population was probably left mainly to its own devices, the occupying troops had little interest in inter-marriage with local women, and much greater concern in levying the extra taxation demanded of non-converts.

Many attempts were made to recover the island from Muslim control, including an expedition mounted in 949 which is fully documented by Constantine VII (945–59) in the *Book of Ceremonies*, and includes a detailed account of the sea route used, discussed by George Huxley, and on the military side, by John Haldon. But just two years after the emperor's death the general Nikephoros Phokas finally achieved the reconquest in 961, and Byzantine control was re-established through a military governor, *strategos*. In archaeological terms this second phase is sadly disappointing, perhaps because (as excavators themselves have admitted) so little dated material is available. In their survey of the Ayiopharango valley, for instance, David Blackman and Keith Branigan point to the lack of comparanda for coarse pottery finds, which might reflect the documented eleventh century habitation. They suggest that some pale green glazed wares currently identified as Venetian might in fact be Byzantine (*BSA* 1977).

Much more light is shed on the second phase of Byzantine occupation by the *Life* of John Xenos, a local Cretan missionary who devoted his life to building monasteries and churches in the southern parts of the island, the most famous being the Monastery of the Theotokos on Mount Myriokephalon. His determination to Christianise the region undoubtedly contributed to the redevelopment of agriculture by clearing land for cultivation, planting crops, establishing beekeeping, for example, as well as constructing a large number of small Cretan churches, all the subject of recent research by Sophia Oikonomou.

Throughout the second Byzantine phase Venice, Genoa, Pisa and other Italian maritime cities were exploring the trade markets of the East Mediterranean and discovering the strategic advantages and economic strengths of Crete. During the Fourth Crusade, which resulted in the sack of Constantinople (1204), the Venetians participated in plans to divide the Byzantine empire, recorded in the *Partitio imperii byzantini*. This reveals their determination to control Crete and the significance they attached to it as a trading centre, which was borne out by the subsequent conquest of the island and its lengthy occupation by Venice.

JUDITH HERRIN

D. Blackman and K. Branigan, *Ayiopharango* (1977), 77–8.

E. Borboudakis, *A.Delt.* 23 (1968), 429 and pl. 398a.

H. W. Catling and D. Smyth, 'An Early Christian Osteotheke at Knossos', *BSA* 71 (1976), 25–47.

V. Christides, *The Conquest of Crete by the Arabs* (Athens, 1984).

W. H. C. Frend and D. E. Johnston, 'The Byzantine basilica church at Knossos', *BSA* 57 (1962), 186–238.

J. Haldon, '2, 44 and 45 of the *Book of Ceremonies.* Theory and Practice in Tenth-Century Military Administration.' *Travaux et Mémoires* (forthcoming).

J. Herrin, 'Crete in the conflicts of the eighth century', *Aphieroma ston Niko Sborono*, 2 vols. (Rethymno, 1986), i. 113–26.

G. L. Huxley, 'A Porphyrogenitan Portulan', in *GRBS*, 17 (1976), 295–300.

K. D. Kalokyres, *Kr. Chron.* 12 (1959), 30–2; pl.12 (4–5), and pl.13 (1).

A. H. S. Megaw, 'A Cemetery Church with Trefoil Sanctuary in Crete', in *Actes du Congrès international d'archéologie chrétienne, Thessalonica 28 September–4 October 1980* (Vatican City – Thessalonica, 1984), ii. 321–9.

S. Oikonomou, PhD Thesis, King's College London (forthcoming).

I. F. Sanders, *Roman Crete* (Warminster, 1982).

S. V. Spyridakis, 'Cretan Ecclesiastical Inscriptions: Notes and Observations', *Kr. Chron.* n.s. 30 (1990), 62–76.

D. Tsougarakis, *Byzantine Crete: from the fifth century to the Venetian conquest* (Athens, 1988).

D. Tsougarakis, 'The Byzantine Seals of Crete', in N. Oikonomides (ed.), *Studies in Byzantine Sigillography*, 2 (Washington, D.C. 1990), 136–52.

A. di Vito, 'Archaeological Reports,' *ASA* 68–69 (1990–1), 481–6.

P. Warren and G. C. Miles, 'An Arab Building at Knossos', *BSA* 67 (1972), 286–96.

THE CRETAN RENAISSANCE

The concept of a 'Cretan Renaissance' is one that has taken shape in the course of the twentieth century, as increasing attention to archival, historical and, in particular, literary researches has extended our knowledge far beyond the vague ideas of nineteenth-century scholars. By 'Cretan Renaissance' we refer particularly to those literary works written in Crete, in the Cretan dialect, in the period from about 1580 until the Ottoman conquest in 1669. This period is a 'renaissance' in the very specific sense that its poets, artists and intellectuals assimilate and draw creatively on Italian Renaissance culture: not as mere imitation, but as a local reception of, and response to, those same dynamic surges that radiated out from Italy to all corners of Europe. One of the compensations of Venetian rule, imposed on Crete from 1211, was that it offered more direct access to Italian cultural developments than was the case for most other parts of the Greek-speaking world. As time went on and the Venetian settlers became increasingly assimilated to the Cretan-Greek cultural milieu, ethnic, and even religious, distinctions were blurred. Much inter-cultural transaction must have occurred. Already from the late fourteenth century we encounter poetry in the Greek vernacular that shows a familiarity with Italian literary fashions and forms. These earlier, fourteenth- to sixteenth-century, works of Cretan literature also have a place in our discussion, although it is the dramatic and narrative works of the last century of Venetian rule that will occupy centre-stage. British scholars have made many major contributions to the study of this body of texts, and most notably perhaps in the fields of editing and literary criticism, not discounting the important role of translation. Research by British scholars in the history and artistic production of Venetian-ruled Crete is slimmer in quantity, but brief mention will be made of the more significant contributions.

At the beginning of the twentieth century remarkably little was known about Cretan literature. Few texts were available in 'modern' critical editions; such editions as existed were unsatisfactory in terms of methodology and based on inadequate textual evidence. In most cases definitive answers to questions of dating, authorship and sources were out of reach. Scholarly opinions about the literary value of the texts were often negative or condescending. J. B. Bury, for example, characterised *Erotokritos* as 'a long and tedious romance [. . .] saturated with Italian influence', although he correctly related its plot and genre to medieval romance (1911). John Mavrogordato later offered the cheeky riposte: 'It certainly has the slowness of a popular and expensive film; but we might reply that it was not written for the entertainment of Professor Bury; and that the same criticism might be applied to Chaucer's *Troilus and Criseyde*, if we did not consider it as a prelude to the noblest age of English poetry.'

Mavrogordato's literary knowledge and sensitivity were second to none. He came from a family of Chiot descent but was himself born and educated in England. His work on Cretan literature, though not voluminous, remains a point of departure: so many good ideas stemmed from his pen that it is always worth checking that he didn't think of it first! In 1929 he published the results of his own researches on *Erotokritos*, the first study of the poem in English. It is a slim volume, containing an extended summary of the poem's plot, with accompanying comment and analysis. In his introduction he gave a critical account of previous research, and accepted the dating proposed by Hatzidakis: the end of the sixteenth century or the beginning of the seventeenth (although elsewhere he was tempted by a dating shortly after 1645). In the final section he suggested affinities with the plot and characterisation of *Romeo and Juliet*. Although we now know that no connection exists, it says much for Mavrogordato's insight that he pinpointed the period in which, according to the current accepted view, *Erotokritos* was composed (1590–1610), while aptly suggesting that Kornaros's relationship with the Italian Renaissance was comparable to Shakespeare's. (FIG. 127)

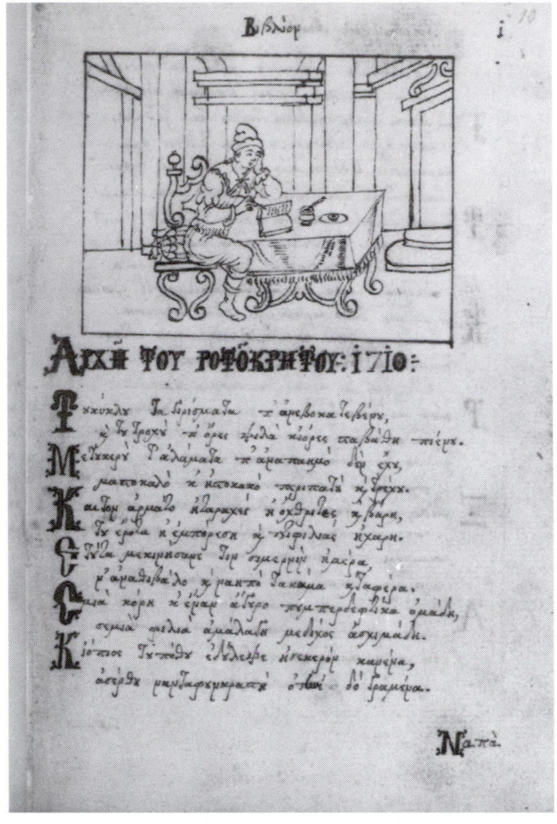

FIG. 127 Title page of the manuscript of *Erotokritos,* (Harleianus 5644, dated 1710; by permission of The British Library)

Mavrogordato was also involved in an effective collaboration with F. H. Marshall, second Koraës Professor of Modern Greek and Byzantine History, Language and Literature at King's College London, which also saw the light of day in 1929. Marshall provided translations, in rather quaint English, of four important Cretan works from the Renaissance period: the religious drama *The Sacrifice of Abraham*, the tragedy *Erofili*, the pastoral comedy *Gyparis* (now known as *Panoria*), and, in an appendix, the pastoral poem *The Fair Shepherdess*. Mavrogordato contributed a substantial introduction, in which he drew on articles he had published in *The Journal of Hellenic Studies* in the previous year. As well as summarising the plots of the works, he discussed authorship, sources and dating, and sketched the broader cultural context. In the second of the 1928 articles he had announced his important discovery of the Italian play from which *The Sacrifice of Abraham* drew its plot: *Lo Isach* by Luigi Groto. The Marshall-Mavrogordato volume was the first scholarly attempt to present a range of Cretan Renaissance texts to an English-speaking audience, and as such represents a very substantial achievement.

Marshall had previously worked on two earlier Cretan texts, an anonymous adaptation of Boccaccio's *Teseida* and the fifteenth-century *Kosmogennesis* by Georgios Choumnos. The latter is a rather naive and pedestrian verse adaptation of the first two books of the Old Testament, though it has considerable linguistic as well as theological interest. The work, which survives in a number of manuscripts and must therefore have been popular in its time, also drew on non-biblical legends. Marshall provided a transcription, rather than a critical edition, of extracts from the British Museum manuscript of Choumnos's poem, together with an English translation, introduction, brief notes, a glossary and photographs of some of the illustrations of the manuscript. In reproducing the orthography of the manuscript, he believed that it was written phonetically and preserved the spoken language of the time, and consequently had 'a distinct value for the history of the Greek language'. Today we would not be so categorical; but it is worth remarking that philological enquiry motivated a good deal of the research on older texts, until the middle of the twentieth century and even later.

In his preface to this volume Marshall acknowledges the assistance of Professor R. M. Dawkins. Richard Dawkins was, from 1920 until his retirement in 1939, the first occupant of the Bywater and Sotheby Chair of Byzantine and Modern Greek Language and Literature at Oxford. A man of vast and wide-ranging erudition who began his academic career as an archaeologist (he excavated at Palaikastro and elsewhere in Crete and the Aegean), Dawkins devoted himself particularly to the study of Modern Greek dialectology and folk tales. However, medieval texts also occupied him, especially the Cypriot chronicles of Machairas and Boustronios. He did not engage with the major poetic works of the Cretan Renaissance, but nonetheless his contributions to Cretan literary studies are worthy of note: in articles of 1930 and 1948 he presented a hitherto unknown Cretan version of the *Apocalypse of the Virgin*. The manuscript of this fascinating prose narrative is written in East Cretan dialect, but using the Latin alphabet (a widespread practice in Crete, and elsewhere, at this time). Dated around 1600, this work (or, more precisely, the two thematically linked narratives contained in the manuscript) is a rare example of a literary prose text in the Cretan vernacular. Finally, in an article of 1932 he drew attention to another neglected prose text: a seventeenth-century Cretan translation of *Barlaam and Ioasaph*.

Dawkins, Mavrogordato and Marshall dominated Modern Greek studies in Britain in the first half of the twentieth century. Mavrogordato succeeded Dawkins as Bywater and Sotheby Professor at Oxford in 1939, but by then his interests had moved away from the Cretan Renaissance, back in time to the Byzantine epic-romance of *Digenis Akritis* and forward to Cavafy. What is worth noting is the fruitful way in which these scholars collaborated in their published work and – it is a reasonable inference, I believe – their recognition of Cretan Renaissance literature as an emerging and important field of study.

The mention of collaboration brings to mind the short-lived periodical *The Link*, characterised as 'A Review of Mediaeval and Modern Greek'. Only two issues appeared, in 1938 and 1939, before financial difficulties and, presumably, the outbreak of war cut short its fledgling existence. Under the editorship of the Russian émigré Nicholas Bachtin, who was then teaching Modern Greek at Birmingham, it gathered together an interesting range of articles on medieval and modern Greek linguistic and literary themes. The first issue included a piece by R. J. H. Jenkins, who in 1936 had been appointed as the first Lewis-Gibson Lecturer in Modern Greek at Cambridge, under the title 'Some notes on Foscolo's "Fortunatus"'. Jenkins offered a number of linguistic and textual observations on the seventeenth-century Cretan comedy, which at that time was available only in Xanthoudidis's 1922 edition. The same issue contained an article by Marshall on 'Lord Guilford and Greece', in which he mentioned the early editions of Cretan Renaissance texts in Guilford's collection (which passed to the British Museum), as well as his manuscript of *Erofili*, (FIG. 128) which was later bought by the University of Birmingham. Thus in the first half of the century the contributions of British scholars to the study of Cretan Renaissance literature could be called sporadic, but not without significance, with Mavrogordato's discovery of the model of *The Sacrifice of Abraham* standing out as the most important achievement. In the 1950s it appears that a single British scholar was carrying the torch for Cretan Renaissance studies: Gareth Morgan. In 1953 he entered the shark-infested waters of *Erotokritos* scholarship with an article discussing which version of *Paris et Vienne* had served as Kornaros's primary source for the plot. His major contribution appeared in 1960 – a detailed study of the early period of Cretan literature, based on his Oxford doctoral thesis. Published in three parts in the journal *Kritika Chronika*, it examined in depth a variety of Cretan, or allegedly Cretan texts, such as the Escorial version of *Digenis Akritis*, the poems of Sachlikis, and the *Anakalima tis Konstantinopolis*, as well as versions of *Erofili* and other texts which survived in oral tradition. It is a wide-ranging and ambitious study which is still frequently referred to, even though subsequent research has altered the dating of some of the texts. Morgan later took up a post at the University of Texas, but maintained his interest in Cretan literature. In particular he suggested an interesting new approach to *Erotokritos* by relating its imagery to Western European emblem literature of the time, although not all of his ideas have found favour.

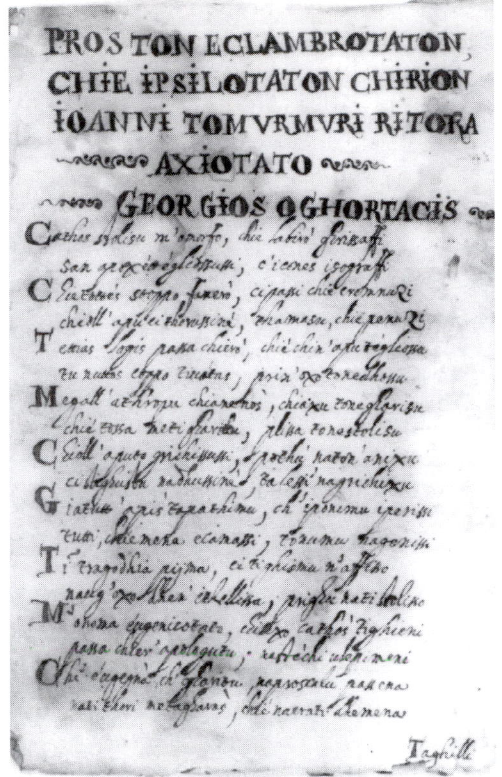
PROS TON ECLAMBROTATON
CHIE IPSILOTATON CHIRION
IOANNI TOMVRMVRI RITORA
AXIOTATO
GEORGIOS OGHORTACIS

FIG. 128 Title page of Chortatsis's tragedy *Erofili*. The manuscript, written in Latin characters by the comic playwright Markos Antonios Foskolos, offers the best text of the play and has detailed stage-directions. (MS 13/i/17; by permission of the Library of the University of Birmingham)

Morgan's work heralds the arrival on the scene of a younger group of scholars who developed closer links with scholars in Greece and began to be more concerned with the stylistic and literary qualities of the texts. First among this group was Alfred Vincent, whose research has engaged with a number of Cretan dramatic and poetic texts, as well as with their intellectual and social background. He discovered and published important biographical evidence about the playwright Markos Antonios Foskolos and identified him as the copyist of the Birmingham manuscript of Chortatsis's *Erofili*. Subsequently Vincent published his edition of Foskolos's comedy *Fortounatos* on which he had worked for his Cambridge Ph.D. This careful edition is a vast improvement on Xanthoudidis's 1922 attempt, which it has replaced as the standard text. In collaboration with Nikos Panagiotakis he published new evidence about the activities of the Academy of the Stravaganti, in particular about its founder Andrea Cornaro and his brother Vitsentzos Kornaros, now regarded by most scholars as the author of *Erotokritos*. Since taking up a post at the University of Sydney in the 1970s, Vincent has continued his fruitful research on Cretan literary texts and published several important articles.

Drama has also been the main focus of the work of Rosemary Bancroft-Marcus, who completed an Oxford D.Phil. (1978) on the playwright Georgios Chortatsis. Her published articles have dealt with topics ranging from the identification of sources to the depiction of women in Cretan texts and Cretan society, and she is preparing a substantial volume of texts of the Cretan plays with an English translation. Margaret Alexiou has also provided a penetrating analysis of how the themes of marriage and death are treated in Cretan drama. The increasing interest in style and literary criticism is demonstrated by the work of David Ricks; in particular he has pointed to the need for a literary commentary on *Erotokritos* and offered a specimen of what it might contain.

A collaborative volume edited by David Holton was the first attempt in English to offer a comprehensive study of Cretan Renaissance literary texts in relation to their historical, cultural and social context. In the book's ten chapters the work of British scholars is represented by Vincent (on comedy), Bancroft-Marcus (on the pastoral genre and interludes), Alexiou (on the reception of the Cretan Renaissance and interactions between literature and popular tradition), and Holton (on romance, with particular reference to *Erotokritos*). Holton has also published an introduction to *Erotokritos* and several articles on various aspects of that text, in particular its overall structure, its relations with earlier texts, and its mythological allusions. Under his supervision two young Greek scholars have completed Cambridge Ph.D. theses on Cretan subjects: Anastasia Markomihelaki-Mintzas on the Cretan comedies and their theoretical background (1991), and Natalia Deliyannaki on the versification of *Erotokritos* (1995). Since returning to Greece both these scholars have published articles on aspects of their work in Greek journals. A useful tool for further linguistic and stylistic research on *Erotokritos* and other Cretan texts is the concordance to *Erotokritos* made by Dia Philippides (of Boston College) and David Holton, with the technical collaboration of John Dawson, Director of the Centre for Literary and Linguistic Computing at the University of Cambridge, where the computing work for the undertaking – the first complete published concordance of a Cretan text – was carried out.

A complete English translation of *Erotokritos*, accompanied by illustrations, including several from the British Museum manuscript, was made by Theodore Stephanides. Although one could point to shortcomings in the translation, which is in rhymed verse, it contains a concise and reliable introduction by C. A. Trypanis (Bywater and Sotheby Professor at Oxford from 1947 to 1967), reproduced from the section on Cretan poetry in his substantial study *Greek poetry from Homer to Seferis* (1981).

Finally, mention should be made of the forays of two archaeologists, both with extensive Cretan experience, into the period which concerns us here. Richard Hutchinson made the interesting suggestion that the hostile figure of the Lord of Patra, who appears in the tournament in *Erotokritos*, alludes to the Albanian presence in the Peloponnese (although most scholars now agree that he is more likely to be a Turk). Peter Warren examined the writings of British travellers to Crete between the late sixeenth and eighteenth centuries, and drew attention to the wealth of historical, archaeological, topographical and cultural information to be garnered from them.

Compared with the scholarly work on Cretan literature, British historical research on the period of Venetian rule is limited in scope and seems to lack a proper tradition. Whereas British scholars have done distinguished work on other areas of the Greek world in the later Middle Ages, such as the Peloponnese, the Cyclades, Cyprus, and of course Byzantium, Crete has had little attention in its own right. Most of the works which mention Crete treat it in a broader context: the Frankish Aegean, Venice's overseas possessions, the break-up of the Byzantine Empire. William Miller's work on the Latin East is of fundamental importance. He devoted a whole chapter to Crete under the Venetians in his *Essays on the Latin Orient*, examining in some detail its political and social history as well as certain aspects of culture. Nicolas Cheetham's chapter on Crete has a similar aim; he was able to incorporate some of the findings of more recent scholarship, with a fairly general readership in mind. More scholarly are the volumes by Donald Nicol, Koraës Professor at King's College London from 1970 until 1988 (*Byzantium and Venice*), and Peter Lock (*The Franks in the Aegean*), in both of which frequent references to Crete form part of the complex broader picture that concerns their authors.

The situation we observe in art history is rather similar: a lack of detailed original research on specific aspects (such as one would expect to find in doctoral theses, monographs and journal articles), but some highly successful – and original – discussions of Cretan art in works of a wider compass. (Most of the voluminous research on El Greco is essentially outside our subject.) In this case the larger entity is Byzantine art. The magisterial work of David Talbot Rice has numerous mentions of Cretan painting, but a unified discussion is lacking and the period after 1453 is barely considered. Robin Cormack makes amends, in his recent book *Painting the soul*, by devoting considerable space to a discussion of Cretan painting in the Venetian period. Cormack offers a subtle and original analysis of the meeting of East and West in Crete, and examines its consequences both for the techniques and styles of the artists and for the expectations of viewers.

To conclude this survey, two very different books should be mentioned, one about the landscape of Crete, the other a wide-ranging analysis of the island's history and culture. In the course of their multi-disciplinary study of how the Cretan landscape has developed, Oliver Rackham and Jennifer Moody draw on documentary and other evidence from the Venetian period to produce an objective account of man's relationship with the natural environment. Finally, Michael Llewellyn Smith's personal view of Crete through the ages, besides being very attractively written, includes four extremely useful chapters on the Venetian period: there are lucid narratives of the early rebellions against Venetian rule and of the war of 1645–69 which culminated in the Fall of Candia. In addition Llewellyn Smith offers both factual information and a personal appreciation of the art and literature of Venetian Crete. Although some of the facts have been revised by newer research, the book has not been bettered as a sensitive expression of the intellectual and spiritual fascination of Crete for so many British scholars from diverse disciplines.

DAVID HOLTON

M. Alexiou, 'Women, marriage and death in the drama of Renaissance Crete', in M.M. Mackenzie and C. Roueché (eds.), *Images of authority. Papers presented to Joyce Reynolds on the occasion of her seventieth birthday* (Cambridge, 1989), 1–23.

R. E. Bancroft-Marcus, 'I pigi pente kritikon intermedion', *Kritologia* 5 (1977), 5–44.

R. E. Bancroft-Marcus, 'Georgios Chortatsis and his works: a critical review', *Mandatoforos* 16 (1980), 13–46.

R. E. Bancroft-Marcus, 'Literary cryptograms and the Cretan academies', *Byzantine and Modern Greek Studies* 8 (1982/3), 47–76.

R. E. Bancroft-Marcus, 'Women in the Cretan Renaissance', *Journal of Modern Greek Studies* 1 (1983), 19–38.

J. B. Bury, *Romances of chivalry on Greek soil* (Oxford, 1911).

N. Cheetham, *Mediaeval Greece* (New Haven and London, 1981).

R. Cormack, *Painting the soul: icons, death masks and shrouds* (London, 1997).

R. M. Dawkins, 'A Cretan *Apocalypse of the Virgin*', *BZ* 30 (1930), 300–4.

R. M. Dawkins, 'A Cretan translation of *Barlaam and Ioasaph*, with some notes on the transliteration of Greek in Latin characters', *Medium Aevum* 1 (1932) 109–25.

R. M. Dawkins, 'Kritiki Apokalypsis tis Panagias', *Kr. Chron.* 2 (1948), 487–500.

N. Deliyannaki, 'To chioumor tou poiiti ston *Erotokrito*', in *Oi poiites tou G .P. Savvidi. Diimero sti mnimi tou G. P. Savvidi* (Athens, 1998), 143–60.

D. Holton, '*Erotókritos*, and Greek tradition', in R. Beaton (ed.), *The Greek novel AD1–1985* (London, 1988), 144–55.

D. Holton, 'Pos organonetai o *Erotokritos?*', *Cretan Studies* 1 (1988), 157–67.

D. Holton (ed.), *Literature and society in Renaissance Crete* (Cambridge, 1991; revised Greek edition Irakleio, 1997).

D. Holton, *Erotokritos* (Bristol, 1991).

D. Holton, '"Irakli ton elegasi": O Vasilias tis Athinas ston *Erotokrito*', *Cretan Studies* 3 (1992), 113–29.

D. Holton, 'The function of myth in Cretan Renaissance poetry: the cases of Achelis and Kornaros', in P. Mackridge (ed.), *Ancient Greek myth in modern Greek poetry. Essays in memory of C.A. Trypanis* (London–Portland, Oregon, 1996), 1–12.

R. Hutchinson, 'The Lord of Patras', *Kr. Chron.* 10 (1956), 341–5.

M. Llewellyn Smith, *The Great Island: a study of Crete* (London, 1965).

P. Lock, *The Franks in the Aegean, 1204–1500* (London, 1995).

A. Markomihelaki, 'The relation of the three Cretan Renaissance comedies to the Italian Cinquecento theories of laughter', *Cretan Studies* 3 (1992), 131–48.

F. H. Marshall, *Old Testament legends from a Greek poem on Genesis and Exodus by Georgios Chumnos* (Cambridge, 1925).

F. H. Marshall, *Three Cretan plays, the Sacrifice of Abraham, Erophile and Gyparis, also the Cretan pastoral poem The fair shepherdess* (London, 1929).

J. Mavrogordato, 'The Greek drama in Crete in the seventeenth century', *JHS* 48 (1928), 75–96 and 243–6 ('A postscript').

J. Mavrogordato, *The Erotokritos* (London, 1929).

W. Miller, *Essays on the Latin Orient* (Cambridge, 1921; reprinted Amsterdam, 1964).

G. Morgan, 'French and Italian elements in the Erotocritos', *Kr. Chron.* 7 (1953), 201–28.

G. Morgan, 'Cretan poetry: sources and inspiration', *Kr. Chron.* 14 (1960), 7–68, 203–70, 379–434.

G. Morgan, 'The emblems of Erotocritos', *The Texas Quarterly* 10 (1967), 241–68.

G. Morgan, 'The model of Erotocritos – a review', *Kritologia* 12–13 (1981), 93–9.

D. M. Nicol, *Byzantium and Venice: a study in diplomatic and cultural relations* (Cambridge, 1988).

N. M. Panagiotakis and A. L. Vincent, 'Nea stoicheia gia tin Akadimia ton Stravaganti', *Thisavrismata* 7 (1970), 52–81.

D. M. L. Philippides and D. Holton, *Tou kuklou ta gyrismata: o* Erotokritos *se ilektroniki analysi* (Athens, 1996–2000), 4 vols.

O. Rackham and J. Moody, *The making of the Cretan landscape* (Manchester, 1996).

D. Ricks, 'The style of Erotókritos, *Cretan Studies* 1 (1988), 239–56.

D. Ricks, 'Sources of Cretan literature: some remarks', *Praktika tou Deuterou Diethnous Synedriou 'Neograeca Medii Aevi'* (Venice, 1993), ii. 633–40.

T. P. Stephanides, *Vitzentzos Kornaros. Erotocritos, circa 1640 AD.* (Athens, 1984).

D. Talbot Rice, *Byzantine art* (revised and expanded edition, Harmondsworth, 1968).

A. L. Vincent, 'O poiitis tou "Fortounatou". Anekdota engrafa gia ton Marko Antonio Foskolo', *Thisavrismata* 4 (1967), 53–84.

A. L. Vincent, 'Nea stoicheia gia ton Marko Antonio Foskolo. I Diathiki tou kai alla engrafa', *Thisavrismata* 5 (1968), 119–76.

A. L. Vincent, 'A manuscript of Chortatses' "Erophile" in Birmingham', *University of Birmingham Historical Journal* 12.2 (1970), 261–7.

A. L. Vincent, *Markou Antoniou Foskolou Fortounatos. Kritiki ekdosi, simeioseis, glossario* (Irakleion, 1980).

A. L. Vincent, 'I Vlachia kai oi Vlachoi ston *Erotokrito*', in *Loivi. Eis mnimin Andrea G. Kalokairinou* (Irakleion, 1994), 51–92.

P. Warren, '16th, 17th and 18th century British travellers in Crete', *Kr. Chron.* 24 (1972), 65–92.

THE BRITISH SCHOOL AT KNOSSOS

This section seeks to explain and emphasise the rôle of the British School at Athens in Crete in helping its members conduct their individual programmes of research, as well as large-scale field- or study-programmes in the School's own name. It will focus upon Knossos, where the School has responsibilities and privileges unlike any other it enjoys in Greece. Since 1924, the School has borne responsibility for maintaining and, where possible, improving the residential facilities at Knossos, partly with the Sir Arthur Evans Fund, partly from its own resources and those of its benefactors. That work (apart from the hiatus of the Second World War) has continued uninterruptedly, notwithstanding the transfer of property to the Archaeological Service in 1952. Until 1980, the School responded to the invitations of the Service to undertake rescue excavations in the Knossos archaeological area, and the results were published in the *Annual*. The establishment during the 1960s of the Stratigraphical Museum at Knossos, in partnership with the Service, has provided ideal storage and study facilities in close proximity to the Taverna, the School's excavation house. The School has a share in the management of the Stratigraphical Museum, and employs both expatriate and locally engaged staff to fulfil its responsibilities. The School delegates the management of Knossos to the Director in Athens and, with the exception of a hiatus between 1953 and 1977, through him or her to a Curator at Knossos (1977–80, Knossos Fellow). For the Director, with or without a Curator, frequent visits to Knossos are essential, as are regular meetings with the archaeological authorities in Herakleion.

Archaeology in Greece is conducted according to the terms of a comprehensive antiquities' law, at present administered by the Ministry of Culture. Work by foreigners is enabled by an application by one of the Foreign Schools to the appropriate Greek authority. For British research, this means the British School at Athens, founded in 1886, with Director and staff operating in premises built on land given by the Greek Government, on one hand, and a Council (formerly the Managing Committee) in London. The School exists to facilitate and encourage, through its staff and students, all aspects of the study of the Hellenic world, ancient, mediaeval and modern, with the help of a base and library in Athens.

The towering rôle of Sir Arthur Evans in the early stages of the archaeological exploration of Crete, especially of Knossos, is well known. Through its rôle in the Cretan Exploration Fund, the School shared at the start of Evans's excavation at Knossos and published his preliminary reports in the *Annual*. The School was also active elsewhere in Crete in those early years. In order to excavate at Knossos, Evans had bought substantial parcels of land at, and in the vicinity of, what he would call 'The Palace of Minos'. In

1906 he built the Villa Ariadne as an excavation house, and laid out its garden on part of this land. He owned significantly more Knossian land than he was actually able to excavate.

Not long after the First World War, Evans handed all his property at Knossos to the School, a development the long-term significance of which neither he nor the School can have foreseen. The gift was completed in 1924; with it came an endowment, and further money from Evans for a Curator to look after the School's new responsibilities on the spot, including management of the Palace. The transfer brought the School the privilege of regular invitations from the authorities to investigate chance finds in the Knossos archaeological area. In view of the delicacy of this arrangement, where, inescapably, archaeology and politics rub shoulders, it has reflected great credit on the host country that, for more than half a century, the matter of the archaeological area was handled with great generosity and propriety.

So matters stood until the Second World War, Evans retaining a paternal interest in his former property. First John Pendlebury, then Richard Hutchinson were appointed Curators, their duties included care of the Palace and conduct of 'rescue excavations', under the general supervision of the Director and the Managing Committee. Evans paid for the transformation of a small house on the edge of the Villa grounds into what is known as the Taverna, which has played a key rôle as a hostel and library. In the final years before the war, chance finds investigated by Hutchinson included the tholos tomb on the Kephala ridge, and the tomb at Khaniale Teke with its splendid Orientalizing goldwork. John and Hilda Pendlebury, freed from Knossian duties, were working in Lasithi, notably at Karphi.

The end of the war exposed the problems Knossos now brought the School. While its objects remained the same, and interest in Knossos (where Piet de Jong had been installed as Curator in 1947) showed every sign of a rapid post-war revival, the economic constraints under which the School was attempting to meet all its obligations made the financial burden of the property at Knossos apparently unbearable. Whatever the rights and wrongs may have been, the School felt compelled to relinquish its Knossos property and its administrative and financial burdens, but in such a way that Evans's intentions for the continuation of British research at Knossos were not compromised. In 1952 an agreement was signed between the School and the Archaeological Service that transferred ownership of the Knossos property to the Greek State. Certain privileges were conferred on the School, including exclusive use of the Taverna and the land attached to it.

Continued ownership by the School of the excavated remains of the Palace and its dependencies would obviously have been wholly inappropriate. It is less plain that no other solution could have been found for the Villa and the untouched land, even if the salaried post of Curator could at that time no longer be sustained. But what was done, was done; the record of subsequent British work at Knossos suggests that there was no real harm.

As things have turned out, though the transfer brought immediate financial relief in one sense, this was replaced, in another, by the post-war intensification of the School's Cretan activities, of which Knossos was at the heart, where there has been a succession of major research excavations from 1956 to the present. Expenditure at Knossos has steadily grown, assisted by increased British Academy grants and the generosity of institutional and individual sponsors. And, virtually from the end of the war, the Greek authorities continued to invite the School to undertake 'rescue' investigations in the archaeological area. Even while there was a Curator in post at Knossos, such excavations as often as not also needed the experience of the School's Director or Assistant Director, so that it became accepted practice that an urgent rescue call from Herakleion meant the direct involvement of a number of the School's senior staff. Such rescue excavations yielded particularly important finds during the construction of the Venizeleion Hospital, north of the Palace, but there were many others up to and including 1978, the year of the huge North Cemetery rescue.

The general pattern of the School's work since the last war has ensured that for successive Directors, the administration of Knossos has been their largest single responsibility, and, probably, their greatest headache. This arises directly from the School's passion for Cretan, particularly Knossian, archaeology. This passion has been shared by many of the School's most distinguished members, for many of whom, indeed, Knossos was their entry-point into Greek archaeology, the scene of their apprenticeships in the many skills required of them, and the source of the raw material that has subsequently lain at the heart of their scholarship. They have returned again and again to that source; it has been the responsibility of the Athens staff, particularly of the Director, to ensure they meet no obstacles.

The transfer of property at Knossos in 1952 left only the Taverna and its garden plot under the School's control. The Herakleion authorities have been generous in allowing *ad hoc* use of the Villa Ariadne, but the School has learned to rely upon the Taverna, complete with catering facilities, accommodation and library. Improvements have been made, including an extension to the Taverna itself, a separate excavation store and workshop in the garden (later converted into living accommodation) and a separate dwelling, originally for use of the foreman/caretaker, now used by the Curator since the post's revival.

A vital development was the construction of the Stratigraphical Museum on a site near the Villa, the expenses of which were shared by the school (structure) and the service (fittings). Originally devised by Sinclair Hood while School Director, the scheme was finally realised in 1966 through the efforts of members of the School and the Service. Its prime purpose is to house, in the systematic and accessible form of Mervyn Popham's arrangement, the retained pottery from the original excavations of Sir Arthur Evans, first ordered and catalogued by John Pendlebury and stored in the Palace. It also provides storage for Knossian material from more recent excavations, and generous room for study and conservation. The porticoed internal courtyard offers space for even the most prolific deposit of pottery to be studied at one time, and was the scene of days and days of devoted work by the School's vase-mender, the late Petros Petrakis, Hon. MBE, notably following the 1978 North Cemetery excavation. More recently ancillary structures include a lapidarium, a store for pithoi and bone, and a store for heavy excavation equipment. Finds from at least one British excavation elsewhere in Crete have also been allowed to be stored and studied here. The Stratigraphical Museum is entirely the property of the Archaeological Service. Since its creation, enlightened ephors in Herakleion have allowed the School unimpeded access to its resources, so that study of its contents has gone on apace, the benefits of which are to be seen in several of the School's major publications. The facilities include a draughting office, scene of much of the basic work for other major Knossian publications.

Chief credit for this achievement since the war belongs, of course, to those who have surveyed, excavated, studied, reduced their material to order and published their results. They invariably acknowledged their indebtedness to the Archaeological Service, to their financial sponsors – and to the School. This last recognises the vital rôle of the School in everything that happens at Knossos, and the permanent concern felt for Knossos by the School's officers. The School's property at Knossos has to be maintained – the Taverna and its dependencies must be in acceptable structural condition – equipment and amenities must be adequate for residents' needs. In the Stratigraphical Museum responsibilities affecting security, concerning care and maintenance and adequate record of the contents must be fulfilled.

There must be cordial relations between the School and the Archaeological Service, both in the Ephoreia in Herakleion and in the Ministry in Athens. The host country must feel comfortable with all aspects of British activity at Knossos. The prime responsibility for this rests with the Director, backed up by the Knossos staff, and supported by the behaviour of all those who work there. A recurring theme in Greek-British relations has for long been the School's rôle in the archaeological area of Knossos. At the transfer of property in 1952 it was agreed that the School might undertake research excavations on what had been Evans's land, now the property of the Greek State, without compensation, provided an appropriate permit had been granted. It was also understood that the arrangement should continue whereby successive Ephors might invite successive Directors of the School to undertake rescue work in the archaeological area, as it had been defined before the war. The pages of the *Annual* are eloquent testimony to the generosity with which our hosts interpreted this understanding, and the seriousness of the School's responses, and the use made of this unique opportunity by a succession of members of the School.

With the passage of time, the delicate balancing act demanded of both the Greek authorities and the School in sustaining this arrangement in the archaeological area became (and was seen to become) more and more difficult. The greatly increased pace of building and agricultural development in the Knossos area brought a corresponding increase in the demands of rescue archaeology. There was also a change in local attitudes towards foreign archaeological activity. The former could place the School in the invidious position of being unable to respond to every invitation, and thus appearing to pick and chose. The latter had implications which it was imperative not to ignore.

The scale of the problem was mercilessly exposed in 1978 when the new University of Crete was about to develop an extensive olive grove north of the Venezeleion Hospital, and thus right within the archaeological area. The Herakleion Ephoreia invited the School to test the archaeological potential of the site ahead of construction. The School had no chance of assembling a special team to meet the Ephoreia's invitation, but did the best it could. Work began in March under the Knossos Fellow, Jill Carington Smith, helped by the Assistant Director, Christopher Mee, by the School's Honorary Surveyor, David Smyth, and several students. It was soon seen that this was a huge burial ground in continuous use from *c.*1050 to *c.*650 BC, and again through Hellenistic and Roman times into the Early Christian period, including the almost entirely robbed remains of a basilican mortuary church with associated osteothekes. It took nearly a year to complete the excavation. With great generosity, the Archaeological Service paid the expense of the work-force, led by the late Antonis Zidianakis, the School's Knossos foreman. The University of Crete paid for essential earth-moving equipment. The School shouldered the remaining costs. At one level, there is no doubt that the immense efforts demanded by this excavation were fully justified: see, for example, J. N. Coldstream and H. W. Catling (eds.), *Knossos North Cemetery: Early Greek Tombs I-IV* (1996). But there was a price.

The then Director spent ten weeks or so at the excavation, working in the field, and many more in subsequent years in study at the Stratigraphical Museum, and in preparing his share of the publication. Members of the School at all levels of seniority dropped what they were doing to help, whether in the field, at the Museum, or the desk. Other School activities (including at least one programmed School excavation) suffered in consequence, the effect of the North Cemetery excavation still leaving its mark on their progress. It was clear to the School management in Athens, where the full cost was most apparent to those upon whom it had fallen, that the School could not sustain the demands of another similar Knossian rescue, should the circumstances ever recur.

The 1980s brought many changes to Greece, including a fairly critical look at the activities of the foreign Schools, a look for which there was strong, occasionally vocal popular support. For a time, non-archaeological voices in Herakleion called into question the School's use of the Stratigraphical Museum. Responsibility for the School's handling of a potentially hostile situation had to be left in the Director's hands. Not everyone to whom the School's position at Knossos was important necessarily shared the Director's view of what was still possible and what was not.

As things have turned out in the twenty years since the end of the North Cemetery excavation, the School has continued to enjoy a privileged position at Knossos, especially in the Stratigraphical Museum, all important for successful research. True, there have been very few invitations for rescue excavation in the archaeological area, but this owes as much to stringent controls on any kind of development as to reservations over foreign archaeology. A succession of young scholars has worked as Curator at Knossos, refining the arrangements of the Stratigraphical Museum, directing their own excavations, sometimes at Knossos, sometimes elsewhere in Crete. A series of research excavations has been authorised by the Ministry of Culture, some in the Palace and its immediate environs, some further afield on what was once Evans's land. The School, in short, continues to fulfil its obligations to the great site of Knossos – it is hard to believe that Sir Arthur, apprised of all the circumstances, would have found great fault with the School's stewardship.

HECTOR CATLING

ARTISTS and CRAFTSMEN

Over the past century in Crete there have been many men and women whose practical skills have helped to make it possible for the archaeologists to test the validity of their theories. The crucial importance of their expertise with measuring and surveying equipment, with pencil, watercolour and camera, with pick and shovel, in mending and restoration of artifacts, in man-management, in organisation and catering, has perhaps not always been fully appreciated.

When Arthur Evans began excavations in the Palace of Minos at Knossos in the spring of 1900, David Theodore Fyfe (1875–1945) was the current Architectural Student at the British School at Athens. He soon found himself coopted, at the age of twenty-five, as architect to the Cretan Exploration Fund, which had been established to help with the financing of the early excavations at Knossos. (FIG. 129) As assistant to Evans at Knossos he was occupied in making plans, elevations and drawings of the Palace then being dramatically revealed by excavation. As well as making watercolour paintings of the many fresco fragments, he found time to plan the early houses which David Hogarth, then Director of the British School, was digging on the neighbouring hill of Gypsades.

By the second campaign in 1901, it became clear to Evans that 'various supplementary operations connected with the shoring up and underpinning of the walls of the large halls' had become necessary before further digging could be risked at lower levels on this sloping site. It was also essential to put a roof over the Throne Room to protect the throne itself, the benches round the walls, the paving slabs and the revetting of the attached lustral basin, all of them made of gypsum, liable to dissolve when exposed to the winter rains. Fyfe made plans for this construction which was carried out under Duncan Mackenzie's supervision.

Conservation of the remains became almost as important a concern as their excavation and in these first five years Fyfe advised Evans on the

FIG. 129 The early years at Knossos. *Left to right:* Arthur Evans, Theodore Fyfe and Duncan Mackenzie. (Ashmolean Museum Oxford)

restoration of many areas in the Palace. No doubt he had a hand, in 1903, in the erection of a wooden watchtower in the Central Court so that the excavators and visitors could gain an overview of the Palace site. Crete made an indelible impression on Fyfe, revealed in his later publications, as it has on many of those who have worked there. In 1922 he became Master and subsequently Director of the Cambridge School of Architecture. There he became known for his somewhat unfortunate remarks, and a book of his inauspicious sayings was published. He died in a skating accident at the age of seventy.

In 1904 Fyfe was succeeded as architect to Evans by Christian Charles Tyler Doll (1880–1955) (FIG. 130), educated at Charterhouse and Trinity College, Cambridge, and then articled to his father, Charles Fitzroy Doll, whose firm designed the Russell and Imperial Hotels in Bloomsbury. He rendered 'signal service' to Evans at Knossos in helping to solve the problem of the restoration of the Grand Staircase. (FIG. 17)

In 1906 Doll built the Villa Ariadne for Evans as a residence to accommodate the excavation group while at work in Crete. The somewhat damp, lower ground floor bedrooms are cool to sleep in and the building has remained proof against earthquakes, but its atmosphere is

FIG. 130 *Left to right:* Evans, Christian Doll, and Mackenzie with local guides. *Far right:* Manolis Akoumianakis. (Ashmolean Museum Oxford)

gloomy, owing little to any vernacular architecture in Crete. Doll was left in charge of this feat of organisation at the age of twenty-five, and describes the daily problems in his diary for that year. In February he ordered 320 quoins, 29 cills and 29 lintels from the quarry. Enormous quantities of cement were imported from the Portland Company in Trieste. Ironmongery for the building was sent from England – all these necessities had to be cleared through Customs. Doll lived in Herakleion (Candia, as it was then called) and walked daily to and from Knossos, often adding to his collection of butterflies on the way; once he caught a particularly fine Swallowtail in his cap. Life in Candia was eased by the presence of the Inniskilling Fusiliers. Doll, who lacked company at Knossos, made friends with the colonel and some of the officers. He often dined in their Mess and was eventually made an honorary member of it. He frequently read the lessons in the church they had established at their camp. In return he showed them round the excavations.

Doll continued with reconstruction work in the Palace, but on a reduced scale, sometimes hampered by the fact that he could not get his measurements to tally with those of his predecessor, Fyfe. When work on the Villa eventually came to an end, he had had to 'speak his mind' to the plasterer about the quality of his work. Doll 'tried to clean [his] revolver' before handing over the cartridges to Major Fleming. On that note he returned to England after fifteen months exhausting and exacting work. There public service gradually assumed more importance in his life than architecture. He became surveyor to the London estates of the Duke of Bedford and, in 1950, Mayor of Holborn, though he still found time to play cricket for the MCC.

1903 saw the re-creation by Émile Gilliéron (père) of the Priest King relief fresco with his fleur-de-lys crown, adorned with peacock feathers. Gilliéron was a Swiss emigré, entranced with Greece, who became drawing master to the royal family. His son, Émile Gilliéron (fils) was equally gifted as draughtsman and mender. Evans was grateful for the manual dexterity of the younger Gilliéron: 'To Monsieur E. Gilliéron (fils), I have been continually indebted for his valuable assistance in piecing together painted plaster panels and his skilled restorations of the frescoed designs . . .' (*PM* ii p. xii). Father and son together made a business of producing metal replicas of Minoan and Mycenaean artifacts at the Wurtemberg Electro Plate Co., and selling them to museums throughout Europe.

While Evans was making spectacular discoveries at Knossos, the British School was also conducting exploration in East Crete, under R. C. Bosanquet at Praisos and Petras where R. Douglas Wells, an architect from Trinity College, Cambridge, made surveys, plans and drawings. At Palaikastro, the scene of extensive excavations lasting several years under R. M. Dawkins, C. Heaton Comyn (1877–1933) did all the architectural work. While in Athens he had designed the Penrose Library and the pleasant terrace outside the Finlay Library. Both he and Wells were architects of originality with subsequent, flourishing careers in England.

Evans pays early tribute to the intelligence and capacity for hard work of the Cretan workmen. He deliberately employed, at a wage of about 6 pence per day, a mixed team of Muslims and Christians in order to give an example of cooperation under the new régime in the island, recently freed from Turkish rule. 'Considering that a few months earlier', he says, 'both parties had been shooting each other at sight, the experiment proved very successful.' Conditions before the First World War were a good deal harsher than today, and Evans mentions 'fever', malaria and the appalling 'Notios' or South Wind as hindrances to his work. There was also the difficulty of keeping men at work as the exigencies of the harvest drew near. Dawkins, digging at Palaikastro, in 1905, displayed sang-froid when 'the prevailing disorders caused some inconvenience. On one occasion a party of malcontent workmen armed with rifles tried to terrorise the rest into striking for higher wages. Helped by the loyalty of the men from the mountain villages, . . . Mr Dawkins was able to keep his people in hand, . . .'

Outstanding among more recent men, in the period just before and after the war, was Spiros Vasilakis (FIG. 131), a person of great distinction, and Grigoris Kritsalakis who always worked as shovelman with him. Successive foremen deferred to the wisdom and experience of Spiros who gave great assistance from his knowledge of the area to Sinclair Hood during the preparation of the first edition of the Knossos Survey, published in 1958. His son, Antonis Vasilakis, is an official of the Archaeological Service, working in the Herakleion Museum and specialising in the exploration of Early Minoan sites.

FIG. 132 Evans's foreman, Grigorios Antoniou, drawn by Theodore Fyfe. (Courtesy of Mrs Lilah Clarke)

FIG. 131 Spiros Vasilakis, *left*, and Grigoris Kritsalakis carry pithoi down from Middle Minoan Tomb VI on Ailias in 1953. (M. S. F. Hood)

All excavators in Crete have been dependent on the expertise, authority and negotiating skills of their foremen. First in an impressive line of men came Grigorios Antoniou from Cyprus, introduced by Hogarth, and qualified for the work by his early experience as a tomb robber. (FIG. 132) He was Evans's foreman at Knossos and in 1905 started the tradition of first class Cretan men supplying a demand for their skills on excavations in other parts of Greece. He was soon taken on as foreman at the British School dig at Sparta. The skills of Cretan workmen are valued to this day on other archaeological sites in Greece.

Iannis Katsarakis, born and bred in Palaikastro, became pot mender there on the excavations for Dawkins. He went as foreman to Perachora with Humfry Payne, and in 1937 to Ithaca. He also worked with James Brock at the Early Greek-Iron Age Fortetsa Cemetery. He passed on his deft craftsmanship to his son, Stelios (FIG. 133), whose wise counsel as well as his practical abilities at the pottery table as a young man were much appreciated by the Directors of the School in the years after the Second World War, John Cook at Smyrna in western Turkey and Sinclair Hood at Emporio in Chios.

Manolis Akoumianakis (FIG. 134), 'whose lynx eyes nothing Minoan escapes', succeeded Antoniou as foreman in Knossos during the inter-war years until his death in 1941 during the Battle of Crete. After the war, Manolis Markoyiannakis (1903–67) from Lasithi, who had worked with Evans as a post boy, took on the mantle of foreman to the British School (FIG. 135). He and his wife, Ourania, lived in the rambling servants' quarters of the Villa Ariadne and provided meals for the various excavation parties in the 1950s and 60s. Meat was considered an expensive luxury. Sometimes a delicious and unexpected sweet would be produced and the popular song *zacharoplastis itan o babas mou* would be hummed round the table. On the death of Manolis in 1967, Antonis Zidianakis, who had begun as a barrow boy for Evans and Pendlebury at the Temple Tomb, conducted operations especially for Hector Catling's excavations at the Knossos North Cemetery and served as foreman for Mervyn Popham at the Unexplored Mansion. He was probably among the last of the village people to be clothed in a hand knitted, unbleached woollen vest under a shirt made of the thick, strong cotton woven by Mrs Kastrianoyiannis in Herakleion and an even thicker, long cummerbund to keep chill from the kidneys, as well as the traditional black, fringed kerchief on his head. Workmen are now more likely to be found shirtless under the broiling sun and deeply bronzed after the manner of tourists. Nikos Daskalakis, from Makryteichos, whose intelligence and cultivated interest in archaeology has been of the greatest help to the many excavators with whom he has worked, both in Crete, and

FIG. 133 Stelios Katsarakis. (M. S. F. Hood)

FIG. 134 Manolis Akoumianakis.

on the mainland, is the latest holder of this distinguished post.

The architect whose work has perhaps made the most lasting impression on the appearance of the Minoan Palace at Knossos was Piet de Jong. He was a Yorkshireman of Dutch extraction employed by the Greek government in 1919 on reconstruction work in Macedonia. He was introduced to Evans by Alan Wace, who, at Mycenae, found him 'a very nice man to have on an excavation'. For nine years, from 1922, de Jong collaborated with Evans on planning and restoring the palace at Knossos.

In 1923, in repairing the Stepped Portico and its upper floor, Piet (FIG. 136) began to use true reinforced concrete technique, the materials for which were then becoming widely available in Crete. Peter Kienzle, of York University, who has kindly allowed us to read the relevant parts of his as yet unpublished thesis on the history of restoration at Knossos, makes many interesting points. He notes that Evans had two purposes in mind, first 'conservation', that is to protect the decaying remains from further depredation by the weather, and secondly 'explanatory reconstruction', or the presentation of the site in a manner comprehensible to the public. Kienzle also remarks that de Jong favoured a 'pseudo-ruined' style in his rebuilding, whereas Fyfe and Doll had used horizontal top courses which failed to disguise the reconstruction. In 1928 work reached a crescendo when Evans 'decided to roof over the Hall of the Double Axes'. About one hundred carpenters and masons were employed for six months on this major effort. Work on the North Lustral Basin was completed in 1929 as well as the restoration of the North Entrance Passage. Evans felt that the public should be able to appreciate the grandeur of that approach to the Palace, as he conceived it, with

FIG. 135 Manolis Markoyiannakis. (M. S. F. Hood)

FIG. 136 Piet de Jong making notes on the back of a cigarette box. (M. S. F. Hood)

its plaster relief of bull hunting reconstructed from fragments by Émile Gilliéron (fils) to look as it might have done in antiquity. De Jong planned and supervised these major enterprises.

At the age of sixty, in 1947, Piet was appointed Curator of the British School's property at Knossos and he and his Scottish wife, Effie, lived in Crete for the next four years where he combined archaeological rescue work with looking after the Palace site and the olives and vines on the land which had belonged to Evans before he gave the property to the British School. The Director of the Museum in Herakleion, Dr N. Platon, employed Piet to make repairs to the Palace in 1952, including the erection of a concrete roof over the Royal Magazines (Corridor of the Bays and Magazine of the Medallion Pithoi). He also commissioned Piet to make the vivid watercolours depicting Minoan life in the Palace which now hang in the Museum galleries. His last archaeological work in Crete was done with Sinclair Hood in the 1950s. At that time he designed a functional workroom in the grounds of the Taverna at Knossos, since converted to pleasant, airy bedrooms. The series of cartoons that Piet made of his colleagues to cheer them up when things were not going too well on excavations remain as a lasting gift and barbed warning to future generations of archaeologists. Among those caricatured in this rogues' gallery are Arthur Evans, Duncan Mackenzie, E. J. Forsdyke and Émile Gilliéron (fils), all of whom worked at Knossos. Piet was a most congenial companion, and raconteur of great skill who devoted his life to the furtherance of archaeology conducted by both British and American excavators in many parts of Greece and Turkey. (FIG. 137)

David Smyth (1925–95) was the stocky, bronzed, surveyor for most of the School's work in Crete during the 1970s and 80s (FIG. 138), notably on Hector Catling's excavation of the North Cemetery. Taking early retirement from work as a surveyor in the Middle Eastern oil industry, Smyth came to live in Greece and to indulge his interest in archaeology by using his skills to produce plans and surveys, first at the Menelaion in Sparta, subsequently at Myrtos (Pyrgos). He also made the new map which accompanies the second edition of the Knossos Survey, and worked on nearly all British undertakings during those years in Crete. He was renowned on the one hand for his patient kindness with students, and on the other for his uncompromising ability to call a spade a spade. His aptitude for crosswords, his hacking cough and his intense professionalism endeared him as a friend.

FIG. 137 Piet de Jong with some of his cartoons. *Left to right:* Humfry Payne, Georg Karo, Dilys Powell and Virginia Grace. (Private collection)

William Taylor (1921–) came to Greece in 1957 as one of the last holders of the Athens Bursary for architects before it was abandoned in favour of subjects more connected with 'social reality'. His aim was to study at first hand the Classical Greek architecture he had long loved and taught as part of his duties as Senior Tutor in the Department of Architecture at the Oxford Polytechnic. A continuing interest in all aspects of Greek architecture put him in touch with Sinclair Hood, and a long session at Knossos in 1977 provided measurements and information for a complete redraughting of the Knossos Palace Plan which was published in 1981, the fiftieth anniversary of Evans's death. Subsequent frequent visits and close co-operation with Hood have made it possible to record the position of the many hundreds of signs known as Masons' Marks visible in the Palace. It is hoped that their more recent work in making sections throughout the Minoan building will help in the study of its structure and chronology.

Petros Petrakis, who succeeded Stelios Katsarakis as the British School's vase mender, is perhaps one of the most affectionately remembered characters. A metal fitter by trade, he came into the archaeological orbit in the early 1950s by marrying Eleni Kandaraki, cook in the Director's House in Athens. A change of career

FIG. 138 David Smyth. (BSA Archives)

was initiated when the then Director, noting the excellence of his handiwork, asked him to mend a clay dish. Training in this skill followed at the Athenian Agora. Thereafter, for thirty three years, Petros worked on countless excavations for both Greeks and foreigners mending pottery with exceptional speed and accuracy. In 1964–5 Petros and Eleni spent almost two solid years at Knossos where he mended pottery from the Royal Road excavations of 1957–61 and they made many long-lasting local friendships, notably with disabled Michalis, the owner of the kiosk in the village, and his family. Thereafter Petros was an essential member of all the British excavations in Crete. Perhaps his most difficult reconstruction was an LM IB globular alabastron from Myrtos (Pyrgos) put together from 1200 pieces. Each break was swiftly cleaned, daubed with a drop of shellac, heated with a burner, then dabbed with a cold, wet sponge, causing a satisfactory fizz and setting the glue. He may have been the first mender to use wire rivets (for which he drilled holes with a power drill) to join the thick fragments of pithoi (FIG. 139). His constant good humour and zest (*kefi*) enlivened all the digs in

FIG. 139 Petros Petrakis with pithos after he had finished mending it. (P. M. Warren)

FIG. 140 Petros Petrakis in the Stratigraphical Museum. (P. M. Warren)

which he took part. Eleni contributed her unrivalled gift for providing a sudden culinary treat, her knowledge of the Greek countryside, its herbs and practices, and her great kindness, as well as occasional forays into pot-washing with water and acid. As a boy Petros had worked in a café and knew no less than thirty-two ways of making Greek coffee, the most refined of which was *metrio kai ochi* (medium yet not). His skill as a bar tender, dapper in a white jacket, never left him. Later in life, after Eleni's mother died in Euboea and they had no stomach to return there for holidays, they took to worldwide travel, visiting among other places Russia, Rumania, Bulgaria, Switzerland, France, England (twice), Scotland, and much loved Italy where, in Venice, they listened to the gondoliers singing. They always took their own food and were among the early advocates of take-aways. In 1987 Petros died in the full enjoyment of life, at the age of sixty three, of a heart attack while dancing. His loss is still mourned (FIG. 140).

Many draughtsmen and women (in private life mostly artists) have worked on excavations and the subsequent preparation for publication during the past century in Crete. Jeff Clarke (1935–) has made numberless visits to Crete resulting in a series of paintings and etchings of the island (FIG. 141). Many of these pictures have been exhibited in London, Oxford and Cambridge. Clarke, who was a Rome Scholar, trained at Brighton College of Art, is a draughtsman of the first water whose talents have been put to good use by Gerald Cadogan, Peter Warren, Hector Catling, Sinclair Hood, Hugh Sackett, Alexander MacGillivray and others. His resurrection of a fine Kamares pot with its fugitive pattern in red and white on a black ground, is a masterpiece which took many hours of work. Pat Clarke, on secondment from the Ashmolean Museum, spent two years in Crete drawing pottery and small finds from the Royal Road excavations.

In turning over the publications of important British work in Crete during the latter quarter of this century, a certain family element creeps into the acknowledgements. Elizabeth Warren did all the drawing, and typing of the manuscript, for Myrtos (Phournou Koryfi) excavated in the south of Crete by her husband. Elizabeth Catling played a major rôle, drawing as well as sorting the pottery, for the work on the Knossos North Cemetery Tombs edited by her husband Hector, and Nicolas Coldstream. Much other drawing was done by Nicola Coldstream and Diana Wardle, both scholars in their own right, as well as being the wives of archaeologists.

Unrelated to the excavators is Sue Bird

FIG.141 Jeff Clarke at the Villa Ariadne. (Rachel Hood)

(1943–) who, after art school in Cambridge, had travelled as far as India, returning overland and catching a glimpse of Greece *en route*. The glimpse urged her to make enquiries of Joan Thornton, then London Secretary of the British School, about the possibility of archaeological drawing there. At her suggestion, Sue presented herself at the School in Athens where Mervyn Popham sat her in front of a Mycenaean kylix, saying 'draw that', adding darkly 'the proof of the pudding is in the eating'. He was pleasantly astonished by the speed and accuracy with which the job was done, and she was taken on the excavations directed by Popham and Hugh Sackett at Lefkandi for two weeks' trial. Her previous experience with David Stronach in Iran and with Richard Tomlinson in Elis stood her in good stead. After Lefkandi, she made frequent visits to Crete in the 1970s to take part as draughtswoman in the excavation and publication of the Unexplored Mansion at Knossos with the same excavators. Spare time was spent sketching the countryside and its inhabitants. Sue is now retiring after twenty years as illustrator in the Greek and Roman Department of the British Museum including four years work on the Teiresias Project, a book of Braille drawings of the Parthenon Frieze for the visually impaired. She hopes to give more time now to her second career – the throwing and decorating of pottery.

A consuming interest in birds, and her skill in painting them, led Emma Faull (1956–) to revisit Crete after reading Geography at Oxford. She wisely approached Sue Bird at the British Museum beforehand for training in archaeological draughtsmanship. Her first experience of work in Crete was under Hector Catling in 1979 drawing five hundred lamps from his North Cemetery excavations, a tough exercise in accuracy, as she put it. She took part, as draughtswoman, in Peter Warren's Stratigraphical Museum excavation. She spent two winters in Knossos while Jill Carington Smith was Curator, painting and drawing the country and the birds in it. In 1983 Mrs Goulandris allowed her to make drawings of the birds in the collection at the Natural History Museum in Kifissia. Further work on bronzes in Crete and for David Wilson in Kea completed her archaeological experience. She regards the accuracy, on which her archaeological mentors insisted, as the cornerstone of her work in depicting birds. There have been many exhibitions of her paintings in London. Her most notable recent commission, from the Commonwealth Heads of State, to mark the Golden Wedding of the Queen and Prince Philip, was for two pictures – a green peacock for the Queen and a golden pheasant for the Prince.

This brief record has not allowed the inclusion of a great number of artists and craftsmen and women (to whom we apologize), whose work has made many an important contribution to excavation or publication of British work in Crete during the past century.

RACHEL AND SINCLAIR HOOD

Annuals of the British School at Athens, *passim*.

British Architectural Library, RIBA Information Unit.

Christian Doll's Diary for 1906 (Ashmolean Museum, Oxford).

A. J. Evans, 'Work of Reconstitution in the Palace of Knossos', *Ant.J.* 7 (1927), 258.

A. J. Evans, *Palace of Minos,* i–iv (London, 1921–35).

R. Hood, *Faces of Archaeology in Greece. Caricatures by Piet de Jong* (Oxford, 1998).

INDEX

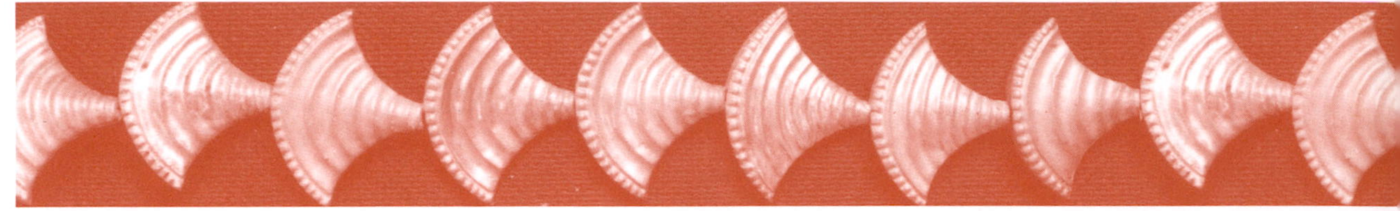

British excavation and survey sites

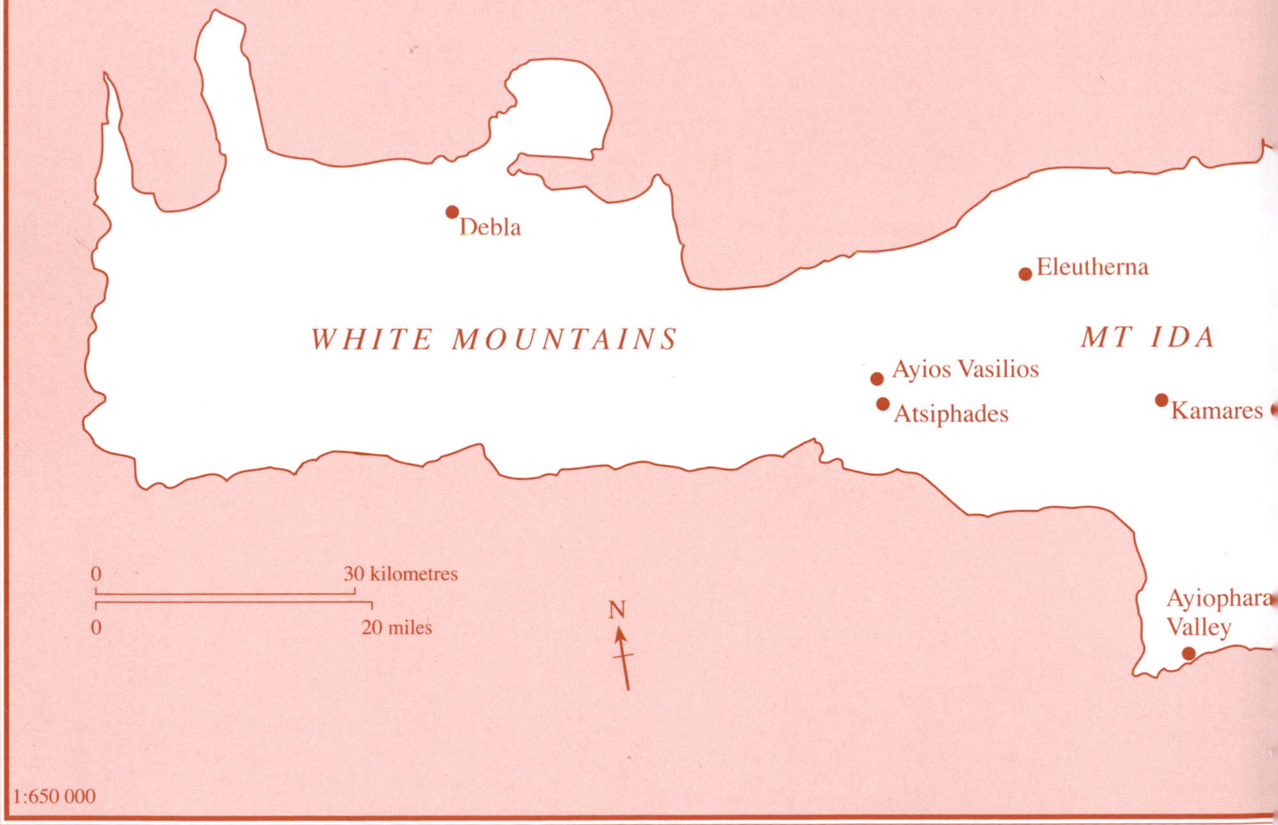

Debla

Eleutherna

WHITE MOUNTAINS

MT IDA

Ayios Vasilios

Atsiphades

Kamares

0 30 kilometres

0 20 miles

N

Ayiophara
Valley

1:650 000

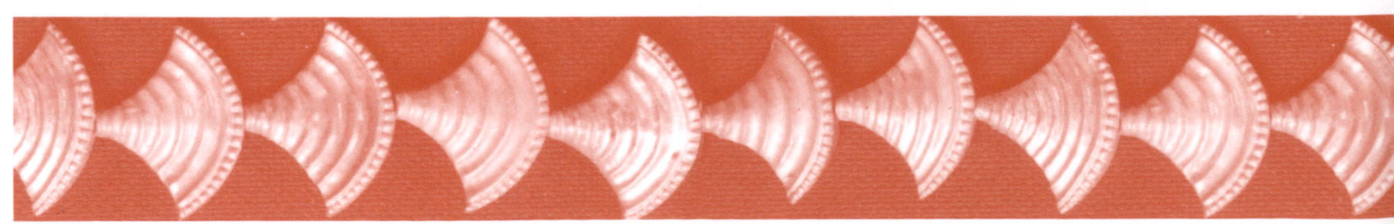